ROY CHOI

WITH TIEN NGUYEN AND NATASHA PHAN

PHOTOGRAPHS BY BOBBY FISHER

L.A.

AN ANTHONY BOURDAIN BOOK

ecco

An Imprint of HarperCollins *Publishers*

HarperCollins books may be purchased for educational, business, or sales promotional use. For information, please e-mail the Special Markets Department at SPsales@harpercollins.com.

FIRST EDITION

Designed by Suet Yee Chong
Photographs by Bobby Fisher

Library of Congress Cataloging-in-Publication Data has been applied for.

ISBN 978-0-06-220263-5

21 22 PC/LSCC 11

I DEDICATE THIS BOOK TO MY AMAZING WIFE
AND DAUGHTER, JEAN AND KAELYN, WHO I DON'T WRITE
ABOUT MUCH IN THIS BOOK BECAUSE THE MOMENTS
WE SHARE TOGETHER ARE OUR OWN. I LOVE YOU GUYS
FOREVER AND EVER AND EVER AND EVER.

"FOR IT IS EASY TO CRITICIZE AND BREAK DOWN THE SPIRIT
OF OTHERS, BUT TO KNOW YOURSELF TAKES A LIFETIME."

"THE POSSESSION OF ANYTHING BEGINS IN THE MIND."

—BRUCE LEE

CONTENTS

ACKNOWLEDGMENTS   IX

INTRODUCTION   1

1. MOTHER SAUCES   5

2. SILVER GARDEN   27

3. NECK FROZE   47

4. NOLAN RYAN   73

5. GROVE STREET   93

6. CRACK   123

7. YOU VERY LUCKY, MAN   141

8. EMERIL   175

9. NEW YORK, NEW YORK   199

10. THE PROFESSIONAL   229

11. FISH SAUCE   271

12. WINDSHIELD   293

13. VEGETABLES 1-2-3   311

THE RULES   323

INDEX   333

ACKNOWLEDGMENTS

THANK YOU TO ALL OF YOU IN AND OUT OF OUR LIVES.

GRACIAS POR TODO.

THIS BOOK IS A PART OF YOU, TOO.

—ROY, TIEN, AND NATASHA

INTRODUCTION

HELLO. I'M ROY. Get in. We're going for a ride.

Right around the time I started writing this story, I picked up a book about tribal tattoos, written by a Samoan chief. The opening line began, "I had to write this book." That first line was so powerful to me. It struck me then, as I started putting the pages of my life together, and it strikes me now, as I sit here writing this introduction after, funnily enough, having finished this book. He wrote that line because he was compelled to tell the story of his tribe and his islands. Because he thought it was his destiny to help keep former generations alive by documenting the folklore, the information, and the stories that are passed down through the art of the tattoo. So it wasn't that he wanted to write that book. He had to. It was his spiritual duty.

In a small, weird way, I feel the same about this book.

I had to write this book. To tell the story of my journey from immigrant to latchkey kid to lowrider to misfit to gambler to a chef answering his calling. To tell a story of Los Angeles and the people who live here. And to preserve it all on wax.

But before we get knee-deep in the messy yet beautiful chapters of my life, maybe it'll help to have a little map in your pocket. L.A. is a huge place, and sometimes the glare of stereotypes and television screens blinds visitors to its true character, the amazing cultural diversity of our residents and the food. That muthafuckin' L.A. food.

So let me play tour guide for a minute and show you around.

We'll start in the same place I started when I immigrated here with my family from South Korea in 1972: Olympic Boulevard and Vermont Avenue. This

is a big intersection in the middle of a neighborhood that's now the hardworking community of Koreatown, where the smoke from the Korean BBQ grills will stick to your hair for days no matter which fancy shampoo you choose and where you'll wash down your beers with crispy Korean fried chicken before hitting a multitude of other bars. A few miles north of here is Hollywood, and a dozen miles to our west is Sawtelle Boulevard, a little street with some of the best ramen and sushi in the country. Keep going west to see the canals of Venice and to kiss the sands of Malibu. UCLA and Beverly Hills aren't too far from the beaches, and if we hop northbound on the 405 and 101, we'll hit the San Fernando Valley—Granada Hills, Burbank, Tarzana, Sherman Oaks. Or if we ride the 405 southward instead, we'll drive right into the cradle of the South Bay—Torrance, Gardena, Carson, Long Beach.

East of Koreatown is Downtown proper, where Hill and Broadway split like wooden chopsticks through Chinatown and the wind tunnels of Pershing Square whoosh us through the Jewelry District. Farther northeast of Downtown is a whole other world: the hills of Pasadena, the tacos and burritos and families in East L.A. and Boyle Heights, the amazing noodles and phở and soup dumplings in the San Gabriel Valley.

And there's so much more: from the SGV, we'll jump down the 710 or 605 freeway and drive through Commerce or Bell Gardens, passing factories and a casino or two along the way. Roll down your window and smell the sweet drippings of lechón and carne asada smoking in backyards as we swing by Cerritos or Whittier. Keep going south, and there they are, our neighbors, Orange County and Riverside.

To loop back to L.A., we'll head up the 110 freeway, pull off in South Central and Inglewood for a hot minute to ride the wide streets and grub on BBQ and soul food, and then swoop west on the 10 freeway, through Downtown, to end up right back where we started—right here on the corner of Olympic and Vermont, the heart of Koreatown.

I know. We covered a lot of ground. But don't sweat it. I got the wheel and a full tank of gas. All you have to do is sit back and trust. In the pages that follow, you'll see a little bit of this magical city through the lens of my life and through the food of the people who really live here. Through all of that, you'll start to understand this amazing place that I was raised in and taste the flavors of the streets of L.A.

Thank you for picking up this book. Thank you for joining me on this ride through the crooked journeys of my life. L.A. welcomes you, and I welcome you, with love.

Oh, by the way, are you hungry?

Let me cook for you.

I got that, too.

You're riding shotgun with Papi now. What could possibly go wrong?

> NOTE:
>
> BEFORE DIVING INTO THE RECIPES, FLIP TO PAGE 325 AND CHECK OUT INGREDIENTS YOU MIGHT NEED TO STOCK UP YOUR PANTRY.

CHAPTER 1

MOTHER SAUCES

Seoul, South Korea, 1970. A hospital room in the heart of downtown Chongro-gu. A baby with a big Frankenstein head, drenched in his own blood, with more spewing out through his upper cleft like lava erupting from a volcano. Wailing, crying. Yeah, they stitched me up all right, but when the rumble in the jungle was over, I had a fat lip and a Harry Potter scar between my mouth and nose. One hell of a hectic entry into this world, huh?

MY PARENTS ACTUALLY MET IN
Los Angeles in 1967. They were in
Korea before then, on opposite sides
of the country in fact. My mom's
from the most famous province in
the North, Pyung-An Do. It's cold
up there, where the country meets
China. I don't know too much more,
as Communism has washed away a lot
of history, and it's taboo to talk too
much about it in the South, but I do
know that the herbs and plants there
would make even Humboldt County
blush. And I know that my mom's
family took those raw ingredients
and turned them into something

pretty spectacular. As family legend had it, they had a magic touch: *Sohn-maash*.
Flavors in their fingertips. Flavors that had been passed down over thousands of
years, from generation to generation to generation, flavors that were now part of
their very spirit. My mom grew up on things like mandoo, dumplings filled with
mountain herbs mixed with ground meat and seafood. And naeng myun, cold
buckwheat or arrowroot noodles, done two ways, both cold. One's served in
ice-cold beef broth with mustard and vinegar. The other has dried skate mixed
in with the deadliest of the deadly chile pastes and filled with garlic, leaving your
dragon's breath stinking for days. Fucking delicious.

My mom was sister number four and child number five, right after my first
uncle. She actually was supposed to be a boy but came out a girl, so they flipped
around a Korean boy's name. Nam Ja is man in Korean; make it Ja Nam and you
got my mom. She went to the second-best all-girls school in the country, Jin
Myung, and even though her grades weren't the best, she was the queen bee
of her crew, and she ruled the school. She continued on to Hangyang University.
Then, in 1966, when she was all of twenty years old, my mom decided to take
herself to the next level and head to America. The story was, she was going to
the United States to attend "art school." If you saw a photo of her at the Gimpo
Airport, though, ready to cross the great Pacific, you'd see her outfit showing more

art than school: Jackie O. gear, big stunner shades, a beautiful handbag. She was young, sassy, and pretty. How could the City of Angels be all that tough?

MY DAD, MEANWHILE, is from Chollanam-do in the South. That's a province known for its food and the temper of its people: all that spicy, pungent, funky stuff you may associate with Korean food—from kimchi to pickled intestines and even to bi bim bap—comes from this province. Now don't get me wrong—the rest of Korea has kimchi, too. It's just this southwest region has the stinkiest, and it's the most brash. And, like flamingos pink from plankton, the people are what they eat: tough, rude at times, abrasive, dominant, vivacious, conniving. Everybody hates the Cholla people, sometimes in envy and sometimes for good reason. But the freakin' food no one can deny.

That's where my dad's from. It's proper, then, that he was a badass muthafucka.

Even at ten, my dad was smart and tough as nails. He had to be. His mom had died by then, and so it was just him, his dad, his stepmom, and his older sister. And when the North invaded the South in 1950, the whole family had to flee the stampede of North Korean armies pushing southward. Eating scraps and old, cold rice, they fled from Seoul, going farther and farther south through Busan and Gwangju, settling down and then taking off again when the fire got too close. For my dad, that meant enrolling in a new school every time they moved, and *that* meant he was always the new kid, picked on and bullied by the local kids. But, really, all that just toughed him up more. As the family bounced from town to town, he bounced the local competition: with the same strategy that rules any street in the world, he would find the toughest dude on campus and challenge him to a shil-lim-style wrestling match. Shil-lim's like sumo, but without the weight and with a sudden-death point system: first on his back loses. My dad never was first on his back.

Then he went gangsta in the classroom, Pac-Man eating up the competition. Kyunggi High School, the Phillips Exeter of Korea. Check.

Seoul National University, the Harvard of Korea. Check.

First commander as liaison with the U.S. Army. Check.

He got so high up the chain of command that in 1963 he was sent abroad to an Ivy League school to study diplomacy, international politics, and the Western way of life. With no money and no firm grasp on the English language except for a slippery handle on what he got from memorizing the fucking dictionary, he got through the University of Pennsylvania's master's program. Just so he could be that perfect foreign policy diplomat of the future. And as if that weren't enough, he ran the mail room at ABC for Dick Clark. Mr. Incredible.

He wasn't done yet. Like other Korean students sent to the United States to study, he was heading to another university to finish his education and get some more perspective on this new Western life of his, so he could take home what he knew and become a leader. He started his Ph.D. program at the University of Colorado at Boulder, then transferred to the land where the weed is green and the sunshine sets on the hydraulics, slow and low. This was Los Angeles, UCLA, Lew Alcindor. 1965.

In the land of sun, he had jobs in shadows: washing dishes at Lawry's, janitorial duties throughout the city and on the north shore of Lake Tahoe during ski season. It was rough work, but he did what he had to do to survive. I think this was when he also started to party a little more, and he, the perfect Clark Kent,

NO TEETH? MAN UP, BOY! YOU GOTTA BE STRONG AND HEALTHY. THE FOOD HAS TO BUILD YOUR BRAIN!

slowly transformed into a real man. A real man who wasn't perfect, who was okay with having a little dirt under those properly trimmed nails.

That's when he met a party girl. My mom. He pulled down his Wayfarers, lit a cigarette, and ripped straight game on her. They moved in together in an apartment off Crenshaw Boulevard and got married in a church on Jefferson and Vermont near the University of Southern California. He in a white tux, she in a simple, beautiful white gown with a veil centered with flowers. He never finished his Ph.D.

The late 1960s was a cool-ass time in Los Angeles. The Beach Boys, total Mod skinny tie shit, big long Chevys in cobalt blue cruising under bright green palm trees and the amber glaze of the California sunshine. They soaked in the L.A. sun and honeymooned in Europe. They returned to L.A., but this time it wouldn't stick. Just one year after walking down the aisle, they bid UCLA good-bye—art school? what art school?—and off they went *back* to the country they had worked so hard to leave. In 1969, this meant returning to a country ruled by a dictator, Park Chung-hee, and an economy marked not by the flat-screens, semiconductors, and other bomb-ass toys of today but by heavy, raw industry. They took a step to the First World, then took two steps back to the Third. That's Korean guilt and Confucian good son shit in play right there.

ONE YEAR AFTER COMING HOME to Korea, they welcomed me into their world. Stitched up as I was, you'd think I would have been treated differently, but in Korea it doesn't matter if your mouth has one hole or two. You don't baby the baby, and there was no such thing as "baby food." So as soon as I got off my mom's milk, they had a whole kitchen going for their little boy. No teeth? Man up, boy! You gotta be strong and healthy. The food has to build your brain!

So we'd get our Elton John on with electric griddles and butane burners surrounding my mom and aunts like pianos and keyboards. They'd feed us straight from the pan, straight off the griddle, always straight out of their fingers: try this, taste this, eat that. Chap chae, vermicelli noodles layered with julienned vegetables, egg, and marinated beef as complex and fly high as a J Dilla track. Daikon soup, abalone porridge, blended mung bean, soybean, and tofu soup mixed with rice, spinach, anchovy broth, and noodles. I slurped raw kimchi from stained Rubbermaid gloves. I was hand-fed bits of savory pancakes filled with pureed mung beans and scallions, sometimes studded with oysters. Flavor after flavor. *Sohn-maash.*

Life was tough, though. Money wasn't flowing. My mom had married the "perfect" man, but the gravy train was starting to derail. My dad initially left Korea ahead of his class, but he came back behind the times. The classmates he had once eclipsed now shone in powerful positions in the government and universities. He was forced to kiss the ass of the people he had run circles around just a few years earlier.

And still nothing. Then there was the indignity of it all: even if he was given a decent position, how could he work for the guy he used to boss around?

And then me. In a land of conformity, what of the boy with the deformity?

I don't know how it exactly went down, but after almost two years back in Seoul, with no money, no job, and that lingering cognac lipstick film on their lips from the amber sunshine and cool palms of Los Angeles, they must have started to prepare. And in 1972, they finally packed it all up, snuck on a plane, and said, "Peace out, muthafuckas." I would have, too.

IF YOU COUNTED all the Asians living in Los Angeles in 1970—Vietnamese, Koreans, Chinese, Japanese, an entire continent of ethnicities clumped together as one—the total number would have been 240,000. That was just 2 percent of the population of L.A. at the time. Thanks to a federal law that lifted immigration restrictions in 1965, people from all over Asia streamed into L.A. in significant numbers in the early and mid-1970s. When the Koreans got here, they didn't *intend* to take over the part of town that was once Old Hollywood. It just ended up happening that way.

Old Hollywood, along Olympic and Wilshire Boulevards, was where the entertainment industry partied in Hollywood's glory years. But by 1950 or so, the party shifted westward, and the big Jewish and European populations living in the area transplanted west, too. The buildings and apartments in the historic core of L.A. emptied, and whole city blocks became run-down and scruffy. Old Hollywood faded, a ghost town in a themeless park.

By the 1960s the real estate in the area was cheap, dirt cheap. The Koreans coming into the city in the early 1970s discovered the low rents and hunkered down. And while they didn't start out with much, they managed to transform the dilapidated three-square-mile neighborhood into a bona fide bustling Koreatown, now home to the largest Korean population outside of Seoul.

It all started with a pot and a bunch of people. There had to be some trust in the group, or it was all for nothing. Every month everyone met and shared stories and dreams, and, in the course of all that, everyone decided on an amount. Then everyone anted up. Each month, one person got the jackpot and opened a business. A liquor store, dry cleaner, gas station, small restaurant, trophy shop, golf store, whatever. Something. As each person built a business, his or her share of the pot increased so new families could get on their feet. It was thanks to these *kyae* meetings that the ghost town came alive.

When our day came to take the pot, my dad snatched up that Johnnie Walker. He opened a liquor store on 9th Street and Vermont Avenue in Koreatown, and he was so proud of it. So proud. He polished and cleaned till the place was so shiny you couldn't turn around without catching your own reflection. I remember the candies and liquor bottles. I remember the glass storefront. My dad's proud smile.

At home my mom was possessed by a brilliant compulsion to cook. Every morning she was up at 4:30 A.M., and a huge breakfast feast would be waiting for me when I woke up. But in those early days you couldn't walk down the street and take your pick of kimchis. No, we trekked across Southern California to find certain ingredients. We went to Santa Barbara for abalone that would be in that night's bowl of porridge. Goleta for dandelion greens for crab and tofu stew. Indio for bean sprouts to complete my mom's bi bim bap. The piers in Newport for rock cod, but only if we got there by 6:30 A.M. and only if we were first in line. At the very least, we would get freshly caught fish and hang them, salted, on our porch like laundry drying on the line.

And all the while, every night, my parents fed me from their fingertips. The *sohn-maash* had made it stateside.

CLOSER TO HOME, we took in the City of Angels. We took in America. I started watching *Happy Days,* and the Fonz became my idol. He was everything to me. He was the guy who never fit in, but only because he was too cool for school. He would say his "Ayyyyye," laugh, and give a thumbs-up to all those things he approved. I loved his touch: he could just be holding a float or a milk shake, and it was better than how anyone had ever held a float or milk shake. Or he could just hit something that was broken, and it not only worked again but worked better!

The Fonz had Arnold's for his hamburgers and shakes; we had Tommy's. We drove our faded blue Peugeot with ripped upholstery to the original redbrick Tommy's on Beverly and Rampart. Any trip to Tommy's was like sinking into a plush movie theater seat with a fresh tub of popcorn with real butter or lying down on clean sheets after a long day: time was frozen at the exact moment when everything was just right. I was protected, safe. I loved the look on my dad's face when we were standing in line for goopy chili tamales, no tomato, extra onions, and an ice-cold orange Crush. I loved the open air, the sun as it hit our car hood. I loved the people around us, standing single file before scurrying off to the rails to stand and eat. I loved the hills as they sloped down from Rampart to the north and Beverly to the east.

We hit Dodgers games in Echo Park with other Korean families, all of us in the bleachers, watching the fabulous four of Ron Cey, Bill Russell, Davey Lopes, and Steve Garvey. We saw the same families over and over again at Dong Il Jang on 8th near Western, one of the first grand, opulent restaurants in Koreatown. Up until then, most places had been just small mom-and-pop joints, places to grab a seat, eat your thing, and go. Dong Il Jang, though, was a big place cloaked in elaborate Chosun period architecture, bamboo, and rice paper. Inside there were big booths and a big party room. At the same time, though, it was, and is, still a place you could imagine your grandfather sitting, with a newspaper, slurping on some noodles, gnawing on some short rib bones. From those rib bones to the bubbling stews to the kimchis to the Korean-style floor seating, you could devour what amounts to a whole cow here and then wash it all down with fried rice swirled in meat juices and kimchi stains. Classic.

My parents took me with them to the movies at night, and I remember watching *Midnight Express* and afterward chowing down on chili spaghetti at Bob's Big Boy. My dad used to be a fruit stocker and janitor at Grand Central Market, a smaller version of Seattle's Pike Place in Downtown. I was at my dad's hip, tasting and squirreling apples, pineapples, scallions, garlic, carrots, boysenberries, rhubarb, dried beans, and nuts away in my pocket. I thought I was real slick. And of course we hit all the important landmarks: whirled in the teacups at Disneyland, screamed on the Log Jammer at Magic Mountain, and clapped when Shamu leaped high out of the water at Sea World. I dreamed of being a tour guide and showing people all these places I was seeing.

And the birthday parties! The parties celebrating my birth at four, five, six, seven, eight, nine, ten years were banging! You know how Western tourists go

to Asia and just have to participate in the sacred, mystical Oriental ritual known as a tea ceremony? Because they think this is what we do, even if we don't? For my parents, throwing birthday parties for their son was their tea ceremony, their attempt to connect spiritually to their new American culture. They had no idea what the fuck they were doing or why, but somewhere they learned or read or saw or heard that that was how American kids in the 1970s celebrated their birthdays. This explains the magicians—goddamn magicians—at my birthday parties, and the clown with tricks up his billowy sleeves, and a man on stilts walking with rented-by-the-hour animals. And a pool party one year, Chuck E. Cheese's another. They were creating memories that were as new and foreign to them as they were exciting to me.

I HAD A KEY
NO LOCK ON MY
WALKED TILL I PUT

But the clouds were gathering.

I was five years old when my dad's liquor store sold its last bottle. My parents still kept on with the rented birthday magicians, the big smiles on their faces, the big breakfasts every morning, but I could sense the magic disappearing. By then they had started drinking at home, just a little at first, then a lot more. On those nights I always tried to be a good son, memorizing the English dictionary like my dad told me to do. I'd look up from the words and definitions, though, and watch my parents. They were about sober enough to hand-deliver a hard whack if they heard Korean coming out of me instead of English, but they also were starting to drink enough for their eyes to hollow, their faces to turn that devil's red. I didn't need the dictionary to learn the difference between sober and drunk.

With the family business closed, we moved. And moved again and again as my parents hustled all over town, working at their friends' gas stations, wig shops, video stores. We bounced around South Central and back up through Crenshaw before finally ending up in West Hollywood in a rent-controlled property that my uncle managed. We were on the second story, surrounded by single mothers and hippies, in a duplex filled with moving boxes torn open as needed.

My parents tried to dig up a new life in the jewelry business. They went straight to the source, taking dusty field trips out to the local mines to check out the turquoise, fossils, agate, and big mineral pendants that matched the huge sunglasses, long linen dresses, and bell-bottoms that were so popular in the mid-seventies. My dad even studied up at the Gemological Institute of America and became a certified gemologist. Together, he and my mom peddled their wares door-to-door, from our neighborhood all the way up to the boutiques on fancy Sunset Boulevard.

It's hard to make a sale with a kid on your back, so my parents left me behind. For two years, until I was about seven, I had a key around my neck but no lock on my life. So I wandered. I walked until I put holes in my soles. And the more hours they clocked, the longer I was alone, ready to be adopted by the city streets. I discovered the urban forest of old palms and sycamores right below Olympic Boulevard. Made my way into alleyways and onto their broken sidewalks. Got lost in the dull lights of the 7-Eleven and swiped candy, chips, beef jerky—why not? I hopped on and off buses, getting off in Koreatown, where I discovered tamales and sniffed out kimchis, some in jars, others in plastic bags. I found hot dogs and carne asada being grilled at the park, studied the jars of soybean paste stocked in market aisles. I rode my way down to Little Tokyo and tasted fish-shaped pastries filled with red beans, grabbed aluminum foils filled with savory pancakes. I saw kids, but most weren't Koreans or any other type of Asian. Mostly black or white instead. I wondered why I wasn't them.

I always managed to get back home before my parents did. When they did finally turn the key in the lock, it was like spinning the wheel of fortune. Sometimes my parents would grab me for a grand trip, like to Oxnard for vegetables. Other times we'd just go to the market for a carton of Marlboro Reds and a handle of Cutty Sark. Or maybe we wouldn't do either, and they'd just go straight to the bottles and yell and sometimes smack me to blow off some steam, then tell me

what a great son I was and cook up a grand feast. I never knew what was coming until it was already done. Whatever we did, our nights usually ended with their friends dropping in and empty bottles and red cigarette boxes littering the coffee table. Food, booze, smoke, and chatter. Just a little weeknight get-together. Nothing wrong with that, right?

Truth is, I didn't know what was right or wrong. The English-only rule was supposed to turn me into an American, but that alone didn't spell out how to actually *be* American. I still ate kimchi and porridge but got a beat-down if I spoke Korean, so, fuck, I didn't even know how to be Korean either. Everything was all a jumble.

So what does a bewildered, lonely boy who can't find the right words do? Throw up the Bat Signal, of course. Get some outside help. And the Fonz, my great American superhero, answered the call. He swooped in with his Fonzie touch, his thumb of approval, and gave me some confidence.

This being the city where dreams are made, it just so happened that my neighbor's mom worked at Paramount Studios, where *Happy Days* was filmed. She got us special passes to meet him.

I was so fucking excited.

On that great day, we went through the famous gates. Walked onto Paramount's famous studio lot. The Fonz was busy when we found him. I know my friend and I were probably the least important things on Henry Winkler's agenda that day, but he was the Fonz, man. Classy above all, a drink of water for a parched soul. He stopped what he had been doing and did all the niceties for us. But beyond that, he looked at me and said something without words. He somehow told me that shit would get deep, but to hang in there, because I had an interesting road ahead.

And he gave me the thumbs-up.

Fuck, the Fonz read my palm when all I was looking for was his thumb.

That was it. Whatever my parents were going to do that night suddenly didn't matter. Something inside me unjumbled and fell into place, like a code had been cracked. I looked at that thumb, and a deep part of me saw the flavors in our fingertips. On a level I wasn't even aware of, I was encouraged to make that a part of my life. Touch of gold. Everything's better. *Sohn-maash.*

KIMCHI

A car needs gas; as a kid, I needed kimchi. Everything I am comes from kimchi. Kimchi plus a bowl of rice equals a meal for me. Hot dogs and kimchi? Sure. The La Brea Tar Pits in Los Angeles bubbled slowly throughout my life, and they always reminded me of the jars of fermenting kimchi that filled our refrigerators. In a way, all that kimchi took this long to ferment within me.

Always slurp the first batch from the bowl with your fingertips before it goes into the jar. Industrial gloves for mixing are optional but recommended.

MAKES 1 BIG JAR

PASTE

1 cup kochukaru

1 cup peeled onion

½ cup water

15 garlic cloves, peeled

¼ cup peeled and chopped fresh ginger

2 tablespoons kosher salt

2 tablespoons sugar

¼ cup plus 2 tablespoons fish sauce

2 tablespoons oyster sauce

2 tablespoons natural rice vinegar
  (not seasoned)

1 tablespoon soy sauce

VEGETABLES

4 cups water

1 tablespoon kosher salt

1 large napa cabbage

½ bunch fresh chives, cut into 1-inch
  batons

½ cup jarred oysters

1 tablespoon salted baby shrimp

Put all the ingredients for the paste in a blender, puree, and set aside.

In a bowl large enough to hold the cabbage, mix the water with the salt. Split the cabbage in half and soak it in the salted water for 2 to 3 hours at room temperature.

Drain the cabbage. Mix ½ cup of the paste, the chives, oysters, and salted shrimp and layer between the leaves of the cabbage. Coat the exterior of the cabbage with the remaining paste.

This is when you cut off a leaf and slurp.

Stuff the cabbage into a gallon-size glass pickle jar and seal tightly. If it doesn't fit, you can cut the cabbage in half again.

Keep the jar at room temperature for 2 days, then put it in the refrigerator. It will be ready to eat in about 2 weeks and can be kept refrigerated indefinitely.

ROCKY, YOU CAN DO IT. A RAW EGG IS LIKE A SLURRY. IT'LL COOK GENTLY IN THE PORRIDGE AND PULL THE WHOLE DISH TOGETHER.

ABALONE PORRIDGE

The island of Cheju is famous for its abalone porridge, and Los Angeles has a place called Mountain Cafe on 8th Street in Koreatown that does the best version of the dish. But people who eat abalone porridge on a regular basis know it's best eaten at home with family, especially when you have a toothache. This is how I do it. Hope you enjoy.

For the anchovy stock, homemade is best, but you can also use canned anchovy stock, fish stock, chicken stock, or even instant dashi broth.

SERVES 4

ANCHOVY STOCK
1 cup dried anchovies
13 cups water

PORRIDGE
8 cups cooked white rice

2 tablespoons plus 2 teaspoons minced peeled fresh ginger

2 tablespoons Asian sesame oil

2 tablespoons roasted sesame seeds

8 ounces Santa Barbara abalone, pounded and diced, or chopped fresh or canned clams

Big pinch each of kosher salt and freshly ground black pepper

4 eggs

1 tablespoon plus 1 teaspoon thinly sliced scallions

Bottle of soy sauce for the table

To make the anchovy stock, combine the anchovies and water in a medium pot over low heat and simmer for 1 hour. Drain through a sieve and set aside. You should have about 3 quarts.

To make the porridge, combine the rice and stock in a large pot and bring it to a boil. Reduce the heat to a simmer and cook until the rice starts to become bloated, about 10 minutes, stirring the rice often. Add the ginger, sesame oil, sesame seeds, and abalone.

Over very low heat—lower than a simmer; you're looking for one bubble to pop on the surface every now and then—cook until thick but still viscous, about 20 minutes. Season with the salt and pepper.

Pour the porridge into 4 bowls, crack an egg into each, and top with scallions.

Splash in soy sauce as desired and GET DOWN.

TWICE-COOKED DUCK FAT FRIES

As a kid, I loved going to Tommy's Burgers with my dad, the sun setting low and slow as we pulled up to the tiny shack and got in line to order burgers and fries. Those were such simple things, but sometimes the things that look the simplest take the most care. And these duck fat fries using potatoes, sweet potatoes, and yuca are a take on that—yeah, they might take a little while, but the process of making these isn't a burden as much as it is hidden dedication. Do it with care; then the fun will come from eating it. Things that come in threes must be good, right?

SERVES 4

2 cups canola oil

2²/₃ cups duck fat

8 ounces Idaho potatoes, peeled and cut lengthwise into ¼-inch-thick batons and held in water

8 ounces sweet potatoes, peeled and cut lengthwise into ¼-inch-thick batons and held in water

8 ounces yuca, peeled and cut lengthwise into ¼-inch-thick batons and held in water

Sea salt

Limes, halved

1 bunch Thai basil leaves

In a deep fryer or a very large, deep pot—whatever you got, man—heat the canola oil and duck fat to 250°F. If you don't have a food thermometer, you'll know the fat is hot enough when you drop one test fry in there and it sizzles slightly.

Line a sheet pan with paper towels and grab a big metal spider strainer for scooping the fries out of the fat. Dry the potatoes and yuca after removing them from the water.

Dump the Idaho potatoes into the fat, in batches if necessary to avoid crowding, and, moving them constantly, cook until they're slightly colored, about 3 minutes. Transfer them to the paper-towel-lined sheet pan. Repeat for the sweet potatoes and yuca; look for a light, light beige color, letting the fat come back to 250°F between batches.

Once all the tubers have been par-blanched, bring the fat up to 350°F and fry each batch again until crispy, 4 to 5 minutes, or a deep golden brown color. Scoop each batch onto the paper-towel-lined sheet pan. Sprinkle with sea salt and squeeze limes all over.

Fry the Thai basil leaves in the fat until crispy, about 2 minutes, and toss with the fries.

EAT NOW.

CHILI SPAGHETTI

Chili spaghetti at Bob's Big Boy, milk shakes, root beer floats, late-night movies, repeat—that was our family fun. My parents took me to some raw-ass movies: *Midnight Express, Taxi Driver, The Godfather, Apocalypse Now, Jaws, The Deer Hunter, The Exorcist, Dog Day Afternoon.* Man, I was only five years old, homie! I don't know what they were thinking, but those movies were great! I felt so alive being up so late, watching crazy movies, and eating spaghetti topped with chili. I wasn't in bed by eight—ya know what I mean?

SERVES 4 TO 6

¼ cup plus 2 tablespoons vegetable oil

2½ pounds ground beef

1 large onion, minced

5 garlic cloves, minced

12 ounces tomato paste

1 tablespoon cider vinegar

2½ cups beef stock, homemade if you've got it, canned if not

One 4-ounce can diced green chiles

1½ jalapeño peppers, minced

1 tablespoon ancho chile powder

1 tablespoon cayenne

3½ tablespoons ground cumin

1 tablespoon plus 1 teaspoon dried oregano

1 tablespoon plus 1 teaspoon canned crushed pineapple

3 tablespoons chopped fresh cilantro

Kosher salt

1 pound spaghetti

GARNISH

¾ cup grated cheddar cheese

½ cup minced onion

Bottle of Tabasco sauce for the table

Heat the vegetable oil in a large saucepan over medium heat for about a minute. Add the beef to the pan and brown it. Transfer the beef from a pan to a bowl, leaving the oil in the pan.

Raise the heat to medium-high and add the onions and garlic to the pan. Cook until soft and lightly browned, 3 to 5 minutes.

Add the tomato paste to the pan, stirring and cooking the paste just slightly for about 2 minutes. Add the vinegar to deglaze the pan, then add the stock and the ground beef. Bring to a boil, then reduce the heat to a simmer. Simmer for 30 minutes, then add the green chiles with their liquid, the jalapeños, chile powder, cayenne, cumin, oregano, pineapple, and cilantro. Simmer for 30 more minutes.

Bring a large pot of salted water to a boil and add the spaghetti, cooking until al dente, 8 to 10 minutes.

Drain the spaghetti and transfer to a big bowl. Pour the chili over the spaghetti and garnish with the grated cheddar cheese and minced onions.

TAKE IT OUT TO THE TABLE TO SERVE FAMILY STYLE, OPEN THE BOTTLE OF TABASCO, AND SPLASH.

CHAPTER 2

SILVER GARDEN

WELCOME TO

SILVER GARDEN

Open 11am – 9pm

We accept Visa, Master Card, American Express, Diner's Club

Please seat yourself

***

Silver Garden was a family restaurant. My family's restaurant. Deep in Orange County, there was no other Korean restaurant around at the time that had food quite like we did. It was in the right place at the right time, until it wasn't.

MY PARENTS DIDN'T CHOOSE the restaurant business so much as it chose them. Sales for their hippie jewelry faded as the seventies switched gears from Peter, Paul and Mary to the Bee Gees, and they had to look somewhere else for work. By then, everyone in the L.A. Korean community knew about my mom and her legendary food and homemade kimchi. Her kimchi was so good that not only family and friends, but also friends of friends and friends of friends of friends, straight up bought it off her. She took orders, cooked up a red storm at home, then packed it all up in Styrofoam containers. I'd pack those into cardboard boxes, and off we'd go to make home deliveries. Everything spilled in the car, my parents fought, but my mom made it happen.

She sold her kimchi and panchan at house parties and bowling alleys and parking lots while pregnant with my sister. She was like the Avon lady, but instead of makeup, it was kimchi calling. Free savory pancake with any purchase. What a deal!

"Open a restaurant," everyone would say to my mom after eating her food. And after their jewelry business went belly-up, my parents realized that, hey, they *should* open a restaurant. Move their underground hustle above ground. There was another *kyae* meeting. They combined their savings with the *kyae* pot and looked south to plant their seeds.

Our restaurant was in Anaheim, California, barely five miles north of Disneyland, on a long, never-ending boulevard called Brookhurst Street. Brookhurst runs almost twenty miles from Huntington Beach north through the Vietnamese ex-pat community Little Saigon in Westminster, up through the OC's own Koreatown in Garden Grove, all the way into the barrios of Anaheim. We were in the western part of those barrios.

When we opened the restaurant there in 1978, West Anaheim was what you could call trashy, a transient hood. Some residential pockets did take root, but for the most part the homes weren't where the heart was. The blood that ran through the veins of the neighborhood was a bit less

PANCHAN ARE LITTLE SIDE DISHES THAT WELCOME YOU TO A KOREAN MEAL. THEY GIVE YOU A GLIMPSE OF WHAT YOU'RE ABOUT TO EAT AND TELL YOU A LITTLE BIT ABOUT THE PERSON WHO MADE THE MEAL: WHAT THE PERSON CAN DO, HOW HE OR SHE THINKS, WHERE THE PERSON CAME FROM, HOW MUCH THE PERSON CARES. IT CAN BE AS SIMPLE AS KIMCHI AND SOME PICKLED CUCUMBERS, OR IT CAN BE AS ELABORATE AS A HUNDRED DIFFERENT INTRICATE LITTLE SIDE DISHES, LIKE YOU'D GET IF YOU WERE FEASTING WITH ROYALTY. AT HOME YOU'LL PROBABLY HAVE FIVE TO SIX PANCHAN. THESE WILL COME OUT FIRST, THEN STAY ON THE TABLE AS THE REST OF THE DISHES COME OUT. THE MEAL IS EATEN FAMILY STYLE, SO BY THE TIME EVERYTHING IS SET DOWN, THERE WILL BE DOZENS AND DOZENS OF SMALL PLATES AND BOWLS AND DISHES ON THE TABLE, WITH EVERYONE PICKING AT WHAT THEY WANT WITH THEIR CHOPSTICKS.

wholesome: dive bars, drugs, Harleys roaring through the parking lot in front of the Humdinger, where girls danced nightly. As for Korean food, there were some noodle joints and a few small sul rong tang joints specializing in beef marrow soup, but that was it. Opening a big, family-friendly Korean restaurant in a place like that was like opening the only Korean restaurant in Hell's Kitchen back when it was *Hell's* Kitchen.

But that's why the area was so cheap. And cheap real estate, as you know by now, is like a ghetto birdcall for Koreans. Our new home was just a few miles from its cultural cousins in Little Saigon and Garden Grove, but it may as well have been a hundred.

I WAS EIGHT when we started work on the restaurant. We called it Silver Garden, after my sister, just born. Her English name is Julie, but her given name is Eun-Jung, which means—well, you guessed it. All the family love was poured into our little girl. It's an Asian thing, y'all. Prosperity and future, pride and no prejudice. Your children's names are the waters that cleanse and sprout new life.

Before we took it over, the restaurant had been an Italian-American joint—emphasis on "American"—and we made it our own right quick. The restaurant's sign was Winnie-the-Pooh yellow, with huge black letters and the Korean lettering—Eun Jung Shik-dang—just to the left of the English translation. "Silver Garden" was just one name crammed on a strip-mall signboard, just one business stuffed onto a strip of concrete with six other businesses, lined up like ducks in a row. We were the odd duck out, though, tucked between a used-appliance store and a silkscreen T-shirt shop. Just a few hops down were a couple of choice dive bars—Sherwood Inn ("Cocktails, Hot Fantasies") and Sugar's ("Beer—Girls—Pool")—plus a hobby shop, a takeaway BBQ rib place, a liquor store, and a nail salon.

The first thing you'd notice about Silver Garden was that almost the entire storefront was floor-to-ceiling plate glass. You know that glass that encapsulates car dealerships? The kind

WALK INTO THE MAIN DINING ROOM. ENTER THE MAGIC.

of glass that wobbles when fire trucks roll by? That kind of glass made up the front of Silver Garden. The front door was glass, too, with a long handle that braced its center like a belt. Rice paper framed by bamboo square boxes tic-tac-toed the bottom half of the front facade. Open the door, scrape. The door always stuck. Pull hard. Boom.

First thing to greet you: a cigarette machine. On the wall to your left, a corkboard pinned with calendars, business cards, flyers, couches for sale. Slope right. Walk into the main dining room. Enter the magic.

Rice paper with bamboo trim covered the walls, and my parents hung up antique tools from Korean farms—brooms, fruit-gathering baskets, hatchets, drying baskets for fish and chiles—for decoration. It was dark in here, but not so dark that it was depressing. A bamboo and rice paper room divider split the dining area into two; on the right side, big leather booths studded with brass buttons lined the wall, and brown Formica tables and stackable polyurethane chairs arranged into four- and two-tops took up the rest of the floor space. On the left side of the divider, larger tables in the same Formica. This side was the party room.

As you headed toward the server area, the place began to lighten up until bright white light swallowed the dark. This was exactly the line where the back of the house met the front of the house; in fact, you could literally stand right on this border, and half your body would be brown and the other half white. Ha!

When you stepped into the kitchen, you'd note how huge it was. There was a soda machine on the right, then the hand sink, water station, ice bin, and a stand-up refrigerator. To the left against the dining room wall, a piano of burners. The grill was on a side wall, and the center was filled with a prep table, stainless steel shelving, and a dishwashing area.

There weren't too many cooks in the kitchen. There was my mom, the chef at Silver Garden, always elbows-deep in kimchi-stained plastic tubs. There was a dishwasher dude, a couple of older ladies helping with the kimchi and marinating meats, a cook putting out stews. Then my dad, doing whatever my mom told him to do. It don't matter whether you are classically trained, a chef is a chef, and you do as the chef says. *Yes, chef!*

It was just this tiny group of people, but the kitchen was constantly busy, and the food never stopped coming.

Every morning before the restaurant opened at 11:00, the kitchen went into overdrive. The back alley was an orchestra of food: Porcelain barrels of fermenting bean paste lined up around the door like pipe organs. Right next to these barrels were salted fish, croakers or mackerels, hung and tied together, accordion style. In the pit of the alley were crates and crates of onions, scallions, garlic, mung beans, soybean sprouts, ginger. My auntie—a distant relative, actually, but the kind of relative you gotta call "auntie"—would strap on rain boots and wash all the vegetables down with a red hose. She was a short woman with a gold tooth and beautifully wrinkled skin. We have a joke in Korea: there are three types of humans—man, woman, and, for certain women of a certain older age, ajuma. She was definitely an ajuma.

The vegetables sun-dried on milk crates and old clothing racks. As they dried, we'd bring them into the kitchen for prep, and they'd inevitably land in one plastic bucket or another. There were buckets on the floor for the marinated spicy crab and sesame spinach. Other buckets for the short ribs marinating in thick black sauce. More buckets for the mountains of kimchi waiting for salted baby shrimp and oysters to be added. On the counter, flat chives laid out alongside big cubes of daikon and young baby radishes painted in red, all diced and cut, ready to be crunched in your mouth. Big blenders overflowed with savory pancake mixes.

Past all the buckets and blenders was the dry storage: cases of soju and beer, bags of dried chile flakes, sacks of unpeeled garlic and onions, jars of unpeeled ginger, kochujang, cucumbers, pumpkins, sweet potatoes, and pounds and pounds of rice. Then there were the cases of oranges and apples; once sliced, they were strictly reserved as our dessert for the guests.

Just off to the side of the kitchen in the very back of the restaurant was an amazing particleboard trapezoidal structure, a little island my parents built for my sister and me, which we turned into the Choi Family Treehouse. Two big couches,

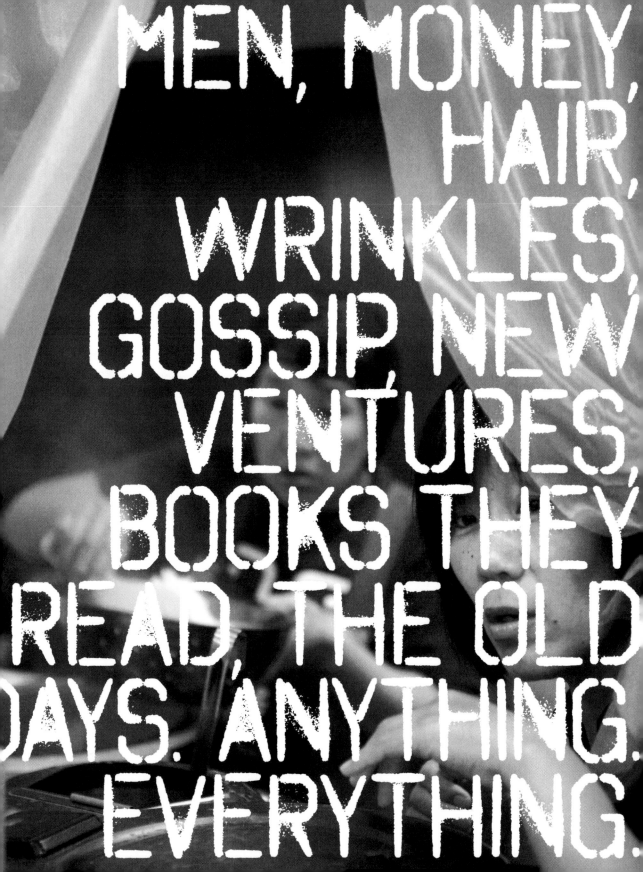

a couple of lamps, a 19-inch television on a swiveling pedestal, a twin bed with striped sheets, a baby playpen, a crib for my sister, a bookshelf, a desk. This was the scene of much of my third- to sixth-grade elementary-school education, where I did my homework, read books, solved multiplication tables, learned my prepositions and adverbs—did everything I needed to do to stay at the head of my class. I'd get out of school, pick up my little sister from day care, maybe take her by the supermarket, where I'd swipe a few candies for us, walk to the restaurant, and, while the kitchen was in full prep mode, settle us down in the Treehouse. She'd take her nap, I'd start on my homework, someone would be hosing the vegetables outside, someone else would be whack-whack-whacking at some piece of meat, everyone working at his own station until . . .

Three P.M. Regardless of what you were doing, everything came to an immediate halt at 3:00 P.M. At exactly three o'clock on the dot, it was dumpling time. Family time. The ladies took off their aprons, plunked down at booth number one, poured flour on the table, and set down a stack of dumpling wrappers and a big mound of ground meat laced with vermicelli noodles, ginger, scallions, garlic, soy sauce, sesame oil, and fish sauce. Time stood still as the women took the tips of their tablespoons, scooped up just the right amount of meat into the palm of their hands, dropped it into a dumpling wrapper, brushed on the egg wash, folded, and pressed. Then again a thousand times more.

And all the while, they talked shit.

"Yah, did you hear that Eun Ja got a new Mercedes? That ho been tricking for a long time, and now she finally got a sugar daddy and thinks she's all that. It's a nice car, though. . . . Yah, what are you gonna do about what Jee Su said about you? She said you left her with the bill and didn't offer to pay because you guys have no money now and she says that you guys are gonna have to file for bankruptcy. She says that your kids are doing no good in school but her kids just got a summer scholarship to UCLA. . . .

"Yah, do I look fat? Yah, I want to get my eyelids done. Do you think I'll look good? Looklooklook—what do you think? Should I get them done? Should I? . . . Yah, does your husband just come home and fart all day and throw his shit everywhere? . . . Yah, did you hear about the new beef soup place in Garden Grove? Wanna go? But I heard the sisters are fighting there now and the food went

downhill. . . . Yah, let's go shopping. That new stuff from Loehmann's is on sale, and we can get some noodles afterwards. Hurry."

Men, money, hair, wrinkles, gossip, new ventures, books they read, the old days. Anything. Everything.

Time went back on the clock around 4:00 P.M. That's when the dinner rush hit. And that rush was almost always for our signature dish, the hot pot.

The hot pot. Twelve bucks for a family-style serving of spicy kimchi-tofu with shiitake mushrooms, vermicelli noodles, pork neck, shrimp, crab, rock cod, leeks, and a raw egg swirled in seconds before you eat it. The hot pot was served in a tin bowl shaped like a flying saucer with a hole in the middle. Heated by a can of Sterno underneath the saucer, the stew swirled and boiled around in the doughnut ring of heat.

To accompany the hot pot, you could get a warm tofu or rock cod dish braised in soy sauce and rice vinegar, topped with shaved scallions and toasted sesame seeds. And some salted croaker fish and the raw spicy crab, too. And of course you couldn't leave without a plate of panfried dumplings and grilled short ribs. Then, as the Sterno began to sputter, you could mash the rice into the bottom of the stew and turn it into deliciously crispy bits. On top of those greatest hits we had our B-sides. There were twenty-five to thirty dishes on the menu in total, divided into sections for BBQ, stews, soups, dumplings, hot pots, noodles, and rice, plus specials like braised kalbi. All between five and twelve bucks.

At its busiest, the restaurant did two hundred to three hundred covers a night. That's fuller than full—lines-out-the-door full. And that's because nobody, I mean nobody, was doing food as good as Silver Garden back in that day. If Yelp were around back then, Silver Garden would have been on the home page with 4.5 stars, there would have been lines out the door, and there would have been food blogs decorated with photos of that hot pot.

But this was the late seventies and early eighties. We had to rely on the original

AT EXACTLY THREE O'CLOCK ON THE DOT, IT WAS DUMPLING TIME. FAMILY TIME.

form of Yelping: old-fashioned word of mouth. And, damn, word got out fast. Our crowd included the occasional white and Indian folks, but the restaurant was mostly crowded with the small but fierce community of Koreans in Anaheim. We had friends who rolled in a few times a week. Then there were Korean groups who came in after work. Korean guys hungry after a few rounds of golf. My dad took care of these crowds, and the two waitresses—usually young Korean exchange students or little sisters of my mom's friends—took care of the orders.

And me, why, I played maître d'. Before everyone came in, I took care to Windex the front door and windows, made 'em real shiny and clean. I checked on all the tables, made sure the settings were right, had a Coke while waiting for the crowd to arrive. And when they did, I posted up by the cigarette machine and said "Welcome to Silver Garden" and told them they could sit anywhere. Then I'd give a wink to the cute waitress cuz I was a cool cat with a cool little crush on a cool little coed. She'd wink back and greet the table. Every once in a while I'd go back to the Treehouse to check on my sister and take a break to watch TV or read a book with her. Then I was back out on the floor, part of the laughter and the roar, refilling the panchan and water glasses.

Honestly, I probably got in the way a lot. But even then I knew that people were at our restaurant, sitting in our booths, to eat and enjoy themselves. So I tried to have a great time, too. For the first time in my life, the cooking that I was so used to at home was part of everything I was doing—no start point, no end point. For two years it was a beautiful blend of all good things. The garden was in full bloom.

THEN THOSE DAMN CLOUDS started gathering again to rain on our parade. I told you this was West Anaheim, right?

The grass was looking greener on the other side of Brookhurst. There Koreans were turning Garden Grove into the next Koreatown, while our end of the street darkened. Drugs trickled in slowly, then flooded the area like water bursting through a dam. Our neighborhood became the seedy motel capital of the West Coast, occupied mostly by increasing numbers of hookers, transients, bikers, and gangs. Disco was out, heavy metal in. These new residents definitely weren't looking for our brand of hot pot. Eventually, nobody really wanted to come to our part of town—not for a visit and especially not for Korean food.

My parents became grumpier and grumpier and worked harder and longer, and I latchkeyed it like I had never latchkeyed it before. They still found time to put me in the Cub Scouts and Little League, but I knew what was up. We were losing customers, our business. Everything was COD now. Electricity bills paid in the morning to have functioning lights during the day and the night. Then paid again tomorrow morning with last night's take.

My parents, trying to keep Silver Garden alive, added bulgogi mixed-rice bowls and spicy mandoo stews; these didn't really make sense for their menu, but all the newer Garden Grove restaurants offered these, so they tried to make them fit. They painted new signage on the window, brightened up the dining room, made flyers. None of these things worked.

And my parents just couldn't see that they were chasing their own tail. My dad was blind to the weeds in the garden, but it was more from pride than denial. He'd have scotch with his buddies in the restaurant, invite them over to share glorious plates of kalbi and soju, as if we were still ballin'. He coped by showing off the most when he had the least. My mom continued to prep as if three hundred covers were coming in each night, stuffing plastic bucket after plastic bucket with marinating meats and her fantastic kimchi. Night after night, these dishes just sat row after row, orphaned and waiting for people who never showed up. Some of the food rotted and decomposed in the back of the walk-in. Sometimes I went in there, quietly, cleaned it all out, and filled our trash cans to the brim with my mom's amazing food. Enough there to feed a small army, if only the war wasn't already lost.

They started to sell Amway and jewelry out of the restaurant.

One by one, the ajumas, the young waitresses, the dishwasher, the cooks were let go. Then it was just us three working the back and front of the house. And then there were none. It was a pink sky at dusk when Silver Garden began dinner service for the last time. My parents worked fifteen hours that day. They were beaten down, smelling of garlic, and hungover from scotch. There was pain in their eyes, but resilience too. We served our last dish to our last customer. The Humdinger whistled its bells; the birds on the wire silently flew away.

For all the things it may not have been, it was the most beautiful time in my life. The prime time of my mom's life. The first time I picked up on the feeling that food was important and not just a meal to fuel yourself to do something else.

This was my family's restaurant.

This was Silver Garden.

DUMPLING TIME

Dumplings will always be a part of my life. They represent those in-between moments when people sit down to make something together and let their real selves come out. I love dumplings panfried and cooked in boiling salted water. Dumplings are the best gift you can give yourselves or your friends on a lazy afternoon. This recipe shows you how to make both boiled and panfried dumplings.

MAKES 50 TO 60 DUMPLINGS

Vegetable or canola oil for frying

FILLING

4 ounces firm tofu, crumbled
4 ounces ground pork
4 ounces ground beef
1 cup minced scallions
¼ cup minced peeled fresh ginger
¼ cup minced garlic
2 tablespoons oyster sauce
2 tablespoons Asian sesame oil
2 tablespoons roasted and crushed sesame seeds

½ cup finely chopped green cabbage
1 egg
1 tablespoon soy sauce
1 tablespoon natural rice vinegar (not seasoned)
Pinch of kochukaru
Pinch of kosher salt

WRAPPING

1 cup all-purpose flour for dusting
50 to 60 dumpling wrappers

Egg wash (just beat an egg with a splash of water)

DIPPING SAUCE

Equal parts soy sauce and rice vinegar
Pinch of kochukaru

GARNISH FOR DIPPING SAUCE (OPTIONAL)

1 tablespoon minced peeled fresh ginger
1 tablespoon thinly sliced scallion greens

1 garlic clove, minced
1 teaspoon sesame seeds

In a large bowl, mix all the filling ingredients together with delicious and motherly intent, until everything is well incorporated.

Dust a clean table with flour. Lay out your spread: the filling mixture, the wrappers, and the egg wash. Grab some tablespoons. Place a dumpling wrapper in the palm of your hand and scoop a teaspoon of meat into the center. Brush the top edge of the wrapper with egg wash and fold over to make a half-moon, sealing the edges. Be sure to press out any air so the meat purse is intact.

Repeat repeat repeat.

Store your finished dumplings on a sheet pan dusted with flour and keep them covered with plastic wrap so the dumplings don't dry out.

Boil a big pot of salted water, just like you would for pasta. At the same time, heat a large sauté pan over medium heat and add enough vegetable oil to reach about $1/8$ inch up the sides.

Drop half of the dumplings—or as many as will fit in your pot—into the boiling water and reduce the heat, keeping the water at a strong simmer. The dumplings should take about 2 minutes to cook; they will rise to the top when done.

With a slotted spoon or a spider, transfer the dumplings to a plate.

For the other half of the dumplings, place as many as will fit with oil in the sauté pan without overcrowding, bottom-side down. Cook on medium heat until the bottoms are a light golden brown, about 45 seconds. Add 2 tablespoons of water to the pan and cover. When the water has evaporated, the dumplings are done. Remove to a plate and repeat for the remaining dumplings.

For the dipping sauce, mix together the soy sauce and rice vinegar, add the kochukaru, and, if you have them, add the minced ginger, sliced scallions, minced garlic, and sesame seeds. Or, if you've made some Splash (page 121), use that.

GO TO FUCKING TOWN!!!

KOREAN CARPACCIO (SORT OF)

Don't be freaked out about eating raw beef. Raw meat has been consumed for thousands of years; in Korea, it can be traced back to the Mongolian invasion at the end of the Goryeo Dynasty (918–1392). For the beef, buy the best you can: grass-fed, aged, from a good farm. You don't need a lot of it for this recipe, and it's a delicious luxury.

SERVES 4 TO 6

5 ounces top round beef

5 ounces New York (strip) steak

¼ cup plus 1 tablespoon soy sauce

4 tablespoons minced scallions

2 tablespoons minced peeled garlic

1½ tablespoons roasted and crushed sesame seeds

1½ teaspoons kosher salt

¼ teaspoon freshly ground black pepper

1 tablespoon Asian sesame oil

1 Asian pear, peeled, cored, and julienned

1 cup simple syrup

1 or 2 quail eggs

5 garlic cloves, sliced razor-thin

1 tablespoon toasted and ground pine nuts

Slice the beef into thin strips against the grain. Mince the meat just a bit.

Mix the meat with the soy sauce, 3 tablespoons scallions, garlic, 1 tablespoon sesame seeds, salt, pepper, and sesame oil. Massage to mix. Chill the mixture for 1 to 2 hours.

While the meat chills, soak the pear slices in the simple syrup.

When the meat is cold, place it on a plate or in a 10- to 12-inch pan and crack the raw quail eggs over the top.

Drain the pears. Layer the pears, garlic, and pine nuts over the top of the meat. Garnish with remaining scallions and sesame seeds.

TO MAKE SIMPLE SYRUP, COMBINE 1 CUP SUGAR AND 1 CUP WATER IN A SMALL POT, BRING TO A BOIL, AND STIR UNTIL THE SUGAR IS DISSOLVED. ADD A SPLASH OF LEMON JUICE, THEN CHILL THE SYRUP.

GRAB SOME CHIPS OR A SPOON AND ENJOY THE SUBTLE AND DELICIOUS FLAVORS.

INSTANT PICKLED CUCUMBERS

I love to snack, but sometimes chips just bore me the fuck out. Then I try the store-bought pickles, and I'm like, really? So what to do when you want a little kick? Make these damn pickles, that's what you do! These are the best snack.

MAKES ENOUGH FOR 2 TO SNACK

4 Persian cucumbers
2 teaspoons sea salt
2 star anise
2 teaspoons Asian sesame oil
2 teaspoons natural rice vinegar
    (not seasoned)

Pinch of sugar
1 tablespoon roasted and crushed
    sesame seeds
Pinch of kochukaru
Freshly cracked black pepper

Rinse your cukes, then dry them well. Slice them into thin rings on a slicer like a Japanese benriner or a mandoline, sprinkle with the salt, and place in a bowl.

Heat a pan over medium heat for 1 minute, then add the star anise, shaking the pan just until you smell the aroma of the spice. Add the cucumbers to the pan.

While the cucumbers are cooking, mix the sesame oil, vinegar, sugar, sesame seeds, and kochukaru in a small bowl, then add the mixture to the cucumbers in the pan.

Crack some black pepper from a pepper mill over the cucumbers and mix again. Cook for 1 minute more. Remove the cukes and sauce from the heat and scoop into a bowl.

Chill the bowl for 30 minutes, then snack.

I BET YOU WILL EAT
THE WHOLE THING
IN ONE FELL SWOOP!

POTATO PANCAKES

When you say pancakes, you instantly think of sweet. But what if it had nothing to do with sweet? What if it was something savory with potatoes and mung beans in a tempura batter? That might fuck your morning up, wouldn't it? Welcome to my life, and now it can be a part of yours. Keep the syrup in the fridge.

MAKES FOUR TO SIX 5-INCH PANCAKES OR 1 HUGE ONE

- ½ cup dry mung beans
- ½ white or yellow onion, roughly chopped
- ½ cup prepared tempura batter, from store-bought mix
- Fat pinch of kosher salt
- 1 Idaho potato, peeled and grated
- ½ cup minced scallions or fresh chives
- Vegetable oil for frying
- Splash (page 121) or equal parts soy sauce and natural rice vinegar plus a pinch of kochukaru

Soak the dry mung beans in water for at least an hour, then drain.

Combine the chopped onion, tempura batter, mung beans, salt, and a splash of water in a blender and puree. Fold the grated potatoes into the batter and mix in the minced scallions.

Add 2 tablespoons of vegetable oil to a griddle or medium-size pan over medium heat. When the oil starts to smoke, ladle about a fifth of the mixture into the hot pan and let it cook, adjusting the heat as necessary. You want crispy and not burned.

After 1 minute, flip the pancake over and cook on the other side for 1 minute. The pancake should plump up just a bit and be nice and crispy on both sides. Remove and drain on paper towels. Repeat for the rest of the batter.

To serve, bring out the Splash if you have it or mix together the soy sauce, rice vinegar, and kochukaru, and your dipping sauce is good to go.

DIP, BABY, DIP . . .
NOW SLIDE.

KIMCHI STEW

I grew up on kimchi jjigae, or kimchi stew, and, to this day it's what gives me strength. It's my real answer to that tired question "If you had only twenty-four hours to live, what would you eat?" because even though I often change my answer depending on how I imagine my death, at the end of the day, it really is kimchi jjigae stew that I would want to eat. I hope it gives you strength, too.

If you made Kimchi (page 19), feel free to use that here; if not, just pick up a jar from the supermarket.

SERVES 4

8 ounces pork baby back ribs
8 ounces pork belly
2 tablespoons Asian sesame oil
2 cups kimchi, chopped
2 teaspoons minced garlic
½ cup thinly sliced scallions
3 cups pork stock, beef stock, or water

1 cup water
Half of an 8-ounce package firm tofu, cut into medium-size cubes
1 cup shiitake mushrooms, stems removed and discarded
Kosher salt

Slice the mushroom caps in half and set aside.

Score the ribs with a knife and cut the pork belly into small cubes.

Heat a large pot over high heat and add the sesame oil. Toss in the kimchi, the pork ribs, and the pork belly and caramelize them just a touch, about 3 minutes. Then add the garlic and scallions and stir just until they start to release their aroma, about 1 minute.

Add the stock and water. Bring everything to a boil, then lower the heat to a simmer for 20 minutes. Add the tofu and shiitake mushrooms and simmer for about 10 minutes more.

Season with salt to taste.

Eat with rice immediately.

CARAMELIZATION SOUNDS DELICIOUS, AND IT IS. YOU DO IT TO INTENSIFY THE FLAVORS OF THE FOOD YOU'RE COOKING AND TO DRAW OUT A LITTLE BIT OF SWEETNESS. TO CARAMELIZE KIMCHI, MEAT, ONIONS, BOK CHOY, WHATEVER, YOU'RE JUST GOING TO COOK IT NICE AND SLOW UNTIL IT STARTS TO BROWN. IT'LL BE STICKY SWEET.

IT SHOULD BE VISCOUS AND DREAMY.

CHAPTER 3

NECK FROZE

It was the first day. A Monday morning right around the summer between elementary school and junior high. The hallway of the eighth floor of an early-twentieth-century building at 6th and Hill in Downtown Los Angeles, kitty-corner from the wind tunnels of Pershing Square.

The plan on this first day was to start at 6th and Hill, walk up to Olive, then down to Broadway, across to 5th, then back down toward 7th. But first we had to take care of something.

It was quiet in the hall. My parents looked around, all suspicious-like. The coast was clear. "Roy. Put these in your pockets."

White paper rectangles with baby blue paper film on the inside, carefully folded and packaged. They'd open up like origami or an eight ball of coke to reveal a select few diamonds, loose. Hundreds of thousands of dollars' worth. We're talking D-flawless, VVS 1–level rocks. Stuffed deep, deep into my pockets.

Now we were ready to roll.

LESS THAN A YEAR after Silver Garden folded, my parents found themselves back in the jewelry business. It was my uncle Edward—Edward Swoboda—who reintroduced them to the industry. He was born in Oakland and raised in L.A.—Eagle Rock, in fact—in 1917, but he didn't stick around too long. No, he was a debonair Sean Connery type with a hunger for adventure and treasure. He traveled the world in the thirties, forties, fifties searching for gems and minerals. Emeralds in Brazil. Tourmaline in Mexico. Dioptase in Africa. It all paid off: his jewelry line sold at all the high-end stores, from Saks to Dillard's to Neiman Marcus. Hollywood stars in the Golden Age blinged out in his gear.

My mom's older sister worked at a jewelry shop in West Hollywood that sold Edward Swoboda gems. They met, married, and settled down. He became part of our extended family, and it really was just like having Indiana Jones for an uncle. He told me tales of fighting piranhas, meeting Amazonian tribes, digging deep, cramped tunnels hundreds of feet underground somewhere in Mexico. He did it all.

So it was only natural that after Silver Garden closed my dad dusted off his GIA certificate and my mom tapped into the family network. Uncle Edward introduced them to two guys deep in his food chain, Rajiv and Deecan. Rajiv sourced the stones; Deecan set them. Both men trusted my parents because they trusted Edward. They agreed to let my parents have the jewels on consignment, believing in the power of the Korean community to bring home the gold. Game, set, match.

YOU COULD WALK through the doors of almost any of the shops in the Jewelry District of Downtown L.A. and island-hop from one vendor's station to another, browsing jewelry, watches, diamonds in the rough. But pretty as they may look from the top down, put them under a microscope and it's only their flaws that shine.

The best-quality gems were stories and stories above street level, behind exclusive double- and triple-buzzer doors.

Thanks to Uncle Edward, we had the golden ticket to get behind those doors. With that access, my parents hatched their plan: rather than trying to make a profit by selling in volume, they would target the "whales"—the trophy wives of the Korean community all over SoCal. And to go after Moby Dick, they knew they had to use the best bait. Only the best of the best for the best. They, meanwhile, would buy the first-class bait at economy prices. Nothing personal, just business. Great business. And the first stop on the way to building this great business was Rajiv's.

Rajiv worked on the eighth floor of that early-twentieth-century building on the corner of 6th and Hill Street in Downtown L.A. We walked up a twisting staircase made of marble and granite to the second floor, then took an old-school elevator with a gate that clanked shut once you were inside.

The elevator opened up to a narrow hallway that took us to the first door. My parents pressed the buzzer; the door popped open. Another door. We waited. The eyes behind the security camera gave us the once-over. We checked out. We went in. High-tech.

Rajiv's office was so peaceful. Quiet. The smell of warm tea in the air. Venetian blinds sifting the sun's flow onto the facets of stones sitting in piles on his desk like paper clips. There were fifteen piles, to be exact, fifteen neat, beautiful piles of diamonds, emeralds, rubies, and sapphires. It was very cool, but I was young and didn't really have a handle on what I was around. Just a bunch of pretty stones, I thought.

There in the middle of all those jewels was Rajiv, a slender Indian man with dark chocolate–brown skin and a dark mustache. He usually wore a rayon shirt, JC Penney slacks, and soft black loafers; he talked with a lisp and always looked tired. Over the years, he'd become a great family friend, my unofficial uncle.

But before we reached that level of kinship, he was just a strong, quiet guy to me. A strong, quiet guy whom my mom steamrolled every time they met. She came to those meetings prepared: she did her research, paid attention to current styles, predicted future trends. She knew Rajiv's business inside out: that he was just one or two degrees removed from his "reliable" contact, so he could source what she wanted. And that he could get it at a good price because there weren't too many dirty hands marking up the cost between the mines and his office. More than anything, my mom knew that though the diamond trade might have looked all bright and shiny, it was just a show backed up with nothing but big talk. Rajiv

was playing like his rocks were flying off his shelves, but my mom knew he was just bluffing. He wasn't selling shit. Combine all that knowledge with her aggressiveness, and she just ran game on Rajiv.

And so Rajiv cracked under my mom's relentless pressure, handing over the best stuff—no, not the neat, beautiful piles of gems lying around his desk, but the stones hidden and locked in a safe as tall as me—at dirt-cheap prices. In exchange, my parents promised that the inventory would sell within three to six months, max.

With damn fine jewels in hand, we left Rajiv's and hid in the hallway or stairwell outside his office for the next phase of the plan: to stuff my pockets with the jewels. Downtown L.A. wasn't a nice place back then, and my mom figured no one would ever suspect that a twelve-year-old kid like me was carrying anything as valuable as jewels. If one of my parents got hurt or was robbed, their kid—and the gems—would be safe. And so they laid it all on me. Take a look, don't see anyone, quick, put this deep in your pockets. Quick, around your neck, under your shirt. Hush hush quiet now.

We left the building with diamonds lodged on me practically everywhere but the soles of my shoes. I knew I'd be bouncing across Pershing Square under all this weight, but I wasn't too nervous. I think I was cool under pressure because I understood that this was the hustle. This was how it was all supposed to go down.

Back through doors number one and two, down the narrow hallway, down the old-school lift, down the twisting staircase, out in the street. HONK!

We crossed streets, dodged traffic Frogger-style, and moved quickly with the Downtown crowds who also were on the hustle. Sometimes the current flowed too fast, and my mom would grab and hold me and the inventory close before letting us go again. We hit up all the stores around the Jewelry District. Picked up gold at Gold Link, where gold chains hung in neat rows like hammers on a workshop tool board.

I WAS COOL UNDER PRESSURE
BECAUSE I UNDERSTOOD
THAT THIS WAS THE HUSTLE.
THIS WAS HOW IT WAS ALL
SUPPOSED TO GO DOWN.

Then past Broadway to see the guy with the opals and pearls. The pearls had just come in the night before, straight from the South Seas, high quality, no blemishes. They were gorgeous black and silver gumballs, swirling with the most majestic tie-dyed flow I had ever seen outside photos of Jupiter.

Then back out to the busy streets, heading to the next X that marked the next spot on our treasure map. More jewels collected and stashed somewhere on me; by the time we completed our scavenger hunt, I would be wearing layers of loot. Before we could unload, though, we had to collect our breaths. Regroup. Figure things out.

The Yorkshire Grill was—and still is—an olde English "pub" with big, tall ceilings, serving Jewish deli food alongside classic American town square soda fountain drinks and pies. The booths along both sides of the space were covered in brownish red vinyl. Dominating the center of the room was a huge horseshoe counter topped in weathered Formica, where bankers and other workers sat, their jackets hanging on the backs of their seats and their ties over one shoulder to keep them safe from the soup of the day. An Armenian man ran the place. He stood in the front, holding a clipboard and calling everyone by name. He always greeted my parents and me with a warm smile, and, even if there was a line out the door, he always seemed to have an open table for me, my mom, and my dad.

Over corned beef, we all discussed strategy as if we were bandits on the run, high on adrenaline and plotting our next move. Quick decisions over Reubens or crusty French dip; matzo ball soup and a root beer float; liver and onions or a bowl of spaghetti. All washed down with Farmer Brothers coffee brewed through big paper filters and poured piping hot into the kind of mug you hold with three fingers through the handle. As our business progressed, the Yorkshire became our place to gawk at our growth and sales: "I can't believe it's happening!" and, in breathless awe, "Today we are selling a four-carat!" It also became our rendezvous point; we'd assign individual tasks—"Dad will go here; Roy, follow me here" or "Dad's going to the pearls, you get the gold, I'll get the diamonds, meet back at three"—then break huddle, disappear into the busy crowds to execute our duties, and return to the Yorkshire to compare notes. We were a three-man team, each scouring Pershing Square, zone coverage all the way.

But back to those first days. We really had no idea what we were doing. My parents were scribbling notes in fake-eel-skin organizers and writing the script on the fly.

"Okay okay okay, we go to Deecan and make the diagrams, right? Let's look at the Tiffany catalog and the Cartier. What do you see is the point? What is the X factor in this ring?"

Pause pause. Think think.

"I think it's the prongs and how they hold the stone. Or it could be the sloped line on the bottom. I have to explain correctly to Deecan. Roy, you help me explain. Okay?!"

I felt the rush. It swept me away. I was in.

The blueprint was drawn. Time to make the play.

DEECAN'S OFFICE WAS "5 ON 5": the fifth story in a building on 5th Street, not too far from the Yorkshire. I loved going to his office, because it was a true man's place. There was nothing remotely feminine or glam about it. Just ugly Yellow Pages directories stacked up randomly around the room, ugly chairs, ugly calendars, and ugly desk lamps blaring their ugly fluorescent light.

The only delicate thing in the room, actually, was Deecan himself. He was the jeweler who set the stones in moldings, an Armenian man with a big round belly, T-Rex arms, and a thick, bushy bristle broom mustache. He always wore a silk rayon shirt, buttoned up to the midtorso only, to let his chest hairs breathe.

He, like every jeweler out there, was a true craftsman. He was a mechanic who lived under the hood of his magnifying glass, holding tiny tweezers ever so carefully to twist and turn precious metals into prongs to project the light of the set stone just right. His workspace was a big desk cluttered with wax moldings, ring sizers, magnifying glasses, and cigarette butts squished in huge agate and quartz ashtrays.

With Deecan, my mom would work out a bunch of fresh, intricate designs for rings, pendants, bracelets, necklaces, anything. Then they would talk business. They argued over price, over quality, over everything. My mom pushed Deecan hard ("Come on, Deecan, don't give me excuse"), and even though he pushed back ("Mrs. Choi, this is too much! My guys need a break, you are asking too much, how can we make this design by tomorrow? You are asking us to do what Tiffany does with just our small team in one day!"), she still ultimately won the day ("So what. Can you do it, Deecan? Or no? Simple question, simple answer." Silence. "Yes, Mrs. Choi.").

Sometimes my mom ran out of English, and she looked to me to finish her thoughts. *"Oi saekki wae dikkae chun chun ee hanung go ya?* (Why the fuck is this guy so slow and doesn't get my point?) Tell him, Roy," and it was my turn to step up to bat. "Deecan, she is trying to tell you to stop complaining" or "Deecan, she doesn't know how to say it, but she appreciates all your hard work but really needs this by tomorrow" and sometimes even "Deecan, she wants to know how old your kids are this year so she can buy a present" to help smooth things over.

Really, though, I was a release valve so my mom and Deecan could blow off some hot air. We would start to talk about the "point"—that little something that differentiated their gemstone setting from everyone else's and made it that much more beautiful and special—but the conversation would inevitably segue into Little League or what I had eaten that day. When things cooled down and they got back to business, it was my turn to clear my head. We would set a time to hook back up, and, with my pockets still full of stones and my neck frozen with gold, I slipped out for my own alone time.

My first stop was usually downstairs at the juice bar. The fruits and vegetables weren't pretty—the carrots were like old rifle bullets from World War II—but that wasn't the point. This place had some sort of kumbaya and was frequented by the most eclectic band of strangers I'd ever found myself around. There were always homeless guys coming in with stories to tell. Armenian jewelers coming out for a refresher. Older Jewish couples pointing at every single piece of fruit they wanted in their blend. Young Latino guys in dark blue jeans and gold pendants. Me, a twelve-year-old kid, watching it all go down.

I usually ordered a carrot-mango-banana-pineapple from a guy with hairy arms and then sat at the long red Formica counter that ran the length of the storefront window. From there I could watch the action inside the store and gaze at the bustle outside on 5th Street. I watched how the older men moved and talked. I listened to them haggle over a certain piece of fruit, heard stories of how life is a mutha. Women would walk in, and I saw how these shit-talking guys would straighten up for just a second, take a whiff of that female energy, then go right back to shit talking.

Next door was a shawarma spot decked out in red and white tiles. Good but not great. The meat was kind of dry, and the pita wasn't the best, so it was the garlic or tzatziki sauce that was your saving grace. There was extra sauce lying around behind the counter, but it seemed to break code to request another tiny plastic cup of it. As if you were really putting that guy out just by asking. *Just give me boatloads of this stuff, so I can drench in peace, man.* They always gave it to me with a sneer and suspicion, but the point was I got some, and I could move to the corner to unwrap the foil and give my shawarma that extra juice.

Once I was I done, it was back into the wind tunnels of Pershing Square, slicing the shaded streets, looking for that soul of the city. I should have just stayed put, waited for my parents, but something about the city kept me moving, exploring. The tall, old buildings always created dark shadows, making Downtown seem eerie even at noon. I linked up with the swarm of people moving between those buildings, briefcases, bags, umbrellas, accordion files in hand. A look, a stare, a bump, a walk, a weave: everything was a riddle that had to be unpacked in a nanosecond. Nobody seemed happy, but we all wanted to be there, going with the flow.

After a few blocks I left the crowds and ducked into the alleys, catching glimpses of all kinds of transactions. Transactions and dudes taking a piss.

Then I dipped into the rush of the Broadway corridor, which was really transforming into *the* hub for Latino commerce. It was also the street that housed all the old retail courtyards from the twenties, little hideaway gardens that took you deep into the belly of the building, populated by stores and Korean merchants selling underwear and toys.

Stores with neon signs flashing "Oro" lined the streets. Delivery trucks rolled by. Big glass-fronted stores advertising televisions and all the audio/video stuff you would never believe could be so cheap but for the snake oil salesman telling you he had the "best bargain, brand new!"

Then right past the old bus terminal, and right to Los Angeles Street, where the city met Skid Row. Somehow I fit in. I felt like I belonged there for some reason; I could just sit down on the curb, jewels and all, and be myself, listen to guys tell and retell stories and relive cons. Or I could sit at the Greyhound Station nearby, enveloped between old food wrappers, dark clothes, ash marks of dirt and tar and the smell of piss, and watch all the movement. The strangers talking to themselves made me feel like they were talking to me, and I somehow connected to these lost souls in transit. For once, it wasn't just me that was in constant flux.

When the sun started to set west over the buildings, I knew it was time to get back to Pershing Square. I cut through the Toy District, weaved through hot dog carts and Spider-Man backpacks, and went back to 5 on 5 and Deecan's man cave. I always hurried, but I was always late and would get an earful for it. Sometimes I wasn't sure whether everyone was worried about me or just about the jewels. Either way, though, at least they cared.

My parents picked out the gems they planned to sell and gave them to Deecan to set, along with a few parting gifts like kimchi and pancakes. What they didn't take off me stayed on until we got home and put them in the safe. This meant I was still loaded when we stopped at Clifton's Cafeteria for an early dinner. Clifton's was a rabbit hole of LSD–laced, Jungle Cruise far-out dreams. The entrance was laid out in mosaic tile and, as we walked through, we had to scurry and get in line.

The room was filled with hanging vines and red booths and chairs. Everyone in there seemed old as fuck, whirling around the brass food island, poking their heads under the heat lamps and sneeze guards to get a whiff of the meat loaf or the corned beef and cabbage or the carrot salad or the sauerbraten or the Jell-O. You paid for everything you put on your tray, so you can imagine how many things I had to put back. And quickly. *Keep moving,* my dad would always nudge, because, man, you had to keep moving. The last thing you wanted was some granny pushing all up on your back, telling you to hurry up.

Finally, the last stop of the day for one last piece of treasure: Chinatown for some almond cookies. Phoenix Bakery's sun-bleached sign has sat on the north end of Broadway for decades. It's a real old-school place with sprinkled cakes, big smiley-face cookies, and shoehorn pastries. The girls working there always seemed like the owners' daughters, just a bit older than me. I crushed on them hard. Twelve to thirteen with a dream— can you blame me?

But more than anything, I loved the bakery for those almond cookies. Glazed and buttery. Dense and filled with sweet aromas of almond paste and extract. I'd run up and take a number, wait for a pretty girl to call me up, and order a pink box filled with the best cookies I would ever eat in my life, ever.

After Phoenix, it was back home to work on the other side of the hustle: the hard sell.

THIS WAS THE EARLY EIGHTIES, and Reaganomics was in full bloom. Koreans were getting rich with import-export businesses, filling up communities out in Palos Verdes, Orange County, La Cañada, and Hacienda Heights. Mercedes S-Classes were in session. Chanel bags. Hermès scarves. My parents knew it. And they worked it.

They went back to hustling, like in the days before the restaurant. My dad's top-of-the-class Kyunggi-Seoul rep still held weight in the community; it opened doors and built trust. Then my mom made her entrance and went into action; instead of kimchi calling, this time it was jewelry on the line. Sketches were shown and the jewelry she took on consignment sold at *kyae* meetings, friends' homes, golf courses, and restaurants. Her jewelry designs were really that fly, but they only sold as well as they did because my mom was the salesperson of all salespersons. The closer, Glengarry Glen Ross with brass fucking balls. She knew you lived in Palos Verdes. She knew your husband was Dr. Kim, the best surgeon in town. She knew you had more money than you knew what to do with. So, you *would* be buying this $150,000 D-Flawless diamond ring with princess setting because no one else had it and *of course* you wanted to be the first to show off when all the wives got together that week. And at only 10 percent markup from wholesale instead of the 60 percent that Tiffany and other retailers charge? Did you really have to think about it? Sold, cash in hand, end of discussion.

It fucking worked. One by one they bought our stock, and they bought it anywhere, every time. The golf-gear- and St. John–wearing, nip-tuck, Givenchy-powdered ladies always wanted what they wanted right here, right now. We sold jewelry on the spot at informal get-togethers. We went door-to-door by appointment. We made sales at saunas. Hell, we even sold out of the back of our car. A three-carat D-Flawless stone set by Deecan, to a lady with Estée Lauder makeup who rolled up in an S-Class.

Sold, a South Sea pearl necklace right off my neck.

Sold, an emerald from Brazil set atop sliced baguettes of yellow diamonds.

These were whales of sales. Our quality became legendary. Word got to Korea, and generals, politicians, and tycoons started buying.

We bought a small storefront in Garden Grove, with tinted windows, a double-buzzer lock, and comfy couches for ladies to meet and gossip, 3:00 P.M. dumpling style. Choi Jewelry wasn't open to the public: if you were there, it was because someone referred you there. And so even though my dad set up jewelry cases on the counter, those were empty. Just decoration. The good stuff—everything, in other words—was in the back, locked safe in a safe, waiting for a whale.

The ocean was full of whales. Within three years, we were millionaires.

Everything was about to change.

LEBANESE BEE'S KNEES

The rush of toasted cumin and garlic runs through me like a needle. Heroin. I don't care much for carousels with horses on them; no, it's the one that has a cone of meat wrapped around it that sings my tune. I make my shawarma out of grilled meat, but by all means, if you have a rotating-spit oven or feel like making a fire and indirectly turning the meat Pampa-style a foot away from the flames, you would be my hero.

2 pounds lamb chops or rib-eye steaks
    or beef hearts or even pork belly,
    thinly sliced

MARINADE

12 garlic cloves, peeled and crushed
½ onion, sliced
½ cup extra virgin olive oil
Juice of 2 lemons
3 tablespoons dried oregano
Three 3-inch cinnamon sticks, broken
1 teaspoon ground allspice

Pinch of cayenne
Kosher salt and freshly cracked
    black pepper to taste
½ teaspoon ground cumin
8 sprigs fresh thyme
½ cup chopped fresh cilantro
½ cup chopped fresh flat-leaf parsley

YOGURT SAUCE

1 cup yogurt
2 tablespoons sour cream
1 tablespoon minced garlic
Juice of 1 lime
Juice of ½ lemon
Kosher salt and freshly ground black
    pepper to taste

1 teaspoon dried dill
1 teaspoon chopped fresh flat-leaf
    parsley
1 tablespoon extra virgin olive oil

SANDWICHES

Pita bread
1 red onion, thinly sliced
2 tomatoes, thinly sliced

FOR THE TABLE

3 lemons, halved
Kosher salt

In a bowl large enough to hold the meat, mix together all of the ingredients for the marinade. Add the meat to the marinade and let the meat marinate, covered, in the fridge for at least 4 hours, but preferably overnight, turning the meat periodically if you can.

When the meat is ready, prepare your grill for medium heat and start cooking your meat, making sure to get a nice charred crust on the outside. Then move it to a cooler part of your grill and cook it low and slow for about 10 minutes, or until the lamb is medium-rare.

While the meat cooks, mix together all of the ingredients for the yogurt sauce in a small bowl.

Grab a few pita breads and throw them over the coals to get them a bit charred and crusty.

When the meat is done, take it off the grill and let it rest for 5 minutes. Once the meat has rested, chop it roughly into bite-size pieces.

Slather the yogurt sauce on the pitas, then fill them with the chopped meat, red onion, and tomatoes. Make sure to have some cut lemons and salt lying around to splash on as you wish.

You might want to triple this recipe and eat more!

CHORIZO FOR BREAKFAST, CHORIZO FOR LUNCH, CHORIZO FOR DINNER, CHORIZO TO MUNCH

On our way to work the gem game in the Jewelry District, or sometimes on our way back late at night, my parents and I would take a break from Clifton's Cafeteria and hit IHOP or another coffee shop instead. My dad always ordered corned beef and hash. My mom had the lumberjack. And me?

Chorizo and eggs, my friend.

SERVES 4 TO 6

3 ancho chiles, seeded
2 pasilla chiles, seeded
2 jalapeño peppers, seeded
¼ teaspoon dried oregano
¼ teaspoon ground coriander
2 teaspoons Hungarian paprika
Pinch of ground cloves
Pinch of ground cumin

½ cup rice wine vinegar
4 garlic cloves, minced
2 pounds pork butt, ground
3 tablespoons extra virgin olive oil
Kosher salt and freshly ground black
   pepper
Enough large eggs for everyone
1 lime, halved

FOR THE TABLE
Corn tortillas
A few avocados, peeled, pitted, and
   sliced
Bottle of Tapatío or other hot sauce

Place a small pan over medium heat and toast all the chiles together, then remove and cool.

In a food processor, combine the chiles with the herbs and spices and grind to a powder. Place the mixture in a small bowl, then add the vinegar and garlic.

In a large bowl, combine the chile mixture and the ground pork and mix it well with delicious intent. Let the meat mixture marinate in the refrigerator, covered, overnight or for up to 2 days; immediately freeze whatever you will not eat.

Pull the meat out of the refrigerator and place a large pan over medium heat. Add the olive oil to the pan and then the meat. Cook, seasoning the meat with salt and pepper to taste.

Into another pan, crack enough eggs for everyone and cook them any way you like 'em.

While you're at it, warm up some corn tortillas and scoop out some avocado.

Plate the chorizo and eggs for each person at the table, adding a squeeze of lime over the chorizo. Eat with hot sauce.

WELCOME TO CALI.

WINDOWPANE SMOOTHIES

My eyes would glaze, and my ears would sonar into the stories: Sucking down on a straw filled with fruit, I was transported to my own private Idaho in the hustle-bustle of Downtown L.A.'s Jewelry District. Feel free to get creative with the fruits.

MAKES 4 TO 5 SMOOTHIES

One 14-ounce can coconut milk, shaken
¼ cup agave nectar
Juice of ¼ lime
½ cup fresh or frozen strawberries, stemmed and hulled
½ cup cubed fresh or frozen mango
½ cup sliced fresh or frozen peach
½ cup cubed fresh or frozen pineapple
¼ cup sliced fresh or frozen banana
Half of a 46-ounce can pineapple juice, shaken

In a large bowl or pitcher, mix the coconut milk, agave nectar, and lime juice.

Place the fruit in a blender and add 1 cup of the pineapple juice and 1 cup of the coconut milk mixture. Blend until smooth, adding more pineapple juice or more coconut milk until it meets your desired consistency and taste. Add some crushed ice if you please.

Pour the smoothie into cups and enjoy with a big thick straw.

CHINATOWN ALMOND COOKIES

I'm not really a big-thick-chocolate-walnut-cookie kind of guy. Instead, I love shortbreads with a passion. Wafers filled with lemon cream make me think devious thoughts. I can also get down with the ghetto market stuff like Soft Batch and the old Flaky Flix. Christina Tosi of Momofuku Milk Bar fame bakes some pretty cool cookies, and who doesn't love an Oreo with a glass of milk? But, really, there are two types of cookies that I can eat for days. Elephant ears—or more eloquently, palmiers—and Chinese almond cookies keep this monster fed. This is a simple recipe for Chinese almond cookies, inspired by my friend John. Cookie, cookie, cookie.

MAKES ABOUT 18 BIG COOKIES
OR ABOUT 36 SMALL ONES

12 tablespoons (1½ sticks) unsalted
    butter, softened
½ cup plus 2 tablespoons sugar
1¾ cups all-purpose flour

1 tablespoon almond extract
Pinch of kosher salt
½ cup toasted slivered almonds for
    garnish

Preheat the oven to 325°F.

Cream the butter and sugar with an electric mixer or a stand mixer with the paddle attachment, then add the flour, almond extract, and salt. Mix until just incorporated and transfer the dough to a clean work surface. Lightly knead the dough, then wrap it in plastic and chill for at least 30 minutes.

When you're ready to bake, remove the dough from the fridge, scoop out golf-ball-size rounds of dough with a spoon, place them on a greased sheet pan about 2 inches apart, and flatten them slightly with the palm of your hand.

Bake the cookies for 18 to 22 minutes, until they're nice and caramel colored.

Transfer the cookies to cooling racks. While they're still warm, stick an almond sliver in the center of each cookie.

PUT IN PINK BOXES
AND COME WITH ME
BACK TO CHINATOWN.

PIE, GIVE THEM PIE! PECAN PIE WILL DO.

I spent a lot of time in coffee shops and delis during this time of my life. Weaving through Downtown and dipping in and out of Clifton's and Yorkshire Grill I found myself smitten with pie. L.A. had some great coffee shops; even the chains like Denny's, Ship's, and Norms had pie carousels. And there was always Marie Callender's, the Jewish delis on the West Side and up in the Valley, plus the *Pulp Fiction*–esque coffee shops of the fifties and sixties all throughout the zones near LAX.

Pecan pie is my favorite thing to eat, period.

MAKES 1 PIE

3 eggs
1 cup dark corn syrup
½ cup sugar
4 tablespoons (½ stick) unsalted butter, melted
1¼ teaspoons vanilla extract

Pinch of ground cinnamon
1 cup pecan halves
1 store-bought 9-inch regular single-crust piecrust, par-baked according to package instructions

Preheat the oven to 350°F.

In a medium bowl, beat the eggs until they're frothy, about 4 minutes. Fold in the corn syrup, sugar, butter, and vanilla extract, and beat again for 2 minutes. Fold in the cinnamon.

Layer the pecans in the bottom of the piecrust and pour the egg mixture evenly over the nuts until it reaches just below the rim of the piecrust.

Bake for 1 hour, until the filling is set.

Rest the pie for an hour. Cut. Eat.

Powdered sugar or a scoop of vanilla ice cream goes well with a slice.

CHAPTER 4

NOLAN RYAN

The rims were wire spokes with a flick of gold. The body, a brand-new royal blue. And I don't even know what you would call that interior. It was royal blue, too, and felt plush, like velvet. Everything was electric, and the trunk was big enough to fit a baby grand piano. My sister and I were in the backseat, smiling at each other as we tinkered with the window controls, fiddled with the hand rest, listened to a stereo fit for an audiophile. In the front, my parents looked like they were a million miles away, laughing and holding hands. It was so lucid and surreal, like a lens filtering a vision of the future through to us. Except the future was what was happening now.

We had just upgraded from our old brown station wagon to this four-door 1984 Cadillac Fleetwood Brougham. Fully loaded, sun roof and everything. I can't remember whether I was there at the dealership when my dad bought it, but I sure as hell remember when he brought it back to our apartment. That shit stood the fuck out! It was a pimpmobile, and my dad was its driver, Fillmore Slim reborn.

That Caddy was taking us from a little month-to-month apartment in Koreatown to our new home on moving day. Other than the fact that we were moving, my dad didn't tell us much, and I had no idea where we were going. But that was fine; by now, stuff like this had become a normal happenstance, a blip in the everyday: we moved eight times before I was thirteen. We'd open a shop, move nearby, see it go out of business, put stuff in storage, find a cheaper rental somewhere else, start a new shop or help friends with theirs, and so on and so on. What was one more time?

But moving in the Caddy was different. In retrospect, it seemed to embody the very world it was transporting us to, but I didn't notice that part of it then. I was too busy getting lost in the *Leave It to Beaver* family fun, in the fantasy of the American dream.

At some point I looked out the window, expecting to see nothing more than strip mall after strip mall crowded with dingy stores. Instead, what I saw made me stare: plaza after plaza of pretty markets covered in Spanish tile. Even the trees looked different. So did the street signs. Each house we passed was exponentially larger and more ornate than the last. There were beautiful lawns and carefully manicured landscapes. Benzes and Beemers parked in driveways, with luxurious, wide streets to accommodate them.

When I glanced up at the rearview mirror, I could see the smile in my dad's eyes. Before I could say or ask anything, he pulled the car into the long driveway of our very own new home. There really was a white picket fence. I was Dorothy for a moment, clutching my sister like she was Toto.

The house was all white, a long, low-slung ranch house with a half-a-million-dollar price tag back in 1983. A brown shingle roof and a three-car garage. The sign on the greener-than-green lawn said SOLD.

I can only imagine what my dad was thinking as he pulled into that swoosh

of a driveway. It had taken him fourteen years, but he had done it. Finally, he could provide the best for his family. Finally, there would be no more worries. It was all clear skies from here.

He tapped us all on the shoulders and skipped excitedly to the front door. I was still in shock, a little confused and, to be honest, a bit annoyed. We had literally packed up the night before, then my dad shows up in the morning with this fancy car, and he's happy, and he takes us to this white house with a picket fence and big driveway. And still, no one had told us what was going on or prepared us for anything. *Where the fuck have you taken me? Why are you so giddy all of a sudden? Where is my real dad?*

The key had a shine to it and seemed to fit in the lock ever so perfectly. I could hear the bolt disengage; the key turned and, with it, my whole soul. He opened the door to a foyer lined with flocked yellow wallpaper patterned in daisies and tulips. To the left a high-ceilinged room, the future setting of nights of drinking, partying, and obscene amounts of food adventures. We swung to the right, still stepping gingerly on our new floors as if we were Goldilocks sneaking around the home of the Three Bears. It seemed like my dad knew his way around; he kept telling us to hurry. Look at this; check that out; that's amazing. But I wasn't in the mood for amazing. I was still wondering what the fuck had just happened to my life.

My dad led me and my sister past the family room and its big redbrick fireplace, past the kitchen, down a long hallway, past a few rooms, finally stopping at the end of the hall. The bathroom. We walked into this bathroom, and he flipped up the toilet seat, placed his foot on top of the rim, and did the most glorious of toilet flushes humankind has ever seen. As the water refilled the bowl, he looked straight at me and asked, "Do you know who took a dump in this toilet?"

"Um, not really, Dad . . ."

"Well, let me tell you! Nolan Ryan. One of the greatest pitchers of all time. A-hundred-three-miles-per-hour fastball. This was his home. He was traded from the California Angels, and now this is *our* home."

"Wow, Dad. That's pretty cool!"

It really was kind of cool. There was a moment there. A tender father-son moment right at the height of my grumpy thirteen- to fourteen-year-old puberty phase, right before my parents became deep alcoholics, right before I started getting deep into drugs, right before it was my childhood naïveté that would be flushed down the toilet.

But for now, it was my dad, his foot proudly on the toilet bowl as if he were George Washington crossing the Potomac, having a moment with his son. I'd be a real dickhead not to go along with the ride and rain on his parade. So I smiled and said, "This is great, Dad. Show me more."

He showed us around each room and said, "You can have this one, and your sister, Julie, can have this one." Our rooms picked out, we all ran to the kitchen to find my mom; she was opening every cupboard, and I could see the wheels turning as she imagined all the kimchi and stew that this kitchen could produce.

Outside, the backyard was huge and wrapped around the house; it was filled with trees, and there was a concrete patio under a wooden trellis. And there, on the side lawn, a long, narrow area lined with grass, set up an awful lot like a pitcher's mound and home plate.

It really *was* Nolan Ryan's old house.

I held on to the dreams of the Ryan Express as I failed miserably throughout junior high school baseball, hoping against hope that by just living and breathing in his home, I, too, would become a major-league pitcher. I'd strike out, but it certainly wasn't for lack of trying.

THE MOVERS WOULD BRING our furniture, but we brought the kimchi. Our priorities were in order. We carried in at least thirty-five Tupperware containers of triple-Saran-wrapped soy-dried beef, radish water kimchi, spicy fish intestine, preserved eggs, cucumber kimchi, oyster cabbage kimchi, scallion soybean paste, dried squid, skate panchan, and pickled garlic to bless our brand-new home, our brand-new neighborhood.

As my mom busily unpacked all the food and my dad twirled my sister in the air, I decided to take a walk. I had to catch my breath and get some fresh air. All that hunky-dory nuclear-family everything-is-perfect-in-the-world shit was making me woozy. I needed to roam.

Outside on the wide, nicely paved streets, everything was so quiet. No one seemed to be around, but sprinklers watered the perfectly trimmed lawns and cars were parked in almost every driveway on our street. I could almost feel the eyes peering out at me from behind the partially drawn curtains, wondering who the new neighbors were, where we were from.

As I made my turn toward the street, a boy came out of the house across the way. He gave me the warmest hello. His name, I'd later learn, was David, and he was a year younger than me. We'd hang out a little, play some basketball. But on this first day I was in no mood to meet the neighbors, so I just nodded back and headed toward the town square. The back of the town square, specifically. I figured I'd walk in through the plaza from the back to check out the alley. There I thought I'd see what really went down in this town.

But the alley was pristine. Everything was neatly stacked. No graffiti, no trash. I went around to the front and realized it was a Ralphs supermarket. It was around October, and the entrance overflowed with beautiful pumpkins. The walls were plastered with drawings of witches and goblins, none of which looked scary—the witches looked like the Good Witch, and there were handsome goblins to match. There were people giving each other hugs, moms chatting away with their young

EVERYBODY WAS WHITE.
WHITE. ALL WHITE.
IT BLEW MY MIND.

kids in tow. Girl Scouts and AYSO tables set up on the sidewalk. Everything was moving in such harmony, so clean, so cheerful.

Something nagged at me. I just couldn't put my finger on it, though, couldn't place it. What was different about this place? There was something. Something beyond all the cleanliness, beyond the birds singing, beyond the smiles, beyond the serenity. Then, right as I caught my reflection in the supermarket security mirror, it hit me.

Everybody was white.

White. All white.

It blew my mind.

I didn't see another Asian, Latino, black, or Indian kid. For days. Literally.

I really wasn't in Kansas anymore. This was Villa Park, Orange County, a small town of 2.1 square miles that, even though it was surrounded by the lower- and middle-class cities of Orange and Anaheim, was populated with doctors and lawyers and CEOs living in million-dollar homes on streets with names like Covington Circle, Peppertree Drive, and Colony Grove Lane. A town that had fewer than a dozen stop signs, no streetlamps, and no lighted signs. A town cut out from the hillsides of the Santiago Mountains. There was no bus system, and trust, if you walked the streets, you would get stopped by Villa Park's finest. Almost every kid got a new car at sixteen, and girls actually attended a debutante ball.

I was doomed.

SEVENTH GRADE WAS ALREADY into its first month when we moved to town, so I had to jump on that moving train while also dealing with all the shit that comes with puberty and pimples. By then I was a geeky thirteen-year-old, with braces and a peach-fuzz mustache, tall and growing taller (from five-foot-six to five-ten in three months!). For all the ups and downs of being a latchkey kid, for all the thrills of hiding jewels on my person across Downtown Los Angeles, nothing could have prepared me for Cerro Villa Junior High School.

Everybody dressed in shorts and flip-flops and had peroxide-blond hair. There were some Goth kids and some rockabillys and a couple Mohawks mixed into the scene. The girls were so pretty with their sandy blond hair, and the dudes seemed so cool talking about surfing sets at Newport Beach and the knee-deep powder at Mammoth Mountain. Everybody listened to Oingo Boingo, Depeche Mode, and the Cure.

Me, I tried to catch up, but I felt like I was a lifetime behind. I had never heard of alt-rock, because I was watching *Soul Train* and listening to oldies. Up until this point I was pretty shy and never had too many friends—we moved too much for me to have anything other than a few school friends at any given moment. And here I was the new kid at school again. I looked for my angle to fit in.

They put me in honors classes with all the smart kids, and I don't know if that was my mom up to her old tricks or if that's where all the Asians just automatically went. Because that's where I saw *all* the Asian kids in the school. All three of them. They were quiet and smart and kept to themselves in their own little group. But that wasn't for me. I didn't want to be another weird Asian kid in an all-white school, a furry new pet orangutan to look at and poke. So I went on the offense first: I became the class clown. I played dumb and cracked jokes in class. And it worked.

The kids in class thought I was hilarious. *Oh shit, did you really just say that!?* Yeah, shit, I really *did* just say that. I was sent to the principal's office a lot as a result of just saying this and that, but I always exited the classroom to a standing ovation. I was laying tracks in this new town, and I sure as hell was going to make sure everyone could hear my beat.

OUTSIDE MY CLASS CLOWNING, I played sports. Offensive lineman on the football team, third baseman on the baseball team, bench warmer on the basketball team. I took up other extracurriculars, too: Home ec. Woodshop. And band. I picked up the trombone because it looked simple compared to the saxophone and trumpet, and it looked real fun, too, with the slide bar and the big mouthpiece. I was curious about how the sound came through an instrument without buttons or signals for the note; I wanted to figure it out. I thought it'd be an easy riddle to crack, but boy was I wrong.

Lucky for me, I sat next to a guy named Rodney, a pudgy white guy with a crew cut and reddish freckles, always with his backpack real high and tight on his back. He was a saxophone man, and together we'd try to figure out how the hell to play our instruments. Just like a real team. We only really hung out before, during, and after class, but sometimes that's all you need to forge a bond. He was quiet and strong, and though he never really laughed, he did have a dry sense of humor, and he always cracked a smile at my clownin' ways.

Rodney was my first real friend in this new Oz, but it wasn't meant to be.

He loved the outdoors, especially dirt bikes and ATVs. One day toward the end of seventh grade, his ATV flipped over backward as he rode it up a sand dune, crushing him. He was the first of three best friends in my life to die too early, and those last few weeks of school after his death were especially awful. A lonely trombone player wailing next to an empty seat.

I MET FRANK in honors English, while I was clowning real hard on Thoreau and *Walden*. I had the whole class in stitches and my teacher really believing my stupid questions about a deer who had feelings. That caught Frank's attention. He invited me over to his house to hang, and we just hit it off right away.

Frank was a kid beyond his thirteen years, a mutt mix of Irish, Mexican, Italian, and who knows what else. He was tall with curly brown hair and a wiry muscular frame. He had a younger sister we called Goo-Goo and a younger brother, Max. He wasn't that rich, and his parents were going through some relationship problems, so he found his release in hard-core heavy metal, the satanic bible, and *Monty Python,* all of which he introduced me to, his captive audience. I often stuck around his place for dinner; his family cooked a lot—mostly some version of home-style Mexican food like chili verde, tamales, nachos, barbacoa—and I really enjoyed eating there and having dinnertime with my new best friend.

But while Frank and I operated roughly on the same level, the other kids at school were playing a totally different game. If I was culture-shocked by all that peroxide and shit I saw on campus, I was electrified when I saw what went on in those boys' and girls' homes. Walking into their houses was like nothing I had ever seen or even knew existed: we're talking 6,500-square-foot mini-mansions with huge spare rooms lined with arcade games, pinball machines, and pool tables. Closets that resembled the inside of a Ralph Lauren store. Interiors decked out in hand-carved mahogany woodwork and Italian marble. Backyards that looked like public parks with their full-sized tennis and basketball courts and fully landscaped rock formation swimming pools. Six-car garages.

And their kitchens! Refrigerators the size of whole walls, masked in the same woodwork as the banisters. Inside, fruit platters. Who the fuck has fruit platters in their fridge just because? On top of that, four different kinds of juice, every flavor of yogurt, ten different kinds of cold cuts, five different kinds of sodas, ice cream in every color of the rainbow. Pop open the freezer: so many frozen TV dinners that they had to be stacked on their sides like books on a shelf.

Their pantries were filled with more cookies than I could count, and if you wanted chips and dip, you had your choice of seven different types of chips and, for dip, anything from bean to guacamole. Then Pop-Tarts, cereals, cookies, fruit roll-ups, two-liter soda bottles. I dug it big-time and went to town.

Let's put those Pop-Tarts in the toaster and unwrap all the fruit roll-ups and paste them together to make one large blanket to eat. Okay, I'll take a chocolate chip cookie, an iced oatmeal cookie, a butter cookie, a Nilla wafer, and a couple logs of Flaky Flix. You got chocolate milk *and* strawberry milk? Bring it.

At first my new friends were a little shocked by my culture shock. But it just took one crazy guy—me—to jump in the pool, and all the racial and cultural barriers were lifted. Then it was like, fuck it. Dive in. All the food they knew as normal became fun again as they watched Tarzan in the City devour it all, fistful by fistful.

BACK HOME, I wasn't disappointed so much as I was reality-checked. Our refrigerator wasn't carved out of teak harvested from an Indonesian forest, and it sure as hell didn't have shingled fruit platters and Brie cheese. Instead, it was filled with bubbling cauldrons of spicy fermentation. Our house smelled like kimchi and sour soybean paste, not potpourri and potatoes. And that was okay by me: sometimes no matter how exciting a new trip can be, all you want to do is get back home, curl up with your own pillow, and sink into its comforting, familiar reality. Even if that reality consists of salted aged fish eggs and grilled pig intestines.

But even as the food in our fridge gave me something to hold on to in my brand-new world, watching my parents navigate theirs set me afloat all over again. They were doing exactly what they thought they had to do for business, for networking, for the family: working every day at the store and in the trenches of Downtown L.A., of course, but also drinking and partying more and more. Staying out late at karaoke bars. Kissing the ass of important politicians and doctors within the Korean community. Just to sell a damn rock.

I watched all this go down and knew they could run circles around half those jokers. I wanted them to run those laps—but, no, they were content to be the ones playing the court jesters just so they could make the sale. I wished they didn't. I wished they could see that they were the kings, not the clowns.

But even though I wished it was different, I knew they thought they were laying the foundation and setting the perfect path for their kids to earn countless achievement awards, score high on the SATs, graduate at the tops of their classes, and attend Ivy League schools. Boom boom boom. Our new life was supposed to be the perfect incubator for my sister and me.

But.

But they were so busy paving that golden road they forgot to check to see if I was ready to go. If they had, they would have found their golden boy slowly heading in the opposite direction, following Frank into the comfort of his world, moving on from K-EARTH 101 ("The Greatest Hits on Earth") to KNAC 105.5 ("PURE ROCK"), swapping Barry White for Black Sabbath, Frankie Valli for Led Zeppelin. And taking that crucial first puff of weed. When seventh grade came to an end, so did my innocence.

Not even the Cure could save me.

MAGIC FISH DIP

The refrigerators of my classmates at Villa Park were stuffed full of all sorts of dip: onion dip, cheese dip, you name it. As for me, our house always had something pink in my refrigerator, but it wasn't fruit punch. No, there were fish eggs. Having fish eggs on hand in your fridge is like having a special pouch of magic dust in your hip sack for whenever and whatevas.

This is a little paste I came up with that's perfect for using up those sacks of frozen pollack roe you may or may not have in your freezer.

MAKES 1 CUP OF MAGIC

½ cup pollack fish roe, crumbled
(you can use salmon roe, flying fish
roe, even caviar or jarred salted
baby shrimp)
½ cup thinly sliced scallions
½ cup minced jalapeño peppers,
seeds and all

1 tablespoon plus 1 teaspoon kochukaru
1 teaspoon roasted sesame seeds
2 tablespoons minced garlic
1 tablespoon plus 1 teaspoon Asian
sesame oil
¾ cup soy sauce
¼ cup water

Mix everything together and store in an airtight container in the refrigerator.

Spread on toast or mix with rice.

FRUIT ROLL UPS AND DOWNS

My mom had a food dehydrator back in the day, and I'd come home from school and find octopus or squid or fish or oysters in that muthafucka. Now, how do you bring non-Asian high school friends home to that? It was a social scar for sure in my teenage years, but I ate that shit. I loved that shit. And sometimes she'd put persimmons and other fruits in there, and they'd end up tasting like fish, too. Ha! This one plays off the supermarket roll-ups you may have grown up with, then gets remixed in the Choi family dehydrator. Trip out.

MAKES ENOUGH FOR 4 TO PEEL AND SNACK

3 cups water

2 cups sugar

2 tablespoons fresh lemon juice

2 star anise

2 kaffir lime leaves

½ teaspoon pink peppercorns

One 3-inch cinnamon stick

2 apples, cored and sliced into thin
    rounds (hold in water with a splash
    of lemon juice until ready)

1 pineapple, peeled and thinly sliced
    lengthwise into wide strips

Preheat the oven to 175°F or prepare a food dehydrator.

Combine the water, sugar, lemon juice, and spices in a medium saucepan and bring the mixture to a boil. Whisk the mixture, lower the heat, and let it simmer for 5 minutes.

Starting with the apples, dip each slice into the simmering sugar liquid, then place gently on a silicone-mat-lined sheet pan or on dehydrator racks, making sure to shingle each slice a quarter over the next one to create a quilt of sorts.

Repeat with the strips of pineapple until the whole sheet pan or dehydrator rack is filled in one single layer. If you run out of room, layer the remaining fruit on a second sheet pan.

Place the fruit in the oven or dehydrator until dry, about 2 hours. Pull out and let cool.

Peel the fruit off the pans or racks and eat like Tarzan.

CHIPS AND DIP

In high school, I loved that onion dip you'd find in the refrigerated aisle at American supermarkets. Man, that was so other world for me. Sometimes my parents would come back from a trip to the supermarket with onion dip and other weird-ass things they pulled off the shelves as they walked down the bright aisles—canned ham, flavored onion packets, pork and beans. And we'd store them all away alongside the fish paste in the pantry and the kimchi in the fridge. Any Asian kid, from Pinoy to Viet to Korean, had parents who did the same thing. For my version of chips and dip, I just wanted to pay homage to how we integrated into American life.

MAKES ENOUGH CHIPS AND DIP FOR 6 TO 8

DIP

2 cups sour cream

½ cup fresh lime juice

¼ cup plus 2 tablespoons prepared
   horseradish

1 tablespoon freshly ground black pepper

2 tablespoons kosher salt

¼ cup grated fresh horseradish

Splash of Tabasco sauce

½ cup chopped fresh herbs,
   any herbs you want

CHIPS

1 pound taro root

1 pound Idaho potatoes

Fine sea salt

2 cups vegetable oil

Whisk together all the ingredients for the dip and set aside.

In a deep fryer or other deep pot, heat the oil to 300°F.

Wash and peel the taro and slice it thinly on a slicer like a Japanese benriner or a mandoline. Soak the slices in water to preserve their color.

Wash and thinly slice the potato lengthwise and store in water.

Layer a sheet pan with paper towels. When you're ready to fry, drain and pat dry with paper towels the taro root and potatoes and start flipping the chips into the fryer, being sure not to overcrowd the basket. Then swirl everything around with a spider spatula.

Swish them around from time to time until the chips are a light brown color all around, about 1 minute; then immediately transfer them to the paper-towel-lined pan and season with salt while hot.

Repeat with all the chips until done.

Make about 30 percent more than you anticipate eating because you will eat that extra 30 percent as you cook them. Leftover dip will keep, covered and stored in the fridge, for 3 days.

Enjoy my sour cream and onion bag of chips.

THAT'S SO SWEET

I've always loved the sauces in life more than the food—maybe that's why I cook the way I do. So it's no surprise that I'm a sauce packet fiend. If I go to a fast-food joint or the mall food court, my tray is like twenty-five deep in the packets. And it's not that I'm hoarding all this shit; no, I have a ritual. I'm real anal about my packet game. I open 'em all before I eat anything, and make my sauces. I blend and mix and create. Then people say, "Oh, he drowns his tacos and rice bowls in too much sauce." Guilty as charged. Drown your chicken or shrimp in this sauce.

MAKES ABOUT 4 CUPS

One 25-ounce bottle Mae Ploy Sweet
    Chilli Sauce or other Thai sweet chili
    sauce
2 tablespoons plus 2 teaspoons roasted
    sesame seeds
1 tablespoon plus 1 teaspoon kosher salt
2 serrano chiles, chopped, seeds and all
5 tablespoons plus 1 teaspoon Sriracha
¾ white or yellow onion, chopped
½ cup fresh lime juice
⅓ cup fresh orange juice
⅔ cup fresh Thai basil leaves

⅔ cup chopped fresh cilantro
6 garlic cloves, peeled
⅔ dried Anaheim chile, chopped
2 tablespoons plus 2 teaspoons chopped
    peeled fresh ginger
⅔ cup chopped scallions
1 teaspoon freshly ground black pepper
2 tablespoons plus 2 teaspoons
    kochukaru
⅔ cup natural rice vinegar (not seasoned)
1 teaspoon chopped peeled galangal

Combine all the ingredients in a blender or food processor. Blend everything until it's all real smooth.

Use liberally on whatever you got cooking for dinner—chicken, shrimp, everything—and pack the rest in Tupperware. It'll store in the fridge for 2 weeks.

GET TOPLESS WOMEN IN HAIRNETS TO PACK THE SAUCE INTO SMALL PLASTIC POUCHES IN A HOUSE WITH BLACKED-OUT WINDOWS LIKE IN *NEW JACK CITY.*

CHAPTER 5

GROVE STREET

The first week of high school. A lot of new faces: unfamiliar kids from the other junior high schools not only in Villa Park but from Anaheim and Orange, too, were all funneled into Villa Park High. Everything was real quiet. That junior high school stuff, I thought, had been just a phase—drugs, heavy metal, typical preteen anger at the world, experimenting with Frank, class clowning. Kids' play. Now this was tenth grade, and I was going to block out all that angst I was having about my parents. I was going to buckle down, be a good kid, and study hard. I joined the Latin and Chess Clubs, even made a new friend in honors English, another Korean kid named Paul Juhn, aka Yogi after some dude pointed out that he looked like the bear. He and I were two Asian kids in a sea of white faces, so there was a natural *Hey, wassup* to our first meeting, as if our spirits had already been introduced and no further explanation was required. What sealed the deal was our shared love for kimchi and hip-hop, and a bit of healthy rivalry that only good friends can have. So, with new clubs and new friends, I resolved to keep my head down and my mouth shut.

That shit lasted for about as long as your New Year's resolution to lose the fat. Barely a day.

It was lunchtime. I was waiting in line, like normal, for my chimichanga and Jell-O, when I felt something dark behind me, barreling through the line like a freight train. Letterman jackets. Jocks. Football seniors. Pushing every Marty McFly out of the way as they made their way to the front.

I was just about to order when I felt the hand on the shoulder.

"Move out of the way, Chink."

Laughter. Hyena laughter. Ugly laughter.

I stood my ground, feet digging into the concrete, fighting the undertow of their aggression.

"Oh, this fucking Chinky gook thinks he's tough."

"Kick his ass."

I fucking started feeling like going Kobra Kai Karate Kid shit on this muthafucka. But I just stood my ground.

They kept pushing. I kept resisting.

Then they pushed too fucking hard.

My face went up against the grate covering the order window, and I stumbled, catching myself before I fell. That was it. I turned around, grabbed the dude from behind his head and threw him into my knee, Thai style. Broke his nose, shoved him into the grate, and rubbed his face up and down till it started bleeding from the cuts. The other dude stepped back and threw a punch. I ducked and kicked him in the nuts.

I got my chimichanga, trembling from adrenaline. As I started to bounce from the scene, I happened to glance over to my right, toward a group of guys hanging out under a tree on a small hill right above the snack stand. The Grove Street Mob.

I FUCKING STARTED FEELING LIKE GOING KOBRA KAI KARATE KID SHIT ON THIS MUTHAFUCKA.

They were all barely sixteen but looked a decade older. Right as I looked over, Martin Ortega, the Pope of Grove Street, nodded at me.

I walked over. He spoke first. "Wassup."

From that day forward, I ate lunch with the Pope and his mob.

THE GROVE STREET MOB wasn't a gang as much as it was a Legion of Leaders that, for miraculous reasons, all ended up together. An All-Star team, if you will. Each guy could stand on his own as easily as he could back you up.

You just met our leader of leaders, Martin. He wasn't just our leader, though; he was the leader of the whole neighborhood, the idol of every young kid on the block, an All-Star wrestler, beer-drinking, gang-related, girl-fucking, Latino superstar. He could do everything: he wasn't more than five-foot-six, but he was built like the Tasmanian Devil, so strong that he could chop down a tree, lift cars, even break bricks. He turned good girls bad and bad girls good. He sheltered drifting souls and kissed babies. His mom, Susie, was an old-time chola from the hood, so no matter what mistakes Martin made or whatever trouble we got in, she was there to house and feed us till we got back on our feet.

Frank Gehr lived right next door to Martin on Grove Street. Frank was a debonair dude, an Italian-looking Guido and fit like a champ. He was always cool to me but started shit with others in and out of the Mob all the time.

Black Mike. Black Mike is no longer with us in this physical world, but the time he did spend here was eternal. You know the kind of dude who looks the same age forever? That dude that looks like he came out of the womb with a goatee? Mike was *that* dude. He must have been twenty-two when we were sixteen. He was about six-foot-one, dark as fuck, eyes as deep as the universe, wore creased Levi's, white T, Chucks, army belt, and some dark shades we call Locs. Proper. He had a Jheri curl, but it wasn't the kind of curl you could pop a joke at. This was a straight Los Angeles double OG curl that bounced like a cheetah. Black Mike was an Obi-Wan Kenobi oligarch of the streets who always had a crisp pack of Newports packed like no other and an ice-cold forty as if he lived in a refrigerator.

Shep. He goes by Big E now but will always be Shep to me. I consider Shep my very best friend for life and beyond. Before the age of fifteen, he was already built like Darryl Dawkins; by sixteen, he was knocking grown men out. I saw Shep hit a guy so hard at a party that it looked like a library shelf of books had collapsed within the dude's body as he fell to pieces. Shep's home was like a halfway house for us drifters. He started dealing weed at sixteen, so we'd smoke a lot together, play *NBA Live,* eat Naugles and Taco Bell and Pizza Hut, maybe even some Chinese kung pao chicken, and share our dreams in between.

Mike Semaza was a born fighter, the best, in fact, that Orange County had ever seen. At seventeen, he became our resident pro boxer: 126 pounds of pure magic. Quick as lightning, ducking in and out and delivering sharp blows to the kidney. He also had a black belt and could beat dudes up, all the while still partying it up with an ice-cold brew in hand. We called him Baby Boom Boom after his doppelganger, Ray Mancini.

Garrett Dean and I were really close. He was built like Fred Flintstone, always barefoot, with feet and hands like cinder blocks. His mom was a truck driver; she was on the road a lot, but always left us food in the fridge and movies on the couch. Garrett would always have me over at the crib to raid the fridge.

Ryan Brown was a small, lanky dude with a big Afro and wide nose. He could bust any dude down hard with Yo Momma jokes; we called it "bagging," and he

excelled. He was from Pasadena—specifically, the Denver Lane Bloods click—and moved down to Anaheim with his mom to get away from that world. But he found himself back on the grind, shooting fierce verbal arrows with the best of them. Ryan was one of my best friends.

Danny Bobbitt was one of the most amazing creatures I had ever met. Freckled face with a long, wiry frame, but tough as fucking nuts. He was like Gumby mashed with Nightcrawler: he could twist any which way; then, bam, he'd go from right next to me to the pole to the roof over to a telephone wire and right back down. All in less than a second. Lightning.

Tommy, Martin's uncle, was all of twenty-something but was like a god to us sixteen-year-olds. He gave us sound advice and, when necessary, a kick in the ass to keep us in check. And even more guys: Carlos Bustamante, our DJ with big long curls as wet as the morning dew. Steve Janzen, the son of a fireman. Curtis and Ken Robinson, brothers and world-class wrestlers who would go on to Atlanta after high school. Pag, our resident scholar and wordsmith. We had Lillian and a few other girls who were down with us, too. And man, there are so many more I left out, and it is not intentional.

And then there was me.

And that, folks, was the Grove Street Mob. We could walk anywhere, anytime; we commanded respect but never had to flaunt it. And we roamed the town: there was always someone in need of a black eye and everyone in need of a beer run. Step up in a fight, drop three hits of acid, 'shrooms, dine and dash, go eat, rob a store, babysit your kid? Sure. Let's go.

Crease the jeans with a whole can of starch. Roll joints with two Zig-Zags. Pack the cigarettes for five minutes, till the tobacco goes down by 30 percent. Comb in some Tres Flores. Sprinkle baby powder on the shoes, which will leave powder puffs when you take off running from the cops. Pack the sawed-off shotguns, 9 mm Berettas, 357 revolvers, rifles, UZIs, butterfly knives, numchucks, chains, bats, brass knuckles, police sticks, big hunting knives, little 22 pistols. Pile in the car, turn on the oldies, and head up to Hollywood, maybe, and deal with some messes along the way.

But it wasn't all small crimes and fisticuffs. We babysat kids, we pulled weeds, we fixed cars. Had keggers and summer bonfires roasting Philippine meats or steaks in Newport Beach. Downed plate after plate of tacos from whatever taquero was nearby—al pastor, carne asada, carnitas, sauced with salsas verde and roja, all eaten with a side of pickled carrots and washed down with a crisp horchata. Sometimes

RYAN BROWN DIED BY CRASHING A CAR AT A

hundred miles per hour into a lube and oil shop just past the Batavia riverbeds in Anaheim, California. I knew he was gonna die that night. And it will always kill me a little each day that I didn't grab him in time to stop him.

I first met Ryan Brown in an alley. He was, as he always was, bagging on some dude with his Yo Momma jokes, and he had my sides hurting with laughter. For almost two years after that, we spent every minute together. I went to his house first every morning and saw him last every night. We had the same physical insecurities—we were both lanky, skinny kids—but more than that, a similar weight hung heavy on our souls.

Ryan had ambition, and if he had been born in another body or in another time, he would have been unstoppable. He would've been able to pantomime the right answers at job interviews, eat with the right forks in the right order, shake the right hands, say the right things the right way at the right time. But no. He was a young, geeky black kid, and all that racism, the burden of low expectations, and other shit wears on a brother. He capped anyone and everyone with his jokes, but inside it wasn't so funny.

I saw his outfit of verbal armor because I was wearing my own chain mail. Outside, I was the tough but quiet kid, down for whatevas. Inside, though, I was just down. Lost and confused. Grove Street was great, but even they couldn't fill the void: I still couldn't adjust to the culture shock of Villa Park, and my parents were drinking more than ever. I never met their high expectations, and, with the drugs, my long hair, and my sneaking around, I justified their shame. When their friends visited with their Harvard-bound sons and daughters, my parents sent their Quasimodo of a son to his room. Out of sight, out of mind.

In my bell tower, I felt like I was in the wrong body, the wrong time, the wrong era, suffocating in a prison of structure. I had to get out. I had to disappear.

I thought about ending it all—knife, wrist; gun, trigger—but, no, that good Asian son heritage pulled me back. I couldn't do it. So, instead, I took off for nights at a time, to a place where nobody knew my name, where I could escape the expectations, the disappointments, the failures, even the accesses. It was a place I knew as a kid. Hollywood. Hollywood then was a free-for-all, a false paradise for transients, drifters, and lost souls. Glam rock and coke, blow jobs on the street. In other words, the complete opposite of Villa Park.

So I'd walk Hollywood Boulevard, panhandle, smoke, and disappear into the concrete. Up and down Hollywood, between Gower and Highland, grabbing pizza slice crusts out of the trash or asking for change to get a shawarma. I slept curled up, head down in my knees, up against a wall then roamed again looking for cigarette butts, drinking water out of the bathrooms. I didn't talk to anyone. I got to know no one. Just fucking walked and walked and walked. I had to know, to really know, that a whole world existed beyond Villa Park.

When the bugs were out of my system, I'd go back home. Reset.

Ryan was the only one who could really understand why I had to get out of Villa Park, the only one who cared about me on a level beyond anyone else. And so he was the only one I told about my Hollywood vacations.

In the last few precious minutes of our time together, we were kicking it at the apartment, like always. Drinking beers, like always. Smoking kush, like always. But over the last few weeks there had been something weird about Ryan. We were mad at each other for something, so we weren't meshing like best friends should. But sometimes guys just trudge through that shit until it naturally gets better, or you fight it out. It was slowly getting better between us.

Eleven P.M. I had my eyes fixed on Ryan. He was sitting on the floor, beer in hand, zoning. He was depressed, sunk in an invisible net.

"Yo, we going to the party or what, Ryan?" I asked. A girl I liked was at this party, and each second ticking away was a second that I could possibly be next to her and maybe get the courage to ask her out.

Ryan waved me away. Said he was just going to kick it there. But there was something about the way he shrugged me off, something about the way he sat on the floor with his back against the wall like he had a stamp and was ready to be shipped, something about it all that was strange. The whole room stopped, and I should have stopped. I should have stopped and grabbed the fucker by the coat like I always did, and dragged him with me. Or I should have stopped and said I was sorry for all the bullshit or for whatever we were fighting about and sat down and kicked it with him. I should have fucking been in tune and not been so selfish. But I wasn't.

Instead, we said "later" to each other as I walked out of the apartment. I took one last look at him and shut the door behind me. Turned my attentions to the party and the girl I had no chance with. And just forgot.

I WAS DRIVING BACK from the party. The road was blocked with cop cars and yellow tape. Something hit me in the stomach, and I jumped out of the car and ran. Two blocks through the jam to the scene. Slowly, I saw guys in stretchers laid out, their car smoking and crushed from front to center. And even though Ryan had never driven a car in the whole time I'd known him, I knew it was him.

It was supposed to be a joke. Ryan had convinced the others to let him drive that night. They were going out for some food, maybe some Taco Bell or McDonald's. Everything must have gone well, because they were on their way back, with food in the car. But then maybe the tire popped and Ryan lost control, or maybe he just stepped on it; either way, the skid marks show he accelerated, turned, and went straight into a brick wall. The others somehow survived. He didn't.

I love you, Ryan, and the lazy mornings listening to the Temptations, getting your braids done, and eating your mom's cooking while we talked about our dreams, together. These are memories hung up like posters in my soul, and I will always kiss them as I venture out, bringing to life all the things we talked about. Making people happy.

RYAN BROWN
R.I.P.

we broke into joints like the Tastee Freez, but not to jack anything other than food: we'd pry the back door open in the middle of the night, bust into that fucker, turn on all the lights, fire up the hoods, ovens, fryers, and just start cooking. Taquitos, chimichangas, burgers, and gyros.

Then I'd go home, crash, wake up, be a good Korean kid and eat kimchi mung bean porridge with the family, go to school, do homework, watch my sister, hit up Downtown L.A. with my mom to pick up jewelry. Then, when the time was right, sneak out into the alleyways and start it up all over again, like a cat with nine lives and counting.

THE MOMENT I BOUGHT that '87 Chevy Blazer, white with gold trim, I knew it was too high.

Back then, everyone had Nissans and Impalas, but not too many were up on the Blazer game yet. And that's why I knew I had to have it.

My boy Matt Kudra had just moved from Compton and brought a swagger to Grove Street that I was instantly attracted to. He was built like an ice block, always with two sawed-off shotguns under the seat and khakis so fresh you'd think he owned a dry cleaner's. He had this canary-yellow VW Squareback dropped to the floor with fifteen-inch Enkeis deep-dish rims. This thing sat so low, you could call it a Landscraper, and it was the illest ride on the scene. I loved riding shotgun with the shotguns under my seat, bouncing throughout the streets. That kind of shit is straight Cali, eyes wide open, scanning everything in sight.

And so I worked hard to get that Blazer. My parents were making mad dough through their jewelry business and would have dropped the allowance on me had I asked, but no. That ain't me. I was stubborn and still not used to riches, so I was on my grind. After school at a toy store, restocking shelves. Washing dishes at Leatherby's ice cream parlor. Busing tables and cleaning the salad bar at a steakhouse called Cask 'n Cleaver.

I eventually made enough to get the Blazer. Then I had to trick it out. At that time in my life, it was the only thing I truly was diligent about. The car became an extension of me. The Millennium Falcon to my Han Solo.

I bought the VW's rims off Matt for $500, including the 50-series low profile tires. I went to the mechanic and dropped my shit, cutting out all the leaf springs till the rubber met the paint. Blacked out all the windows. Then it was time to focus on the system: fifteen-inch Cerwin Vega woofers, a 300-watt Rockford Fosgate amplifier, and midrange speakers in the doors. If you were riding shotgun with me, you could put coins in the cup holders, and they'd jump like crickets. Outside, you knew I was coming from half a mile away, maybe more, and you'd know I was outside your door when the windows in your house started to shake.

I threw some fuzzy dice on the rearview. I was ready to roll.

"WHAT'S UP, AYE? I told my homies about your ride, and they wanna see it," my boy Robert Torres said as I picked him up. I had my fresh creased Levi's on, with a creased white T, gold chain, and hair greased up with a long tail in the back. Pretty fucking fly.

I popped in a cassette and started bumping some Zapp. We leaned back and started to cruise toward Norwalk. Local streets the whole way, going about thirty-five miles per hour, pulling into a liquor store to get a soda and a bag of chips. Then over to the stop sign so Rob could jump out and grab two bags of fruit, chopped fresh from a cart. Cucumbers, jícama, pineapple, mango, strawberries, oranges, and melon chopped and screwed with chili powder, salt, lime juice, all thrown in a plastic bag with a plastic fork, and we were off again.

We cruised slowly down Pioneer Boulevard, looking at doughnut shops and burger stands, catching the eyes of girls. Robert whistled out the window, saying, "What's up? What's up?" to the ladies. I pulled over and over and over, filling his pockets with phone numbers. Me, I came up empty-handed—the girls loved my ride, but the Chicanas in Norwalk and Whittier didn't want to be the first one to date the Chino. All good, though; girls weren't a big part of my life yet. I just enjoyed seeing my friend get some and have fun.

Finally, with one hand on the wheel, I pulled into the lot of the now closed Excelsior High School, creeping up the driveway. Just a tender scrape below, bumping some oldies, filling the whole place with my arrival. Shit, *everybody* was looking as Robert and I cruised in.

All the mini trucks were lined up on one side. Impalas and Bombers on the other. Doors open, truck beds lifted in the air with hydraulics. Girls everywhere and a bunch of veteranos in white tanks and Locs, tatted from head to toe. Geeked-out car dudes in blue T-shirts polishing their rims. Some kids running around. I could smell carne asada and chorizo on the grill, and there was, of course, beer. It felt so right, so good. As we crept through looking for our spot, everybody gave us that Cali head nod. The head nod that is part inquisitive, part code, part whattup, part beware, and all the way L.A.

"What's up, aye?" A guy approached me and put out his hand.

I slid my hand and did the homie handshake. Smooth and glide from side to side, up then down and out, with a snap.

"What's up? My name is Roy. They call me Raw or Chino sometimes; thanks for having me."

"Yeah, Rob told me about you, and once I heard you had a Blazer I knew I had to meet you. Rob's word is golden to me, and everybody here knows you are familia, so don't trip." The leader introduced his crew. "We're the Street City Minis, and we rep Norwalk, Pico Rivera, and Whittier. Let me check out your ride, homie."

The Street City Minis crew was one of the best in central Los Angeles. They had an extremely deep OG network, great mechanics, big family lineage, and a true love for the game. Each ride was unique, too, with each guy specializing in interior or paint or wheels. Lowriding, you see, is all about family, support, respect. It's how the tough guys show their sensitive insides, express themselves and their energies, and how Chicanos celebrate and enjoy time. It looks scary to some folks, a bunch of brown people standing around, but it's our culture. A deep culture, mind you, that has rules and membership: if you have to try to join in, you'll probably be left out cold. Either your soul is a kindred spirit or it's not. That simple.

We walked around the Blazer and checked out the rims. Then the interior, a cool shade of camel suede, and we popped the hood that I kept polished underneath. Wheels to roof, the Blazer had a swagger that could not be denied.

"This ride is firma, Holmes," he said. "Let me introduce you to some OGs and get you some comida and we can see about getting you into our crew," he said. Pop quiz: is that a joke, a threat, a game, or true and genuine? If you're still thinking

A THREAT,
GENUINE?

THE HEAD NOD THAT
IS PART INQUISITIVE,
PART CODE,
PART WHATTUP,
PART BEWARE, 'AND
ALL THE WAY L.A.

about it, you're already way behind. He walked me around and showed me the other cars as I shook hands with countless homies and said hello to girls and kids. They handed me a beer and a plate of tacos and some tamales. I grubbed as we walked, listening and feeling right at home.

We got back to my ride, and he asked me, "So, what do you think?"

"I like it here. You guys really got some fresh rides, and it feels like family."

"Well, what do you think about becoming a part of our crew? We can jump you in later . . . nah, just fucking with you, eh!" Still with that devilish grin of his, halfway being serious to see where I came from. "Really, though, we approve of your ride and think it is Street City worthy. And Rob is family, so what you say?"

I looked around. This was 1987, and I would be one of, if not the only, Asian dude hanging with the deepest clique in the game in the deepest culture of our city. And yet I felt right at home and saw myself as nothing less than a straight muthafuckin' G. And they saw it too. Game recognizes game.

The spirits clicked.

"Let's do it." Cool as a cucumber. I was officially part of the tribe.

He made an announcement, and all I could see were genuine smiles and whistles, head nods, handshakes, and "Orajale, Chino. Welcome to the familia."

Over the next few weeks, we took my whip to the garage and airbrushed the plaka on the back window—"Street City Minis, Norwalk, CA"—ride and shine. Man, I was so damn proud to rep Norwalk all throughout Pico Rivera and Whittier and La Mirada. Shoulders out, head high. Sometimes that's the most important thing on the streets of L.A.

We'd cruise every Friday and Saturday night down Pioneer up to Whittier Boulevard, through Pico Rivera, always one homie in shotgun and the backseat empty but for the girls you hollered at to jump in. A mini-parade to show off our feathers, if you will, fluffed up with hormones, wet lips, Budweisers, and "Hey, hey, qué onda, girl? Where you going, aye?"

My homies were making babies in the back, but I was just fine cruising with the back window flipped up, bumping EPMD, grinding on my Slim Jims, and eating chicharrón chips. I was having the time of my life even though I wasn't getting laid or even getting hickies.

This was Los Angeles 1987–88, Papi Chulo in the making.

CARNE ASADA

There are few foods more emblematic of Los Angeles than carne asada. In fact, the phrase has become so recognizable that you don't even have to translate it to English: just say it out loud, and most people will know it's marinated beef, thinly sliced and grilled to a char on a sunny Cali picnic day. I have heavy roots with carne asada: I grew up around it in Koreatown and ate it almost every day as a lowrider. I love that it's a wet marinade but somehow dries the meat just right. Whenver you eat carne asada, it feels like L.A. Wash it down with some fresh horchata (page 120). *Orale, carnal.*

SERVES 4

MARINADE

¼ cup garlic cloves, peeled

¼ onion, peeled

¼ cup chopped scallions

¼ cup ancho chile powder

1 tablespoon freshly ground black pepper

2 jalapeño peppers

½ bunch fresh cilantro

¾ cup Budweiser or any other beer you got in the fridge

Juice and grated zest of 1 orange

Juice and grated zest of 2 limes

½ kiwifruit, peeled

¼ cup mirin

Good pinch of kosher salt

Good pinch of sugar

1 pound skirt steak

Combine all the ingredients for the marinade in a blender or food processor and puree.

Rub the marinade all over the steak and marinate the meat in the refrigerator, covered, for at least an hour and up to 2 days.

When you're ready to grill, heat the grill to medium heat, brush with oil, and cook the steak for 10 minutes, until it's nice and charred on the outside and medium on the inside.

Rest the meat for 5 to 10 minutes; then eat. **YUM**.

BEEF JERKY

Liquor store runs with the Grove Street Mob. Camping trips. Car trips. Drinking snacks. Beef jerky fit into every facet of my life, especially during high school. To this day I trip out on the old containers in the corner stores in plastic tubs, just sitting there like it's normal to have meat in a tub next to doughnuts. Funny shit.

MAKES ABOUT 1 POUND

1 pound flank steak, cut into large cubes
1 cup garlic cloves, peeled
1 cup natural rice vinegar (not seasoned)
4 serrano chiles, split lengthwise
2 cups sugar

2½ cups soy sauce
2 cups water
1 yellow or white onion, sliced
1 cup chopped scallions
Pinch of red chile flakes

Combine all the ingredients in a large pot and bring to a boil. Reduce the heat to a simmer and skim the scum off the surface of the liquid every so often. Cook until the garlic becomes soft and golden brown, about an hour.

Using a slotted spoon or a spider, remove the meat from the pot and scoop it onto a wire rack set over a sheet pan (to catch drips). Let it rest in the refrigerator overnight. Strain the liquid and set it aside on the counter, where it'll stay while the meat is refrigerating.

The next morning, remove the beef and shred it.

AFTER REMOVING THE MEAT FROM THE POT, DON'T DISCARD THE LIQUID! SPLASH SOME ON A BOWL OF RICE OR PICKLE SOME EGGS: HARD-BOIL 6 EGGS, PEEL, THEN THROW 'EM IN THE POT AND LET THEM SIT IN YOUR REFRIGERATOR OVERNIGHT. ANOTHER DELICIOUS SNACK.

BEEF JERKY
LIKE NO OTHER.
FO DAYS.

YELLOW RICE AND GOAT STEW

When I was in high school, me and the Grove Street guys used to break into a Greek shop called the Mad Greek late at night and cook ourselves up a feast. The goat the shop used in the gyros was amazing, and I've liked the taste of goat and saffron and turmeric ever since. There is something very grounding about these flavors, and I put them in a stew here to make it that much more homey. I hope you and your crew can enjoy them and fill your party with smells that seem to stick to the walls.

SERVES 4 TO 6

MARINADE

3 dried chiles de árbol

1 dried California chile

¼ jalapeño pepper, charred

1 teaspoon kochukaru

1 Roma tomato, charred

3 cloves garlic, peeled

3 sprigs fresh cilantro

⅛ onion, charred

2 scallions, charred

¼ cup cubed mango

Juice of ½ lime

Juice of ¼ orange

2 tablespoons cider vinegar

2 tablespoons vegetable oil

½ teaspoon ground turmeric

¼ teaspoon ground allspice

Pinch of ground cumin

Kosher salt and freshly ground pepper
  to taste

MEAT

3 tablespoons canola oil

1 pound goat meat, cut into chunks

RICE

2 cups jasmine rice, rinsed

¼ cup coconut milk

¼ cup fresh lime juice

5¼ cups water

Good pinch of saffron threads

Good pinch each of kosher salt and
  freshly ground black pepper

½ cup chopped fresh cilantro, chopped

1 tablespoon butter

Combine all the ingredients for the marinade in a blender or food processor and puree. Coat the goat with the puree and marinate it in the fridge, covered, for 2 hours.

Heat a heavy pan or Dutch oven and drizzle in the oil, heating until it's smoking lightly. Remove the goat from the marinade, reserving the marinade. Sear the goat on all sides, then pour in the marinade, adding enough water to cover the meat completely. Simmer everything until the meat is nice and tender, 1 to 2 hours.

When the goat is almost done, combine the rice, coconut milk, lime juice, water, saffron, salt, and pepper in a rice cooker or in a saucepan. Cook, covered, over low heat until all the liquid has been absorbed and the rice is nice and fluffy, 20 to 30 minutes. Fold in the cilantro and butter.

Taste the goat stew and adjust the seasoning if necessary.

Pour the goat stew over the rice and **EAT SLOPPILY.**

PORK AND BEANS

My parents came home from American supermarkets with a lot of random-ass canned food, so we had everything from onion dip to Spam to corned beef hash to cream of mushroom soup to Vienna sausages to pork and beans. And when I popped open that can of pork 'n' beans, I always tripped on that little piece of white lard that would swim in the mix. It was like a toy in a cereal box. I hope you enjoy my version and find your own imaginary toy within it.

SERVES 4 TO 6

1 pound dried pinto beans, soaked in cold water overnight and rinsed
1 pound pork belly, cut into cubes
3 tamarind pods
½ cup garlic cloves, sliced
¼ onion, chopped

2 jalapeño peppers, chopped
1 cup chopped fresh cilantro
Kosher salt and freshly ground black pepper
2 tablespoons roasted sesame seeds

Put the soaked and rinsed pinto beans in a large pot, cover with water by at least an inch, and bring to a boil. Reduce the heat to a simmer and add the pork belly, tamarind pods, garlic, onion, and jalapeños.

Simmer everything until the beans are tender, about an hour. Add the cilantro, reserving a bit for garnishing the bowls, and season with salt and pepper to your liking. Simmer for another 30 minutes.

Ladle the beans into bowls and garnish each with some roasted sesame seeds and chopped cilantro to make it look pretty.

KUNG PAO CHICKEN, PAPI STYLE

I love kung pao chicken, and we—me and the Grove Street crew—ate loads of it because it was cheap or we were stoned. I love it in any way, any form, mall food court to fancy to hole in the wall to family home. This is my little homage to the steam well that exists in every city in every 99-cent-egg-roll storefront. Use equal parts chicken and vegetables

SAUCE

2 tablespoons oyster sauce

2 tablespoons chili garlic sauce or sambal oelek

1 tablespoon Chinese chili oil

2 tablespoons fish sauce

1 tablespoon Tapatío, Cholula, or other hot sauce

2 tablespoons natural rice vinegar (not seasoned)

3 garlic cloves, peeled

2 tablespoons roasted garlic

2 tablespoons fresh orange juice

1½ teaspoons sugar

1½ teaspoons kochujang

1½ teaspoons kochukaru

2 tablespoons soy sauce

½ jalapeño pepper

¼ cup fresh Thai basil leaves

¼ cup roughly torn fresh cilantro

2 tablespoons minced lemongrass

⅛ onion, peeled

¼ cup chopped scallions

1 tablespoon Sriracha

1½ teaspoons roasted sesame seeds

¼ cup Asian sesame oil

FOR THE WOK

Canola oil

Dark-meat chicken, diced

Dried chile de árbol

Bell peppers, julienned

Onions, julienned

Scallions, julienned

Baby bok choy, julienned

Watercress

Chinese water spinach, roughly chopped

Eggplant, julienned

Fresh Thai basil leaves

Roasted peanuts

Fresh cilantro, chopped

Lime, halved

Combine all the sauce ingredients in a blender or food processor and puree the shit out of them.

Heat a wok or large pan over high heat and add the oil, heating until it starts to smoke. Add the chicken and move it around until the meat is lightly caramelized and cooked almost through, about 4 minutes. Transfer to a paper-towel-lined plate.

Add a touch more oil to the pan and turn the heat up full blast. Add the whole chile de árbol and swirl it around the pan. Then add all your veggies in whatever batch size you decide to make, but add them in equal portions.

Immediately after you throw in your vegetables, add ¼ cup of the pureed sauce for every two cups of chicken and/or vegetables, plus a splash of water to thin it all out slightly.

Add the chicken back to the pan and cook the stew together until the chicken is cooked through, about a minute. Turn off the heat.

Add the Thai basil and peanuts. Garnish with more Thai basil and cilantro. Splash it with half a lime if you have one around, then serve with rice.

SALSA VERDE

There are two sauces that define L.A. and OC: salsa roja and salsa verde. It's who we are and who we've become. I could eat anything with salsa verde; now so can you.

MAKES ALMOST 2 CUPS

¼ cup mirin

½ cup natural rice vinegar (not seasoned)

½ cup fresh mint leaves

1 cup roughly torn fresh cilantro

¼ cup fresh Thai basil leaves

3 garlic cloves, peeled

½ shallot, peeled

2 serrano chiles

1 jalapeño pepper

Juice and grated zest of 1 lime

2 tablespoons roasted sesame seeds

2 tomatillos, charred

½ cup canola oil

½ cup olive oil

½ avocado

Pinch of kosher salt and freshly ground
   black pepper

Combine all the ingredients in a blender or food processor and puree.

DRINK.
BURP.
SMILE.

HORCHATA

Big Styrofoam cup the size of a football, fútbol playing on the tube, the sound of extraction coming from the tube when poured out of the machine, tacos about to be eaten . . . nothing could be better. The sweet flavor of cinnamon on your lips and the viscous milk and toasted rice. That moment when you're eating tacos and drinking horchata, nothing else matters.

SERVES 4 TO 6

1 cup white rice, rinsed
4 cups water
Juice and grated zest of 2 limes
One 3-inch stick cinnamon
2 tablespoons blanched almonds

2 tablespoons roasted sesame seeds
½ teaspoon ground cinnamon
1 cup whole milk
¾ cup sugar

Soak the rice in the water, along with the lime juice and zest, cinnamon stick, almonds, and sesame seeds for 1 hour.

In a food processor or blender, blend it all together and let it sit for 3 hours at room temperature.

Strain the rice mixture into a pot, place over low heat, and whisk in the ground cinnamon, milk, and sugar. Bring to a low simmer and keep it there until the sugar dissolves.

Strain again and chill.

SERVE ICE-COLD.

SPLASH

The Latinos I grew up around always had a lime somewhere, anywhere—just to give that extra little boost to whatever they were eating. I like to have this sauce around to sprinkle a little love on my day—and hopefully yours.

1 cup soy sauce

¼ cup natural rice vinegar (not seasoned)

2 tablespoons minced scallions

1 tablespoon minced jalapeño pepper,
    seeds and all

2 teaspoons kochukaru

1 teaspoon roasted sesame seeds

1 tablespoon minced garlic

Mix all the ingredients together in a small bowl. Spoon over rice or even use it to amp up a salad. Add it to anything. Everything.

POUR A LITTLE ON THE GROUND FOR THE HOMIES, TOO.

CHAPTER 6

CRACK

Cruising through the streets of Norwalk with the Street City Minis could go on for only so long. By the time I graduated high school in '88, most of the Grove Street guys had moved either on or out. Without my crew, and especially without Ryan, I was alone, aimless. But good Asian son that I am, I still went through the motions of giving a fuck about my future. I applied to college like I was supposed to, ending up at a commuter school, Cal State Fullerton. I trudged through best I could, even joined some clubs. I got my marching shoes on and tried to save pandas and shit, got political with Amnesty International, joined the Greenpeace club on campus. Changed my major from political science to philosophy, learned logic and Emmanuel Kant, got deep into Vonnegut and Nietzsche, connected with Sal Paradise, Holden Caulfield, Fonny and Tish. I dabbled in theater for a while.

But I couldn't play like I was a good college student. Before too long, I was going to class reeking of weed and staying silent even when called on; I mad-dogged the professors and other students. Ate in the library, stinking up the room while others wanted to study. Bounced around Fullerton Tokers Town houses with cholos, shacked up in a Vietnamese home in Westminster, roamed the streets just looking, hoping to get myself into any type of trouble.

Meanwhile, my parents could only scratch their heads and look for ways to keep their son on track. Finally, in 1990, they sent me to Korea for the summer to attend a program hosted by Korea University in Seoul. It was a wonderful program that focused on connecting twenty-something Korean-Americans to their heritage and identity. My classmates were churchgoing types, the kind who would tell innocent ghost stories while toasting their fucking marshmallows over a perfectly built campfire. They were bright and happy and smart. Pure. And I hated them, because I wished I was just like them. Instead I was me: baseball cap on, pulled low over my eyes, hoodie pulled over the cap, jeans sagging low, sulking during Korean language lessons, refusing to participate while the class learned about Asian history and culture.

Even a field trip couldn't mellow me out. In the middle of the program, we

I KEPT MY HOOD LOW AND
LACED RAP ABOUT KILLING
YOUR MOTHER UPSIDE
MAGGOT

went on a big bus tour of South Korea. It was only about a week, but South Korea is tiny—combined, North and South Korea aren't much bigger than California—so it was more than enough time to see the highlights. And that trip should have been the highlight of the summer: from Seoul, we went east, hiking, camping, and foraging for wild herbs and roots in the hills of Seorak Mountain National Park. Old ladies there would make us herb pancakes in the fields, squatting as they cooked them on little burners and put them on bamboo mats to rest. Up along the freezing cold coast, we met fishermen who gave us live octopus and all sorts of sashimi—fluke and abalone and sea bream and sea cucumber—sliced right in front of us and then dipped in a sweet, acidic kochujang, which you funneled into your mouth with your fingers—or theirs—and washed down with a hot cup of fish cake broth.

After a ride up north near the border to Kangwon-do, we went down to Busan and Taegu in the southeastern corner of the country, the closest point to Japan. Fresh seafood was everywhere here, with mild water-based kimchi all through the region. In the western province of Cheongju, the roots and tubers and herbs and plants were delicately pickled or preserved to create rainbows of flavor, and we had bowls and bowls of bi bim bap. By the time we made our way back up to Seoul, we had visited every province in the country except for the island of Cheju; had we made it, we would have had mandarins, Berkshire pigs, bony fish, and oysters.

The country was a delicious paradise, a giant wonderland.

But no matter where we went, the dark clouds over my head never parted. And the more fun everyone had, the more I was determined to rain on their parade. As we drove from one province to the other, the kids would pass around a microphone, and everyone would take a turn singing a verse of a Christian song or

RIPPED A PROFANITY-
CHILDREN AND FUCKING
DOWN AND STUFFING
DOWN YOUR THROAT.

love ballad. Honestly, a few of them were really good in their own kumbaya way. But they kept passing the mic to me, and I passed it along each time, shaking my head or refusing to even acknowledge it. They weren't going to let me off the hook. They kept passing it over to me so I could join their happy song, insisting I take my turn. They probably thought I was just shy. I wasn't shy.

Finally, I had had enough. I took the mic. I wasn't going to sing no fucking kumbaya. Instead, I kept my hood low and ripped a profanity-laced rap about killing children and fucking your mother upside down and stuffing maggots down your throat.

Silence.

The head counselor said, "Hmmm, okay . . . let's move on."

They moved on. I stayed put.

BUT THEN PARADISE LOST turned into paradise found. There was a girl. There's always a girl.

She was from the East Coast and seemed to be just like me, a fish out of water: no makeup, bohemian clothes instead of shorts and tank tops. Smart, tough, and opinionated, wise beyond her years. I noticed her the first week; a few weeks later, I stepped to her and we clicked. The mean mothafucka became a little puppy in love.

There was nothing sexy about my little dorm room—it was always a mess, always too bright, unless you turned off the pale white light, at which point you'd be shrouded in pitch-black darkness. But we would talk there through the night and into morning, and, as we got more and more intimate, she let her guard down, inviting me to come closer, to be a part of her. We'd clumsily explore each other, trying to figure out how we fit together. We were young and awkward—always bumping our heads against the cinder-block walls. Never quite fitting in the cramped bed, bumping our heads on the bunk bed frame above.

Together we frolicked around Seoul, finding our own souls as we ran, holding hands and exploring the twisted alleys and crowded streets together, finding food everywhere we turned. On the streets, pork belly cooked on steel tables. A drunken crowd folded the pork into lettuce leaves, layering it with soybean paste, kimchi, and radishes. Looks delicious—let's try it! In the Shindang-dong neighborhood, cauldrons of deep red stew bobbed full of rice cakes, fish cakes, and drooping onions. An intrepid bystander would stuff a pack of instant ramen and Vienna sausages into the pot and swirl swirl swirl until it got all sticky and gooey. There were blood stews and beef bone soups filled with handfuls of chopped scallions and wild sesame seeds. Streetside sweet potatoes roasted in makeshift coal ovens. Dried squid charred over an open flame fired by a retrofitted butane can, sold by a guy who also repaired shoes.

Everything was so chewy and delicious and lovely.

It was amazing. I was so happy.

Then the summer ended. So did the program.

Her father picked her up.

It was over.

Before I knew it, I was back at Fullerton for the fall semester, her scent still fresh on me. We wrote love letters back and forth, pumped dimes and nickels and quarters into pay phones as operators told us we had only two minutes left on our call.

It wasn't until months later—January 1991—that I had enough cash to see her. The first chance I got, I jumped on a Greyhound and set sail across the country with one thought in mind: her. I didn't care about the amber waves of grain, didn't take photos of purple mountain majesties. I just had to get there. And three days later I did. I showed up on her doorstep at Brown University in the middle of winter, decked out in Chucks, sagging 501s, an L.A. Kings cap, and a bomber jacket. Heeeeeeere's Johnny!

She had no idea I was coming. What a great surprise this will be, I thought. All I had to do was show up at her door like a bottle of milk, and she would drink it. Brilliant. But Korea was Korea. This was Providence. The second I saw her, and the look on her face when she saw me, I knew it was over. Yet she was so kind to entertain me for even a day.

I held my head high and concealed my embarrassment until I could leave the next day. I had put all my eggs in one basket, and the bottom had fallen out. I had

BUT THEN PARADISE LOST TURNED INTO PARADISE FOUND.

nothing. No best friend. No girl. No purpose. Nothing left for me at home. I looked at where I was, where I could go, and remembered the New York of Salinger, Baldwin, and Kerouac. Holden Caulfield, Fonny and Tish, and Sal Paradise called me out of Providence to work out my troubles with them and the other lost fish in Times Square.

BY THE TIME I crash-landed in New York, I was hurting bad. The heartache of the last few days broke the levee on the heartache I'd been carrying over the last few months. As I walked out of Port Authority and found my way to the YMCA, I went from macho to tender. Let my guard down a bit. Mistakes happen.

The YMCA at Times Square was housed in an old camel-colored brick building. For seven bucks a night, I bought myself a ride up a tiny elevator, a walk down a barren hallway, and a room even smaller than the elevator, with a bed fitted with prison-blue sheets. After I settled in, I headed back downstairs to grab a smoke out front.

"Hey, do you have a cigarette, young man?"

The guy asking for the cigarette was bearded and wearing a Guardian Angels beret and an army jacket. He had a backpack slung over his shoulder and books in his hand. He looked like an educated guy, a little bohemian even. I'm not sure what he saw in me. You'd think some Asian kid smoking a cig in front of a dumpy YMCA wouldn't make for much of a mark. But I guess I was wearing my vulnerability on my sleeve.

I gave him a cigarette, and right there in front of the building we talked. And talked. And talked. He said he was an adjunct professor at Columbia. We talked about Nietzsche; we talked about life and all the things that were important to me. Four or five hours went by. He was earning his keep. He said there was going to be a lecture at Columbia the next night, that he had just happened to be passing through Times Square, on his way to get his ticket, when he ran into me.

"I'm heading up there now to get my tickets. I can get one for you, too. Just stay here and I'll be right back, and then we can get some late dinner. The tickets are $120. Just give it to me and I'll secure our seats."

An Ivy League lecture! I was going to be smart again. Wow.

He took my bounty, darted across the street, and slipped into the darkness.

I waited. And waited. He said he'd be right back, right? Another cigarette, another hour. Twiddling thumbs. Man, he was good. Real good. Got me for everything I had.

Whatever little of that macho shit I had left before that moment was completely gone. *I* was completely gone. Though not angry at the guy—to this day, the sting still amazes me. I tip my hat to him for sniffing me out and humbling me to the quick.

It was almost midnight by then. Numbed by what had just happened, I stared into the night and, just as you find stars in the sky if you look long enough, I started to see figures moving in the shadows. People in trench coats; hookers; dudes with shifty eyes.

Then, as if someone was watching me from the loge seats, I heard, "That dude got you, huh?" The voice belonged to a lanky white guy, maybe twenty-two years old, holding on to a fifth of bourbon and munching casually on a bag of chips. Now that the show was over, he had decided to come out of the shadows.

"You hungry? I got some chips upstairs," he said.

Fresh off the con, I was on red alert. At first I thought maybe he wanted to have sex with me. But there was something about that guy that caught my attention. He was a tiger without fangs. A kindred spirit, in a way. And I had just lost the last thing I had to lose. So, what the fuck. Let's go. Back up the tiny elevator, back down the barren halls, into his room. Lights on. He handed me a pipe.

Crack looks like crack: small clusters of white, chalky nuggets the size of Nerds in a vial the size of a perfume sample. There always seems to be so little of it, rattling around in its tube like a quarter in a pay phone coin slot, but there's always just enough to get you good and high.

He taught me how to take that first hit: back straight, flame to rock, quick puff, chest expanded. It tasted like all the things in the closet of my life, if the skeletons in there had been made of saltwater taffy.

A few hours and hits passed. We needed more. It was 3:00 or 4:00 A.M. when we left his room, went a block or two this way and that way, down empty streets and dim alleys. Then we turned a corner and . . . people. Crowds and crowds of people, hustling—but it was quiet. Dark blankets, tank tops even though it was winter, beards, all moving about in silence. He showed me around like I was his new roommate; through him, I learned how to walk. *Always walk forward. Never stop walking, never give up your position, not even a shoulder. If bodies crash, keep walking. One small move gives up the line, and you've lost the game of chicken. And the vultures will start to circle.*

I was to have his back and keep cool. There were all types of shit being thrown out there to buy, a bazaar for the bizarre. Blow job? No, thanks. Weed? Next time. Pizza? Not hungry. Meanwhile, he was scanning, looking for that elusive right deal. It was like Asian ladies picking fruit: a little bit of superstition, intuition, feeling for the primo spots to find the one that feels just right. Eventually we found him. A few crumpled bucks later, we had the vial. Grabbed some nachos and meat pie and went back up the chute to our penthouse, to lose ourselves in the taste of the taffy all over again. In between hits in the dark, we ate like squirrels: quick nibbles, just a little bit at a time. A handful of chips here, Corn Nuts there, swig of Gatorade, slice of pizza. Hit.

Days passed, but it felt like one long night. The YMCA was full of people, but it was always so quiet, just a bunch of lonely guys minding their own business, talking to themselves, getting high in their rooms, then wandering out for more. We were fish swimming around each other in the same bowl, respecting each other's space. When the sun went down, the stars I could barely make out that first night became clear as day, and I flew with the bats of the night: trench coat flashers; XXX horndogs; other crack addicts; transvestite hookers; hobos; drifters; pimps; hos; invisible joes. People with no homes, no destiny, no hope.

It's not so much that I liked any of this—I didn't like crack all that much, actually. But if it wasn't this drug, it would have been another one: drinking, girls, binge eating. Anything to fill that void in my heart, anything to rub salt in my wounds, anything to make me forget.

I WAS LUCKY. Maybe it was because the drug was just a filler until time could heal my broken spirit. Maybe it was because all that good son/Asian heritage stuff I had in my blood was powerful enough to pull my mind back before it could be pushed too far away. Whatever it was, on the seventh night of this long week, I woke up and remembered my family and heard my mom's voice calling out through the haze in my head. I got up, looked at the mirror, and, for the first time in a long time, recognized the boy looking back at me. I didn't need to be drugged anymore. I could walk on my own now.

Back to Port Authority. Back to the home I had left behind. When I arrived, my mom pulled out all the stops. Everything out of the pantry, everything onto the stove, then onto a plate to feed her son. It wasn't the first time my parents pulled me back from the brink. And it wouldn't be the last.

But I never touched the pipe again.

PERFECT INSTANT RAMEN

You can have almost no money and still have enough to live off this stuff for weeks, months, years. Eat enough and you'll start to look for ways to make it different: add a little more sauce, a little less sauce, cook the noodles less, cook them more, add more water, less water, add an egg, scramble the egg, etc. Me, I've become a freak when it comes to my instant ramen. Don't fuck wit it, don't fuck wit me, let me do my thing. This is how I do my own thing.

MAKES 1 PERFECT BOWL

2½ cups water

1 pack Shin Ramyun or whatever pack of
    instant ramen you have

1 egg

½ teaspoon butter

2 slices American cheese

¼ teaspoon roasted sesame seeds

GARNISH (OPTIONAL)

½ scallion, green part only, thinly sliced
    on a bias

Bring the water to a boil in a small pot. Open the ramen package and add the noodles to the water. Cook the noodles for 2 minutes, then add the flavor pack.

About 30 seconds before the noodles are done, turn off the heat and crack in the egg—but don't mix it in. Just pull the hot noodles gently over the raw egg and let it sit for a minute to poach.

Now get a bowl and gently pour everything slowly into it, being careful to not disrupt the egg.

Add the butter, cheese, and sesame seeds to the bowl. Mix it all around. Garnish with the scallion if you have it.

EGGY, CHEESY GOODNESS. GRILLED CHEESE WHAT?

GHETTO PILLSBURY FRIED DOUGHNUTS

I love doughnuts, but I really love malasadas. And ever since I visited Hawaii, I got up on this game. One day, a friend of mine showed me how he did it growing up in Oahu: take a pack of the Pillsbury biscuits and fry them, then toss them in sugar. "DUDE!!!!!!" I said. Try it and you'll see. You too will say, "DUDE!!!!!!!!!" and deplete your local grocery store of Pillsbury biscuit dough just to make these.

MAKES 8 DOUGHNUTS

½ cup sugar
2 tablespoons ground cinnamon
2 tablespoons roasted and crushed
   sesame seeds

1 tube Pillsbury original biscuit dough
4 cups Crisco shortening

Mix the sugar, cinnamon, and sesame seeds in a medium-size bowl.

Pop open the tube of dough and pull apart the biscuits—they come preportioned, so this will be easy. In a big, heavy pot, heat the shortening over high heat; you'll know it's ready when a tiny piece of biscuit dough sizzles when added to the oil. Fry the biscuit dough until each piece becomes puffy and brown on all sides, about 2 minutes. Flip the pieces over and fry them for 2 minutes more.

Pull out the doughnuts and rest them on paper towels for a minute or two, then toss them immediately in the sugar mixture.

REPEAT.
EAT.
GET BLOATED.

KETCHUP FRIED RICE

Ain't nothing more ghetto than ketchup fried rice. This is a fiend's meal. It's like crackers and aerosol cheese spread. It's like sugar on some white bread or frozen burritos. Basically, some trashy-ass, fucked-up, dumb shit. But it's damn tasty!

SERVES 4 TO 6

3 tablespoons vegetable oil

1 tablespoon minced scallions

1 tablespoon minced carrot

1 teaspoon minced garlic

1 tablespoon minced kimchi (page 19 or store-bought)

2 cups day-old cooked rice

3 tablespoons ketchup

1 egg

¾ teaspoon roasted and crushed sesame seeds

Heat a large pan or a wok over high heat and add the oil. Throw in all the vegetables and the kimchi and sauté for a minute or so, until you start to see a little color on the veggies. Transfer the veggies to a bowl and return the pan to the stove.

Add a touch more oil to the pan and add the rice, stirring it around occasionally. Cook the rice until it gets a bit crispy, then add the vegetables to the rice and mix for a minute or two. Add the ketchup and mix everything around until the rice fully absorbs the ketchup. Remove from the heat and put a small pan over the flame. Fry your egg however you like.

Serve yourself a bowl of the rice and top with the fried egg and a sprinkle of sesame seeds.

WATCH *SESAME STREET* AS YOU EAT KETCHUP FRIED RICE LIKE A G.

CHEESE PIZZA, DOUGH TO SAUCE

I might not convince you to make pizza at home, because most of the time it's easier to just go grab a slice or phone in a delivery, but I'm going to try anyway. This sauce is really, really delicious, and you can work out some stress on the dough. So maybe instead of ordering in one night, you can be the pizza shop. Invite friends over and pile on as much cheese as you'd all like.

MAKES 4 TO 6 PIZZAS

DOUGH

1 cup warm water
2 tablespoons vegetable oil
2 teaspoons honey
Half of a ¼-ounce envelope active dry
    yeast

1 tablespoon plus ½ teaspoon kosher salt
4 cups all-purpose flour

SAUCE

¾ cup olive oil
¼ cup garlic cloves
¼ cup chopped shallots
One 28-ounce can plum tomatoes
1 cup mushroom or vegetable stock
Handful of fresh basil
Salt and freshly ground black pepper

TOPPING

4 cups mozzarella and any other kind of
    cheese you want, shredded

MAKE THE DOUGH

Combine the water, oil, and honey in a small bowl and then add the yeast, giving it a gentle stir. Let the yeast mixture sit for 5 or 10 minutes; until it bubbles. Mix the salt and flour together in a large bowl. Slowly add the yeast mixture to the dry ingredients, then mix in a stand mixer on low to medium speed for 5 minutes.

Transfer the dough to a large, lightly oiled bowl and cover with plastic wrap. Let it rest in a warm place for 10 minutes.

Transfer the dough to a floured surface and form balls; you should end up with 4 to 6 medium-size balls of dough. Let the dough proof again in a covered bowl for an hour. Each ball of dough will make 1 pizza. Take what you'll use immediately and wrap the others in plastic and freeze.

MAKE THE PIZZA SAUCE

Pour the olive oil into a small pan, add the garlic and shallots, and cook them slowly over medium heat until they turn medium brown, stirring periodically, about 40 minutes.

In a medium-size pot, combine the tomatoes and the stock, bring to a slight boil, then reduce the heat to simmer. Add the garlic/shallot mixture, oil and all. Cook for another hour, then stir in the basil. Transfer the sauce to a blender and puree. Add salt and pepper to taste and let the sauce come to room temperature.

MAKE THE PIZZA

Preheat the oven to 450°F. If you have a pizza stone, put it in the oven while it's preheating.

Roll out the dough as rustic or as pretty as you like and lightly brush with olive oil.

Ladle and spread as much sauce as you want all over, from the center of the dough to the edge, being careful to leave a rim around the pizza.

Sprinkle on the cheese. Bake that thing in the oven on the pizza stone or directly on a greased sheet pan for 7 minutes.

I like to top mine with dried oregano, red chile flakes, and hot sauce.

BUTTERMILK PANCAKES

Sometimes, when your whole life, your whole fucking life, is threatening, you need something that comforts you. Pancakes were that thing for me, and I know it's not just for me. Because nothing says comforting in the morning or in a foggy, drug-induced state more than a plate of pancakes: It's just batter, butter, and syrup. Easy as 1-2-3, and maybe enough to help you count back to what got you here in the first place.

SERVES 4 TO 6

2 cups all-purpose flour, sifted
1 tablespoon plus ½ teaspoon sugar
¾ teaspoon kosher salt
1 tablespoon baking powder
¾ teaspoon baking soda
1½ eggs, beaten, or ¼ cup liquid eggs
    (to get ½ egg, beat 1 whole egg and
    use half of that beaten egg)

2 cups buttermilk
¼ cup plus 2 tablespoons melted butter
1 teaspoon olive oil

Mix together the flour, sugar, salt, baking powder, and baking soda in a medium bowl. Mix together the eggs, buttermilk, and butter in a larger bowl.

Slowly mix the dry ingredients into the wet ingredients and beat for 2 minutes.

When all the ingredients are just incorporated, let the batter rest for a little bit while you heat up a griddle or pan. Once it's hot, add a generous drizzle of olive oil to the grill or pan.

Ladle in the pancake batter to make pancakes as big or small as you wish. Cook over low to medium heat until you see a million bubbles on the surface of the pancakes and their undersides become brown and crispy. Once you see that, flip the pancake over. You should get that signature rise.

Cook for about a minute more, and there they are, wonderful pancakes. I like to eat my stack with pure maple syrup and some good, softened butter, and that's about it.

VARIATIONS

For blueberry pancakes, add rinsed dry blueberries to the pancakes in the million-bubble stage, right before you flip them.

For johnnycakes, substitute cornmeal for half the flour.

CHAPTER 7

YOU VERY LUCKY, MAN

"You very lucky, man!"

I didn't mean to get deep into gambling, I swear.

"I told you, he's the best!"

By the time I got back from New York, it was the end of January 1991. I had nowhere to go other than back to school. So there I was, a twenty-one-year-old junior majoring in philosophy and studying logic. I figured I'd try to stay clean now, hit the books, get it right. But try as I might, school was as boring as shit and my mind started to wander. I looked up some guys I knew from high school who were studying at UCLA and ended up moving in with the Korean kid I had met back in honors English, Paul "Yogi" Juhn. Week after week, we wasted time playing video games, trying to get laid, partying hard, drinking harder. Then he and his crew started to hit the casinos. At first, I was just going along for the ride.

"Home run all the way!"

But the instant I sat down at the table and felt the felt, I was jolted out of my routine. Everything suddenly became new, alive, fresh. I could smoke, drink, watch sports, gamble, talk shit, make friends, flirt, and eat. Time didn't exist; neither did judgments. Only possibilities and action. The amenities just made it sweeter: pats on the back, massages, cheers, ladies. And the food. Oh, man, the fucking food.

THE 710 FREEWAY RUNS north to south along the eastern outskirts of Los Angeles, connecting the San Gabriel Valley to the ports of Long Beach. The Bicycle Club—or, as we liked to call it, the Bike—is located just off the 710, in the industrial section south of Los Angeles. On the way there from almost anywhere in L.A., Orange County, or the Inland Empire, you drive past South Gate, Huntington Park, Vernon, Cudahy, Paramount, Gardena, Commerce, Bell Gardens—places that were cattle ranches and farmland before they morphed into lower-middle-class towns submerged in smog and dust, dominated by raw industry. Meatpacking. Smelt. Metal. Rubber. Food processing.

The Florence Avenue exit takes you off the 710 almost directly to the Bike. The lights flash on the sign like any one of the oozing neons lining the Las Vegas strip.

There are three entrances to the Bike: two in the front, one in the back. It should be easy, just to walk into a goddamn building, but when you've gambled so much that it infects your mind, body, and soul, everything feels like Monty Hall asking you for a door number. I'd choose a door based on what the spirits or glow of luck dictated: some days, I knew the Big Deal was hidden behind door number 3. Other days, door number 1 pulled me in like a vacuum.

No matter the door, you instantly feel the sense of the place the minute you enter.

The beetle-black heads of Chinese, Koreans, Vietnamese, Mexicans, and Armenians crowd the tables, populations that have both ready access to the 710 and a penchant for the casino's Asian Pan 9 and Pai Gow games.

There are some old-timers; a handful of fresh new faces, college kids; and blue-collar workers. There are hangers-on—trolls with sunken eyes and furrowed brows—who stand behind rails, overlooking the tables. They throw out sycophantic words of encouragement in hopes of catching crummy tips. Railbirds, squawking at the action.

There's the pulsating white noise of murmuring chatter, chips clicking and clacking, the squeaking wheels of the Candy Girls' carts rolling from one player to another.

The place is huge and separated into three major rooms. The poker room and Asian games room flank the Dragon Room; this room is the home of the big-city gangsters, the Hong Kong and Vegas big shots, or the lucky bastards who won temporary riches elsewhere in the casino and decided to swim here with the sharks. When I first started, you could have found me, day after day, night after night, in the Asian games room, at ease among residents whom many might refer to as social deviants. Prostitutes, drug addicts, delinquents, criminals, gypsies, carnies, bums, drunks sat in those chairs, congregated around those tables, touched those cards.

Say what you will and make your judgments, but understand that there, even in that underbelly of the city, the ethics of the game—the challenge—reigned supreme. You could leave $150,000 in chips on a card table, walk away, take a piss, and come back to find your money untouched, as if it had been insured by the FDIC. Try doing that at a company party.

I WAS DOOMED
FROM THE START.
DDOH MAH.

ON MY FIRST DAY at the Bike, I started with $150.

The game was Pan 9. Ten players are at the table, each with the goal to beat the dealer at his own game. Each player gets three cards, with one more optional; the object is to add up the value of the cards and get to the sum of 9. Face cards are worth zero. If you're Vietnamese and you see a face card, all you say is, *"Ddoh mah,"* which loosely translates as "Fuck me." I won. I won again. And again. I was on a streak fresh out of the gate. I turned that $150 to $500 in 10 minutes. I went from small $100 hands to huge $10,000 hands and never looked back. I should have looked back. I should have reaped my rewards and left behind that room, filled with the hollow eyes and big nostrils of Southeast Asia. But I didn't. Fuck the odds, I thought. Fuck fate.

I was doomed from the start. *Ddoh mah.*

BACK IN THE EARLY NINETIES, you could smoke everywhere, including inside casinos and restaurants. Naturally, then, the Bike was perpetually overcast. But despite the tar, the place smelled like a sweet kitchen, with a menu as diverse as the casino's winners and losers. And more than just feeding your body, the dishes fired up your spirit.

Take phở. The casino cranked out bowl after bowl of the Vietnamese beef soup, full of rare beef slivers, star anise, blackened ginger, cloves, herb stems, beef bones, garlic, pepper, coriander, shaved white onions looking like the lace on white panties ready to hit the floor. The noodles, fresh rice pounded and cut, still warm as they were ladled with the broth. Cilantro and Thai basil danced on top, and a lime wedge grinned like a Cheshire cat. Then the sidecar to the Harley-Davidson: a side plate of green herbs and bean sprouts.

The Vietnamese gamblers usually ordered the phở. They were fucking fierce, aggressive, amazingly deft at switching gears in a hand, and they never hesitated to go all in. And they had no qualms about going all in just before stopping the action to eat. You never saw anything like it: a table full of squatting Viets, talking, mouths full, squeezing limes with the voracity of a vice clip, sweat beading down their temples, making sounds that only a trapped gargoyle would make in a dungeon, their chopsticks clanking viciously at a rapid pace. Nonchalantly slurping up those bowls of noodles even though their lives were on the line: fuck the world for a minute while I finish my bowl.

If you were willing to front, you'd order the phở too, like you knew what the fuck was up. You were Popeye, the phở your spinach—the iron to pump up those muscles and go from weak sauce to hot sauce. It gave you the strength and confidence to take on the Vietnamese players, and, while you were at it, that seasoned poker pro, too, white guy, fifty years old or so, full-on sweatsuit, noshing on a plate of turkey and gravy with cranberry sauce. Your phở would take one look at his bland bird and say, *Your cranberry is no match for my Sriracha. You can't take me. You can't handle my spices.*

And, as your cards continued to hit and your chips began to stack, you would wash it all down with a classic American milk shake. Thick like lava, sweet like a Milky Way. Cheddar, baby.

AFTER ABOUT A YEAR, my lucky streak with Pan 9 ended. And yet, even as my friends deliberately edged me out of the Pan 9 tables, I refused to believe that my run with luck was over. It wasn't, really. We rekindled our relationship in the poker room.

Poker is a game where everything is pistol to pistol. You wait to see who will actually pull that trigger. Sometimes, when you got nothing to lose, and you're twenty-two years old, shoveling away $10,000 nightly in shoeboxes, you get pretty good at making others blink.

While they're blinking, you're building your empire with chips. Colors, like the number of blocks you control on the streets, dictate power. In order, from Youngling to Jedi Grand Master of the cantina: orange chips, blue, green, amber, yellow, black, and multi. That's two quarters, a buck, $2, $3, $5, $100, and $1,000.

It was poker that took me from mild-mannered gambler to rabid addict. I started with $1–$2 stud games, winning with a pair of kings. Then I matured quickly, passing the forty-eight-inch mark on the roller coaster ride, and moved from merry-go-rounds to the big boy rides at the hold 'em tables.

I was called the garbage man. I cleaned up. Even more so than at the Pan 9 tables, luck became a physical and spiritual presence, a dragon whose tail I somehow hitched a ride on. I had a keen Spidey sense with those cards. I could see you. I could feel you. I knew whether I could beat you, and I knew when to fold because I also knew a better hand was just a round away.

Because of that tingling feeling at the base of my skull, I was extremely confident. I'd play hands no one else would play. Nothing could faze me. I could talk to four different people, eat my chow fun, watch the highlights of the Dodgers game, and flirt with the petite Vietnamese dealer with the big breasts, jade bracelet, gold ring, perfect nails, and big full red lips. Like I wasn't paying attention. But I was. I tagged folks the second they cashed in their chips. Now at my table, I saw the sweat drip from a temple or caught a nervous twitch. I knew who counted his chips twice. Who was scared.

Me, I had balls. Two fucking beanbags rested between my legs, and I could not be fazed 'cause I was balls deep.

Oh, it's my bet?

Raise, muthafucka.

On the night of my biggest win, I was talking shit, like I always did. It was a marathon hand, back and forth, back and forth, one volley after another, until the pot reached $34,000. All the while, I walked around. Smoked a cigarette. Talked trash. Every trick in the book. In truth, I was way out of my league—the best thing I had was my high card, an ace—but I knew I could take this guy, just as I knew he knew that I was bluffing about my hand. At that last moment, with all my money on the line, invested, I saw it. I saw the next card in my mind like a lens. I knew it was coming. I knew I had him. The last card flipped. There it was. An ace.

Raked it in. Balls deep.

For almost a year after that, I followed the flame of my cigarette and just couldn't lose. I was, to quote Tupac, *straight muthafuckin' ballin'*. Winning hands followed by exploding roars of joy followed by victorious pats on the back and endless bowls of noodles and celebratory fruit plates.

Mind you, the parade wasn't just for me. When I won, everybody won, from the railbirds on the sidelines shouting, "You very lucky, man!" and receiving my tips in return, to the people who bet on my bets. The dealers loved me; the floor men loved me. Servers and porters were at my beck and call. Fetching a pack of sugar resulted in a $10 tip. I was everyone's personal ATM, the sure stock in that underground market of highs and lows. All chips, no dips.

I kept going, playing heavy games with yellows and blacks. Big bets, $60 to $120 a round. $5,000 pots. This was hard-core pro-level shit. I had to bring it. For myself and for the village that popped up around me.

I hardly ever went back to the Asian games room, but the tale of my rise in poker had taken on mythological proportions there. My old trolls from Pan 9, the same ones who edged me out just months earlier, found their way to my side, giving me pats on the back and lighting my cigarettes. A guy couldn't ask for anything more. My team was together again. I was back.

Eventually, I began to spend more time at the casino than I did in my normal day-to-day life. Two, three weeks could fly by, and I wouldn't even notice. I went through the entire teller-training program at the local First Federal Bank but didn't show up on my first day behind the window. I went through jobs at CompUSA and Pick 'n Save, daydreaming about the moment I could clock out and get back into the action.

All the while, the game permeated my being, and the whole world was filtered through the lens of luck. The number of green lights I hit on the way to the casino. The spot where I parked. The door I entered. The amount of dandruff I saw. The amount of dirt under a fingernail. The marks on a chip. The way an ice cube melted. And the way the flame lit my cig was the direction, I thought, where I needed to find my luck.

I started getting deep.

I grew whiskers at the tables.

I went from the Bike to bigger, higher-limit games at other steel-city casinos. The Normandie Casino was a few streets away in nearby Gardena. Eventually I made it to L.A.'s own Vegas-style big ballin' tuxedo illusion of opulence: Commerce Casino in the City of Commerce.

I took in at least $1,000 a night; many times, much more. I went almost every day. About the only time I wasn't there was when I was having fun with my winnings. That's when I'd be dropping a G a night at Korean nightclubs in Koreatown and East Hollywood. I'd roll up in my Mazda RX-7 that I bought for cash on Robertson Boulevard in Beverly Hills. Red, dropped to the floor, Ricaro racing seats, turbo, see ya!

In my hand, not a beeper, not a pager, but a fucking Motorola StarTAC with a thin battery pack. That shit was unheard of back in '92. If you had the fat battery pack, you might as well stay with yo' momma and bake Toll House cookies at home. If you had a cell phone, you better come correct.

And I came correct.

"Where my waiter at?!" as I rolled up to the club.

I'd valet, light my cigarette, say what up to some other homies, give a hug and kiss to some girls looking all fine in their black miniskirts and low-cut blouses. Then my vest-wearing waiter, Peter Pan, would greet me. Korean waiters go by nicknames; it's how we do.

"Ahnyunghaseo" with a big-ass bow, smile, and warm welcome. Basically, "Welcome, my king, let me take you to your lair."

I would sink into a velvet booth with my boys. There was Yogi, drinking like he was getting ready to hibernate for the winter. Yong Tweezy, who had such a thick Frida Kahlo unibrow that we would tell him to get some tweezers and pluck them fucking umbrellas. Then there were the other guys that rounded out the crew: Davy Baby, Batako, John John Boy, Marty Party, Pong Gil.

Within seconds, three bottles of Crown Royal, a pitcher of ice-cold Coke, a huge platter of fruit piled with watermelon, oranges, grapes, apples, bananas, strawberries, persimmons, and whatever else is in season would arrive. That's L.A. for you: eating local, even after midnight in a K-town nightclub in 1992.

Another silver bowl, this one filled with ice-cold sweetened milk and diced fruit, would arrive, along with the *maru anju,* an octagonal platter filled with dried anchovy, peanuts, wasabi peas, beef jerky, sweet and salty nori, salted plums.

One night after spending almost $2,000 at the club, then going for some kimchi and soup at Hodori Jip on Olympic and Vermont, I was wired. Filled with whiskey, kisses, and phone numbers, I went to the Beverly Center and walked into the twenty-four-hour electronics store. Drunk, full of steam and testosterone, I bought the biggest TV on the floor. Fifty-two inches, signed, sealed, and delivered.

Restaurants were my other indulgence. I initially didn't know much about chefs or what the culinary world was supposed to be. I just knew that I had money, these restaurants were expensive, and I had the means to buy the access and the food. So, off we went.

L.A. always gets short shrift as a culinary city, but if you actually lived here in the early 1990s, you would have experienced food as good as anywhere else—just without a dress code. At first it was eating just to be baller. The Water Grill had a grand space and was, as it is now, one of the best spots in town for seafood. Tiers and tiers of oysters, big shrimp cocktails, lobster tails, crab, clams. That was the first place I tasted a mignonette. It made me rethink lemon and Tabasco. I started to understand that certain people ran these restaurants. Chefs.

Röckenwagner was my first foray into the chef world of L.A. It was a restaurant that blew me away. I picked the spot because I saw Röckenwagner on the cover of his cookbook, hugging a huge stalk of asparagus. The restaurant was a peaceful refuge from the rest of the city, a soothing space with huge, high windows, smooth concrete, pale beechwood, bamboo, and skylights.

I immediately thought I should have dressed up more, before deciding *fuck that.* I had just gone to the Beverly Center and got me them new Jordans, black and Carolina baby blue. New jeans. New Mossimo shirt, worn straight out of the store.

I met my uncle inside. *Hello, hello, hello. We the only Asians up in this muthafucka, man.* "No, no wine, just a Coke for me, please."

The asparagus was so tender and rich, yet felt so light. The potatoes—*man, how did they do that?* I felt like I was flying.

"Can I have more bread, please?"

Man, they are really nice here.

"You are so kind, thank you. Thank you."

I was amazed. I was learning.

I found Mary Sue Milliken and Susan Feniger's City Café and Border Grill, L.A. institutions that helped put Mexican food on the national map. At Matsuhisa, I tasted new-style sashimi for the first time. Before chef Nobu Matsuhisa, it was all California rolls and thick-cut maguros. He flipped that shit around, got the best fish, cut it real thin, and laid it flat on a plate. He'd then hit it with scorching hot sesame oil right before you ate it, splashed with ponzu and jalapeños.

Campanile, in a building originally built for Charlie Chaplin, was unique to me. I was treated like a cockroach that had crawled out of the sewer for a tour of the city, but the food was delicious. If only I could have demanded that we be treated correctly, it would have been different, but no: my pops always told me to reserve my emotions in public, be polite, be humble, shy away from conflict, be clean, respect others. *Fuck that,* I thought, but *thank you very much* is what I actually said as I was dissed, forgotten, told to move aside, seated in the sorriest table in the smallest corner, spoken to s-l-o-w-l-y and loudly.

Despite all that, I loved the food. The table, marooned out in the boondocks, gave me a peekaboo shot right into the restaurant's kitchen, and I saw salt falling out of hands like rain from the sky. I loved how the spoons fit in the cooks' hands, how the chicken glistened. The salmon was moist and earthy; the mushrooms tasted of the forest. *Ragout* was my new favorite word. I felt like I had tasted California.

Things were better next door at La Brea Bakery. The olive bread, baguettes, chocolate cherry bread, pugliese, Pullman loaves, all displayed on rustic wood racks, were revelations. I tasted the crust, the salt, the dense but airy texture, and was hooked. I loaded up my car with the bread and just gave it away, to share the wealth.

No lie, these restaurants, even Campanile, were fucking amazing. The big-screen televisions were great. The girls were gorgeous. At the end of the day, though, the money and the honey weren't the reasons I went home to the tables. The reason was the game's action, its culture, its people, its grind. Rake that shit in, stack 'em, smoke 'em if you got 'em, throw a humble smile, tip the dealer, wink at that girl again.

That was my rotation. *That* was my addiction.

I was a king, right? El muthafuckin' Rey.

What I didn't see then, even though I could see luck and I could channel luck, was that my destiny—and the destiny of every addict—is always to lose.

After about a year of being king of the kingdom, I got stuck, and my luck slowly drained. And with it, my riches became ashes. The rise was all *Goodfellas* Ray Liotta Handycam into the restaurant. The downfall was faster than a ride down the highest roller coaster at Magic Mountain. I lost the game. I lost my friends. I lost myself.

The problem was, I winked at all the pretty ladies in the room, but I never gave that wink to my friend Lady Luck enough. I never listened to the advice and the pleas from the spirit to slow it down, to respect *her* power. I was too selfish. So one day, she got up and left, and I went on as if she had not left me behind. I convinced myself that it was her loss, that it was she who had lost the man of her dreams, that I wasn't the loser. *Fuck her,* I thought. *I run this shit.*

I could hear the little birdie saying Elvis had left the building, but I couldn't stop. That's when things became dangerous. I started to rush hands, force luck, make aggressive, ego-driven moves. Before that, it had all been natural. Swish.

It started innocuously. All the elements were the same. All eyes on me. Big bets. This hand, though, I lost. And that hand, too. A few hundred dollars, gone. The air deflated. The chatter halted. Everyone quieted.

At first those awkward moments of silence dissipated quickly, and everyone got back on my horse again. "You can do it, don't worry don't worry, home run next time, we make it all back, four ways four ways you bet you bet we back we back we all win, ya ya ya ya ya . . ."

So we'd all get back on that horse. I believed that I couldn't let my friends, my investors, down. I had to win. I had to be the man. Always.

Every day was a new day. I'd bring back money from my hiding spots at home and briefly be on top again, only to get greedy and lose. Badly. Hundreds of dollars went, then thousands, then hundreds of thousands.

In the meantime, new kings were crowned, and those new young muthafuckas threw chips at me like I was a has-been railbird troll, like I needed their fucking charity.

They knew of my legend, my reign. But they looked at me as if to say, *Get out of the way, old man. Your time is done. Go read a book or something.*

I couldn't even get in the game anymore. The same floor men whom I had previously tipped thousands of dollars, the same dealers, the same waiters and porters would tell me now, "Players only around game. Excuse me. Don't crowd the area, sir. You can't eat or order food if you are not playing."

And who could blame them? No one wanted to be around a loser. The moment you become a black cat or you walk under that ladder, no one wants to touch you or talk to you. The crowd doesn't hate you or forget about you. It just can't afford you anymore.

I traveled up and down the state looking for games, hoping to find my luck: Fresno, San Jose, San Mateo, San Diego Indian Reservations. But I never found it. The pros knew, even as I didn't, that I was a balloon leaking hot air.

It was more than just losing that was brutal. Without the game, I couldn't breathe. I suffocated in open air; my skin felt pierced by a trillion tiny needles; white noise congested my thoughts. I just needed to get my fix, to get back in there, to feel the felt on my fingers, the chips in my hand, then . . . *ah*. Cigarette, gin and tonic, cards, beef chow fun, Dodgers game, pretty lady, milk shake.

For the next year and a half, well into 1994, I was in freefall, going through the same hungry, repetitive motions. When I ran out of my own money to get my fix, I borrowed it. Asked my cousins for a hundred bucks, spit out of an ATM, taken without explanation. At home, I scrounged around for change. Every pocket in every coat, in every shirt, in every pair of pants. Behind the television, maybe, between the couch cushions, under the bed.

My room emptied as I hit the pawn shops in West Hollywood, selling whatever I could: my Burberry pea coat, a gold necklace from my birthday, my beloved cassette tape collection of Big Daddy Kane, Public Enemy, Eric B. & Rakim, Poor Righteous Teachers. When I ran out of the good stuff, I brought in toothbrushes and other worthless crap. Soon, though, the Russians who owned the shops saw right through me. After a few visits, they asked me what the fuck I was doing and why I was bringing them this shit. Then they locked me out. I remembered Aardvark's on Melrose took clothes. I sold the rest of my clothes and shoes.

When I ran out of stuff to pawn or sell, I searched for shit to steal. With the exception of the rent money I collected from my roommates for our apartment, everything was fair game. That rent was my only anchor, the only thing I never touched, the one place where I drew the line.

Instead, I stole from my parents. They had upgraded from Nolan Ryan's house to a grand Spanish-style stucco house in a gated community on the seventeenth fairway of Coto de Caza Country Club in Mission Viejo. I'd roll right through those gates in the middle of the day, when I knew my parents were at work. I knew they had no idea what was going on with me, where I was going, how I was drowning. My mom's food always was on the table—her kimchi, her salted fish, her fish egg soup—as if she were waiting for her little boy to come home. But her little boy hadn't been home in months. Her little boy ignored the smiling framed family photos and went straight for his mother's closet. Her little boy demanded to know why wasn't there more money in her pockets? In her purse?

Why?

Why??

Why???

Fuck! Fuck fuck fuck.

I swiped my dad's credit cards and used them to buy gift cards, which I used to buy small dollar items, with the balance returned in cash. The cash turned into chips that potentially could be turned into millions.

I looked around and found video games, my sister's harp, old clocks. More things to pawn. Everything will be okay, I told myself. I'll get it all back.

At last, there was nothing left to borrow, find, or steal.

And that was when I finally lifted the anchor and dipped into the rent. A little toe at first, then the whole body, until I was drowning.

At the tables, I went back to the foods that once brought me luck. Milk shakes, fruit plates, Hong Kong–style crispy chow mein with beef sauce, phở. Soon, though, I couldn't waste my money on food. I needed every last chip to survive. Instead I went in with others on an order of chicken tenders. Or stole a bite of a burger, humbly requested a French fry.

I couldn't believe it. In my heyday, I took Telly Savalas for his last chips—that's taking all of Kojak's lollipops, muthafucka. I went from having cigarettes lit for me, eating my beef chow fun, getting my massage, hearing the applause, and winking at that girl to being the guy who lit the cigarettes, gave the massage, applauded the high roller for a fifty-cent chip. I once stuffed tens of thousands of C-notes under my bed, but now was reduced to a pocket empty but for a sawbuck, a fiver, and some change.

I was back to blue chips. And struggling with my $1–2 hold 'em game. I couldn't hold on to anything, really. But I was convinced that if I played my cards

I COUNTED MY CHIPS
ONE BY ONE. IMAGINING,
DREAMING, THAT
EVERYTHING WOULD BE
RIGHT AGAIN

just right, if I treated my short stack of blue disks carefully, I could still win it all back. Have my cigarettes lit for me. Hear the applause. Holler at that girl.

One night a guy won the jackpot and cashed out almost $150,000. Everyone, me included, was in awe. Envious. A few hours later someone came running in, yelling that a person had been killed in the parking lot. That was Mr. Jackpot, who, along with his girl, had been split in half with an ax on the way to his car.

Did I say it correctly, or did you not just hear me???

Split in muthafuckin' half with an ax like a watermelon.

And yet. Even a double homicide couldn't keep me away. I still was at the hold 'em table the next day. I reeked like fungus. I hadn't been back to my apartment in weeks. I had forgotten about my friends, whose rent money I had gambled away.

My head was down. I counted my chips, one by one. Imagining, dreaming, that everything would be right again.

The hand was laid out. I had a king and a seven. On the table, a seven.

I made my bet. Head still down. Then I felt an extra beat in the script that wasn't right. My head was still down, waiting for the next card.

I felt a hand on my shoulder. I finally looked up. Across the room, my friends, angry about being nearly evicted. My mom, an ocean of despair.

Behind me, my dad, his hand on my shoulder. Heavy and cold as ice.

The stop in action was the dealer waiting for my family to make a move. The whole room paused.

I resisted, tried to shake off my dad's hand. It stayed on me like a suction cup. I struggled. I had to finish my hand. I had $14. "Just let me finish the hand . . ."

No.

"Dad, please . . ."

No.

They plunged into the frozen waters and grabbed me with every bit of their might, their souls. The pain in their eyes ran so deep, I couldn't see where it ended.

I stopped resisting. Surrendered. Let them drag me out. For all my big beanbag balls and high fancy rolls, I was still a boy who needed his parents and friends to pull him out of a very, very dark place.

It was over.

As they took me away, someone hit *play,* and the room resumed its murmur, its click-clack of stacking chips, its squeaky wheels. Even then, I couldn't help looking back and seeing the ghost of my body still at the table, head down. $14 in chips. That empty, unfinished hand.

It was daytime out. The sunlight pierced my eyes as my parents walked me to their car and put me in the backseat. The door shut. Silence. Engine, gas, head back, eyes closed, asleep.

And I woke up to a new life.

I was very lucky, man.

PORK FRIED RICE

When I think about pork fried rice, I think about time in slow-mo. But to most people, everything about pork fried rice is quick and fast. A hundred-meter dash in nine seconds fast. But before that starter gun can fire its blank, you have to prep for the race. For pork fried rice, you need day-old rice; leftovers from last night's meal; and cured, smoked, glazed char siu pork cooked for hours in a hot box. The flaming wok is that nine-second dash. The char siu pork belly here is done with a Korean kid's twist to fit your home oven.

At the casinos, this was my go-to dish, served on medium-size oval plates, their edges decorated with Chinese pagodas, a mound of steaming, pale white rice studded with bits of pork, slippery egg, minced vegetables, and soy sauce in the center.

Eat this with a big, frosty glass of Coke, some chili garlic sauce, chopsticks, and a cheap-ass wide-mouth stainless-steel spoon. If you have any leftover pork belly, mix it into a salad—it'll be delicious.

SERVES 4 TO 6

2 pounds pork belly, skin off
Salt and freshly ground black pepper

MARINADE

1 cup kochujang
¼ cup fresh orange juice
5 garlic cloves, peeled

1 jalapeño pepper, chopped
¼ onion, chopped
¼ cup chopped scallions

FOR THE WOK OR FRY PAN

¼ cup canola oil
2 tablespoons minced peeled fresh ginger
2 tablespoons minced garlic
2 tablespoons minced scallions
¼ cup chopped leftover cooked
    vegetables—anything you got, man

Salt and freshly ground black pepper
4 cups day-old cooked rice
3 eggs, whisked
2 tablespoons Asian sesame oil
¼ cup soy sauce

GARNISH

½ teaspoon minced scallion greens

Season the pork belly on both sides with salt and pepper. Place on a rack set on a sheet pan and put it next to the fan in your refrigerator or somewhere cool and let it rest for 3 hours.

Meanwhile, make the marinade. Combine all the ingredients in a blender or food processor and blend until smooth.

Preheat the oven to 200°F. Take out the pork belly and slather with the marinade, barbershop style.

Place the pan in the oven and cook for 3 hours, then turn the temperature up to 450°F and roast for another 30 minutes.

Pull out the pork and let it cool for 1 hour.

Meanwhile, do all your knife work for the vegetables that will go into the wok. Pay attention and take some time to make it right—it ain't that much knife work, and don't act like it's this major fucking deal to mince some veggies.

Chop up the cooled pork into bite-size pieces.

Now organize yourself.

Then heat up a big pan or a wok until smoking over high heat. Add the canola oil and start with the GGS—ginger garlic scallion—and fry them all at once until they're aromatic, about a minute. Immediately add the rest of the vegetables and season with a touch, *just a touch,* of salt and pepper.

Work this muthafucka in and out for 30 seconds, being sure to constantly keep the vegetables moving.

Add the pork, toss toss toss; then add the rice. Pound down the rice with a wooden spoon, stir it up, and make this come together.

Fold in the eggs, sesame oil, and soy sauce. Turn off the heat and mix well.

NINE SECONDS, GOLD MEDAL IN THE 100-METER DASH.

ENJOY IN FRONT OF THE TV WITH A BIG, FROSTY SODA.

MY MILK SHAKE

If I'm anal-retentive about anything, it's milk shakes. I've been making milk shakes since I was a kid in my family's apartment kitchens, using our green Oster blender with the color-coded Chiclet-shaped buttons. Funny thing—my mom used to use that blender for pureeing kimchi marinade . . . ha! Back then, my family used to go to Bob's Big Boy and Carnation on Wilshire Boulevard after the movies and get strawberry shakes. In high school, I visited every burger stand from Inglewood to Anaheim searching for the perfect banana milk shake, full of chunks of banana and the sweet creamy magic of life.

When I moved to Stateline, California, to work at the nearby Embassy Suites, I would hop the California-Nevada border late at night and hit the twenty-four-hour coffee shops in the casinos, just for a milk shake. I couldn't wait for that frosty metal tin and dripping fluted glass. With a long spoon in hand and pounds of maraschino cherries in my stomach, I'd drink it up.

SERVES 4 TO 6

3 cups premium vanilla ice cream
1 banana, chopped
1 cup shaved ice, made by putting
   ice cubes in a resealable storage bag
   and crushing them with a can of soup
   or any other heavy object

3 tablespoons sugar
Microscopic pinch of Maldon sea salt
2 cups whole milk
Frosted Flakes, crushed, and caramel
   sauce (optional) for garnish

Pack the ice cream down into a blender. Add the banana, ice, sugar, and salt. Pour 1 cup of the milk over the top.

Cover and blend everything until it's nice and creamy. With the blender still going, open the top and gently add more milk until the shake gets to your desired thickness. Mine is thick but viscous and drinkable with the ice shavings as a backdrop.

Pour the milk shake into a frozen glass and garnish with crushed Frosted Flakes and a drizzle of caramel, if you wish.

POST THIS NOTE:

PUT EVERYTHING IN THE FREEZER TO KEEP IT ICE-COLD, INCLUDING THE BLENDER, BLENDER TOP, AND THE BLADES, THE MILK, AND THE GLASS.

I USUALLY GAIN A FEW POUNDS, 'CAUSE I CAN'T STOP. . . .

KALBI PLATE

Sometimes sitting tableside with my cards, I'd order a plate of kalbi off the casino menu. They were thin, juicy slices of L.A.–style short ribs, stacked high and crosscut, with the three bones to grab on to like handlebars. Delicately marinated in soy sauce, sugar, garlic, scallions, sesame oil, beef stock, pears, kiwifruit, red wine, and orange juice, these babies were grilled till charred and crusty. They came out of the kitchen a glistening, super deep brown caramel. This is L.A.'s southern comfort, its own version of American BBQ filtered through Korea, which is amazing as anything from Austin to the Carolinas.

SERVES 4 TO 6

MARINADE

1 cup soy sauce
½ onion, cut up
1 kiwifruit, peeled
½ cup garlic cloves, peeled
½ bunch scallions, roughly chopped

½ cup mirin
1 cup fresh orange juice
¼ cup sugar
½ cup Asian sesame oil
2½ tablespoons toasted sesame seeds

4 tablespoons canola oil for the grill
1½ pounds boneless or bone-in short ribs, thinly sliced

ON THE SIDE, IF YOU WANT
Cooked white rice
Macaroni salad
Kimchi

JUST BUY MACARONI SALAD AND KIMCHI FROM THE STORE; THAT'S FINE. OR USE THE KIMCHI YOU MADE ON YOUR OWN (PAGE 19).

Combine all the marinade ingredients in a blender and puree.

Pour the pureed marinade over the short ribs and massage it through the meat with pressure and delicious intent. Marinate it, covered, in the refrigerator for at least an hour and up to 2 days.

Meanwhile, cook some white rice. You know how.

Heat up a grill (or a grill plate if indoors) for 5 to 10 minutes. Season the grill with oil. Grill your short ribs until charred, about 4 minutes on each side. When they're done, they should glisten and have bits of burned but delicious layers.

You can either put everything in a bowl (rice, kimchi, macaroni salad, kalbi) or place each one separately on a paper plate, Hawaii-style, and grub.

SPAGHETTI JUNCTION: THE $4 SPAGHETTI THAT TASTES ALMOST AS GOOD AS THE $24 SPAGHETTI

I've always had this thing for Italians. And in a way they've had their thing for me, too. I went to Italy for a little bit after my dark days of gambling and replenished my soul in Genoa, Milan, and Venice. Then, during culinary school, I had the good fortune of hanging with many friends from the Italian neighborhoods Bensonhurst and Sheepshead Bay in Brooklyn, and Howard Beach, Bayside, and Middle Village in Queens, and even in New Brunswick, New Jersey.

Imagine this: a semi-tall Korean kid from L.A. in his mid to late twenties getting weird looks, then immediate hugs from grandmas and mamas. I'd be thrust into the kitchen with "Oh, you go to culinary school with my girl/boy? Let me show you a thing or two." Then they'd have me cook. This was my icebreaker, 'cause a Korean kid in Howard Beach walking a girl home ain't that easy, son.

Once I cooked, even in my early days, it was magic. Big fat kisses from grandma as she let me stir the pot of tomatoes.

So here you go, my $4 spaghetti. Tastes almost as good as the $24 one.

—— SERVES 4 TO 6

SAUCE
¼ pound button mushrooms, whole
¾ cup garlic cloves, peeled
1 cup extra virgin olive oil

2 28-ounce cans of whole peeled
 tomatoes
Salt and pepper

THE REST (AMOUNTS UP TO YOU . . .)
Spaghetti
Fresh basil, torn
Parmigiano-Reggiano

After a quick brushing off of any dirt, put the mushrooms in a large pot and cover them with about 3 cups of water. Bring to a boil, then lower the heat to a simmer. Strain the mushroom stock after about an hour and a half and reserve.

Meanwhile, combine the garlic and olive oil in a small saucepan and cook over the lowest flame possible, low and slow, for about 2 hours, stirring periodically until the garlic is a dark golden brown.

When the garlic is done, add the tomatoes along with all of their juice to another large pot. Bring the tomatoes to a boil, then add the garlic confit to the pot, including the oil.

Add the mushroom stock to the tomato-garlic mixture, one gallon at first, and blend with a stick blender. You are looking for a smooth consistency. Add more stock if necessary. Season to taste with salt and pepper.

Turn down the heat to the lowest flame and cook for about 2 hours, stirring the sauce periodically. Check for flavor and adjust the salt and pepper if necessary.

Heat up a big pot of water, add ½ teaspoon of salt and a touch of olive oil, and bring it to a boil. Cook the spaghetti just until it's al dente, about 8 to 10 minutes.

Drain and divide the spaghetti among all the bowls. Toss immediately with the sauce—about a cup of sauce for each bowl of spaghetti. Garnish with the basil and Parmigiano-Reggiano.

GRANDMAS WILL KISS YOU, TOO.

CASINO PRIME RIB

From my dad working at Lawry's to going out for fancy dinners with the parents as a kid to having a plate while ballin' as a gambler, prime rib seems to have followed me through my life. When it's done quickly, though, just for the sake of saying "prime rib," the dish can be a waste of an animal and its soul. But when it's done right—thoroughly seasoned and cooked with patience over a low, low heat—it can be one of the wonders of cooking. I hope this one, served with au jus and dip, is more on the wondrous side.

SERVES 4 TO 6

A whole or half rib-eye (bone-in is great
  if you are feeling ambitious)

Aluminum foil
Racked pan

SEASONING SPICES

2 tablespoons coarse ground black
  pepper
2 tablespoons dried rosemary
2 tablespoons dried thyme
2 tablespoons garlic powder
2 tablespoons paprika

2 tablespoons kosher salt
2 tablespoons dried sage
2 tablespoons dried basil
2 tablespoons dried fennel pollen,
  if available

AU JUS

2 tablespoons beef base
2 cups water

Note: You'll need a meat thermometer to make sure the rib-eye is as rare as it should be.

Preheat the oven to 300°F.

To make the seasoning, mix together all of the spices in a bowl.

Liberally cover the rib-eye all over with the seasoning mix, patting it into the meat as much as you can.

Place the rib-eye on a racked pan and cover it with aluminum foil. Place the rib-eye in the oven and roast it gently for about 2½ hours if it's a whole one and 1½ hours if it's a half. You'll know when it's done by checking the internal temperature—you want it to read rare, about 115°F.

When it's rare, remove the aluminum foil and continue to roast it, uncovered, for about 30 more minutes until it is just under medium rare, about 125°F.

Take the rib-eye out of the oven and let it rest for about 30 minutes before slicing. While it rests, make your au jus and the dip.

To make the au jus, combine the beef base and water in a small pot over high heat. Bring it to a boil and turn off the flame. You can also use the veal stock (page 222); just use the strained stock, but don't reduce it to a demiglace, and season it with salt and pepper.

For the dip, use the "Dip" part of the Chips and Dip recipe, page 90.

SLICE, DIP, MMMM. PULL OUT SOME BREAD TO MAKE A SANDWICH IF YOU WANT, OR JUST CHOW DOWN ON THE MEAT AND DIP.

PHỞ FOR DEM HOS

If you're at a gambling table, nothing is better than a bowl of phở. I don't know if it's the fact that you're nervous, that you've been sitting for hours, that endorphins are bouncing around inside you, that your soul is being emptied, dripping and dripping away . . . but eating a hot bowl of phở, tableside, cards in one hand, chopsticks in the other—well, it's the most delicious food you can eat right at that moment. It'll help you shed any feelings of insecurity and grow you the pair you need to take on your opponents.

Eat fast and ferocious. Snorting helps.

SERVES AT LEAST 6

THE BROTH

10 pounds beef bones, rinsed and soaked in cold water for 2 hours, then drained

2 onions, unpeeled, halved

1 bunch scallions

2 big stalks fresh ginger, unpeeled

2 cups garlic cloves, peeled

1 cup star anise

½ cup coriander seeds

½ cup black peppercorns

1 cup beef base

1 big heavy handful of cilantro stems, leaves reserved for garnish

Salt and freshly ground black pepper

THE REST (AMOUNTS UP TO YOU)

Rice noodles, prepared according to package directions

Onion, thinly sliced

Scallion, minced

Fresh Thai basil leaves

Limes, cut in half

Bean sprouts, washed

Sriracha

Hoisin sauce

Fresh cilantro leaves

Rare filet mignon, sliced

Put the beef bones in a big pot and add enough water to cover the bones. There should be at least 3 gallons of liquid in the pot.

On a grill or in a sauté pan over medium heat, char the onions, scallions, and ginger, using little to no oil, until they're blackened but not burned.

Heat the pot with the bones over medium-high heat, then add the charred vegetables, garlic, star anise, coriander, peppercorns, beef base, cilantro stems, and some salt and pepper. Bring to a full boil, then lower the heat to simmer. Let simmer for 3 hours, constantly skimming foam off the surface.

Check for flavor, adjust the seasonings, and drain the broth through a large sieve, discarding the solids. You can keep this broth in your refrigerator for 2 days or freeze it for the future.

To assemble the phở, place the rice noodles in a bowl. The noodles should be soft and at a tepid temperature. Pour the hot broth over the noodles and garnish as you please. If you wanna do like me, then add everything to the bowl.

EAT WITH FRIENDS, SHOES OFF, ONE FOOT ON THE CHAIR, KNEE UP, SLURPING LIKE YOU DON'T CARE ABOUT EMILY POST.

CHAPTER 8

EMERIL

When we left the Bicycle Club, it was light outside. I fell asleep in the car and woke up from an *Avatar* dream and into the detox of infinite Korean love.

There were no words for this detox. My parents and I didn't talk about what had happened. Sometimes, in Asian culture, it is all about the words—the stress and the lectures and the discipline and the heightened expectations. The constant nagging, the torture of never being good enough.

But sometimes, in the deepest of moments, there are no words. There is only food. There is a bowl of rice. There is kimchi. Broiled fish. Soups and noodles. Chopsticks and the newspaper. The only things that truly communicate forgiveness and repair a broken soul.

I was to be repaired at my parents' Coto de Caza house in Mission Viejo, the same place I had stolen from and used as a surplus center to supply my low-life pawns. It looked like a Miami bungalow, painted bright flamingo pink, with shaded palm trees and windows cascading light in from everywhere. Around us were meandering foothills, soaring falcons, families on horseback. The Saddleback Mountains loomed over the landscape, and a creek dribbled water across the fairway—frogs straight out of a Disney movie would ribbet throughout the night. You might see a mountain lion on the prowl, a coyote chasing bunny rabbits, or a golf ball sailing across the sky toward a sea of bright green.

I hated the place from the moment they moved in. I hated how boring it was, and I abhorred the senseless affluence. But the day my parents brought me back from the Bicycle Club was the day I finally saw past all that and discovered the genuine beauty in the nature surrounding Coto de Caza. Besides, I was exhausted, I had lost all my friends, and I had nowhere left to run. At least there on the seventeenth fairway, I could hide from everyone. Everyone, that was, but myself.

The detox took weeks. I was just twenty-four years old, but between my lost week in New York and my lost years at the tables, I had become frail to the bone. Everything in me was sick. My mind was filled with white noise. I couldn't think. I had to come to terms with the fact that I had begged, borrowed, stolen, and lost everything. That I had let everyone down, including my friends and especially my family. For days on end, I stayed in my pajamas and stared at the TV and at the pages of books, trying to relearn how to piece words together to form sentences. When my parents left for work at 9:00 A.M. and returned at 7:00 P.M., I was still on the couch where they had left me, empty bowls of food and crumbs everywhere. Towering over me at the end of the day, my parents could do only what they knew to do: keep feeding me, bowl after bowl, hoping their walking dead of a son would come back to life.

After weeks of my wrestling with my demons, nature and nurture finally got the better of the guilt and shame. The jitters slowly went away, color came back to my face, my cheeks filled out again, and I even had a little spring in my step. I put on some real clothes and decided it was about time to face the world and become a part of society again.

First things first. I had to find some work. Classifieds. And right there in black and white was a listing for an investment banking position at First Investors Corporation, a New York firm with a Los Angeles office on Westwood Boulevard. Fancy. They managed mutual funds and were looking for motivated and talented brokers. You could be successful there. I was motivated. I could be talented. *I* could be successful there.

I dusted off my dad's tweed suit and drove to L.A. to apply.

First Investors was in a small office in West Los Angeles. An older gentleman named Malvin Scherr, direct from a corner office at the New York branch and looking forward to retiring as soon as he had the L.A. office up and running, oversaw things. His assistant, a beautiful older lady with round glasses, had that look of a New York Jewish aunt. And then there was me, without any experience, licenses, or certifications, but young, fresh off some bad times, and ready to succeed. We all hit it off beautifully. I was hired on the spot.

The plan was for me to take the Series 6 and Series 7 broker exams to become licensed to sell mutual funds. If I passed, Malvin would groom me. I'd start from where I was—the bottom of the bottom—and learn about the company's funds and how to run the market. And so I did it. I studied up and took the exams on a computer in some office building in Irvine. Somewhere in me, I secretly hoped to fail both tests so I wouldn't have to work. But I fucking passed. I was a certified banker.

My parents were so proud. To celebrate, they took me and my sister out to Benihana that night. Their son was going to Wall Street! We ordered the hibachi steak and lobster combos. Extra shrimp? Of course! Double the fried rice. And you want the filet mignon, too? Buddha drinks for everyone! My son's going to Wall Street! Hercules, Hercules, Hercules!

Alas, Hercules's first day on the job was not running with the bulls on Wall Street. While my parents thought I was on the top floor of the Oppenheimer Tower in Westwood, I was actually in the basement, in a dark room with a rotary phone and ten stacks of telephone books. Cold-calling 101. What is a brother to do? Not tell his parents and start with the letter *A*, that's what. One by one, I called. Maybe I even called you. Do you remember a guy with a nervous tremble in his voice ringing you up in the middle of the day sometime in 1995, asking if you had ever considered investing in mutual funds, class A shares, then thanking you for your time and wishing you a good rest of the day?

So I wasn't Gordon Gekko. But the job gave me what I needed: a structure and a goal. I wore a suit every day. I carried a briefcase full of investment portfolios. Door to door, I had more.

Beyond the Yellow Pages, I reached into my own Rolodex, hitting up everyone I knew, from people I met during the old days at church to my parents' clients to merchants in liquor stores and video shops. It was a slow start. No one was interested in investing in their future. Then, right around the time I hit *F* in the phone book, I made my very first sale, off a lead from a network of friends within the Korean community. A Class A First Investors aggressive growth fund called Technology sold to a guy who ran an embroidery shop in Costa Mesa.

As soon as I popped my cherry with that first fund, it was on. Boom, another sale, to a family friend who owned a liquor store in Topanga Canyon. These first few clients did so well that they referred me to their friends. And I listened to their stories, examined their lives, and tried my best to give them the right fund to fit their needs. It worked. My picks were gangbusters with incredible returns. It was "You very lucky, man!" all over again.

Things were going good. Over the next few months, I worked my way up, eventually making six figures. I got my step back on the L.A. grind and reconnected with Koreatown, now in full bloom after recovering from the L.A. Riots a few years earlier. But just as I was gathering steam in my new life, I bumped into my old homie and roommate Yogi.

He had graduated from UCLA by then, and his family had high hopes for him. After all, he was the smart kid in his family who was supposed to fly to success and be a doctor, just like his pops. But, to his and his family's disappointment, he just couldn't fly straight. He was drinking a lot when we roomed together, and he kept it up even after he graduated. In fact, his reputation for drinking preceded him throughout the Asian-American college community from UCLA to USC to CSUN to UCI to the Cal States and all throughout Koreatown. And he was still ruling the streets when I ran into him again.

After all that shit with the gambling, though, I was a little reluctant to see him. But time heals all wounds, and beer waters the lawns of friendship. We instantly rebonded like nothing had ever happened and went out for a drink.

Then a few more. And more. And with each bottle, I started to lose my step and fall behind. Then I just lost my footing altogether, and for the next year and a half, he and I each let alcohol fuel the other's anger about unfilled expectations, our disappointments, our fears, the stress, the pressure. And so if you were in Koreatown around 1995, you probably ran into Yogi and me running fucking game, getting into fights and defending our turf. The long nights would start at around 9:00 P.M. at the Dragon for black bean noodles, hand-pulled long elastic chewy threads covered in steaming hot onions, zucchini, and pork. We'd slurp that up, our faces covered in black smudges. If we wanted some classic Korean BBQ, we hit Soot Bull Jeep, a place filled with smoke and hot charcoal. The panchan were decent, but what brought us in were the plates and plates of raw marinated meat ready to be singed over nuggets of smoldering mesquite, which had been fired up outside till they burned lava red and brought inside to fuel the tabletop grills.

When we wanted something more low-key, we went for big bowls of jjambbong, a spicy seafood stew filled to the brim with octopus, squid, shrimp, clams, and onions. Other times we hit Mom's Place on 8th Street for abalone porridge, where the rice is cooked in stock until it breaks and explodes, then simmered until it's gelatinous and soupy. Chunks of abalone and a raw egg are

I GOT MY STEP BACK ON THE L.A. GRIND AND RECONNECTED WITH KOREATOWN, NOW IN FULL BLOOM AFTER RECOVERING FROM THE L.A. RIOTS A FEW YEARS EARLIER.

mixed in, and it's all seasoned with sesame oil, garlic, ginger, soy sauce. And there were so many other options: fried chicken done Korean style—marinated in milk and beer and then fried till the skin broke like stained glass—at OB Bear; potato pancakes and kimchi jjigae at Kobawoo House; or drinks and spicy rice cakes at a bar called Bohemian.

Just as we got our buzz on, it was off to the club for more drinks, showing off for girls, and turf battles, then to the twenty-four-hour Hodori Restaurant for some blood-cabbage soup or El Taurino for drunken spicy tacos and more phone numbers. Then to Yogi's to crash at his pad on Beloit right near Sawtelle Boulevard.

In the mornings, we ate at Hurry Curry, dead hungover, pouring that extra-spicy glop all over the rice and chewing like horses on hay, or went to Junior's or Langer's and ate our pastrami sandwiches in silence, contemplating.

And all throughout, night or day, we'd walk up and down the streets, glaring like mean mothafuckas, sometimes drunk as shit, red-faced and potbellied, breaking windows for the hell of it. Sometimes I'd start fights for the hell of it, bringing my crew into a brawl that would spill into the street and block traffic with our swinging chains, knives, and bats.

Even our own friends weren't immune to our belligerence. I'd pick drunken fights with them just as soon as I'd start pounding on some random guy who looked at me the wrong way. Or I'd grab a buddy's girl and just start making out with her. Then we'd all fight it out, friend and foe. At first my friends laughed it all off. But I kept pushing that line, and they went from laughing to warning to threatening. When that didn't work, they just tried to avoid me altogether. But they couldn't hide: if they were at a booth somewhere, I'd crash it. If they were at a party, I'd show up. Same shit, different day.

Meanwhile, I was clocking into First Investors later and later every morning, reeking of alcohol and pale as the moon. My clients blew up my pager, asking for my advice about their funds. My advice should have been to run from me before it was too late. I stopped going back to Coto de Caza, and my mom's stews probably sat on the kitchen table, steaming under plastic wrap, waiting yet again for her son to come home. The Buddha celebration at Benihana could last only so long.

Six months of compressed chaos finally came to a head one night in 1995. It was almost 3:00 A.M., and I was hanging out with friends and drinking in the lobby of a karaoke club. I looked up, and there she was. Grace. My ex-girlfriend. We had dated back when I was still playing poker; she was beautiful and clever, and she stuck with me through a lot of shit. It had been a few years since I had last seen her, but she was still as fine as fine could be. So I stepped to her again, opening up some old wounds but also cracking some old jokes to help her remember our good times. We were just sinking into a good moment when her boyfriend came up.

He asked her to come with him. I grabbed her arm and said, "She's staying with me." Then I went the fuck off. I thought he was Chinese and started yelling *"Ni hau ma, muthafucka!"* and telling the punk to say hello and to respect me first. I started to shove him, but I was so drunk, I couldn't even stand straight. Then out of the blue, from the bleacher seats, *whoomp!* Coldcocked, and I hit the ground. Maybe ten dudes came out kicking, hitting, punching. I grabbed one guy and broke his fingers, but I was done. Knocked out and down for the count.

Amid this mayhem, I glimpsed my friends shaking their heads at me and walking away. At any other moment, they would have had my back, but the *"ni hau ma"* was the final straw. My act was getting old. As far as they were concerned, I was a beast and a burden, a dead weight who was getting exactly what he deserved.

Meanwhile, I was dragged into one of the karaoke rooms. The boyfriend's goons threw me down on a couch, whipped out their guns, and put the barrels to my head. The boyfriend asked me if I wanted to live or if I wanted to die. It was quiet. I'm sure the other guys were waiting, just waiting, for the signal to pull their triggers. But the boyfriend took his time. Because my old girlfriend was now his girlfriend, he had just the slightest, most microscopic bit of sympathy for me. So he asked me again.

"Do you want to live? Or do you want to die?"

I dripped blood. Slobber drooled from my nose and mouth. My bruised face ballooned like the Elephant Man's. I thought about his question, but the answers just weren't coming into my head. So I stood up. Raised my two fists, clenched except for the middle fingers held sky high into the air. And said, "Fuck you. I'm still standing even after all you punks tried to kick me. *I'm still standing.*"

And I walked out of the room.

WANT TO LIVE?
WANT TO DIE?"

They should have shot me.

But I walked out, spitting and thinking I was such a bad ass, not knowing that if it weren't for the grace of Grace and the love that her new boyfriend had for her at that moment, I'd be dead. Not knowing that I was a piece of shit whose life was spared because a dude got asked by his girlfriend to please not kill me. Some tough guy, huh? Grace drove me back to her apartment in my car as her friends followed her in their cars. I woke up the next morning in the passenger seat and haven't seen her since.

I didn't learn my lesson. The stupid cycle continued a little while longer, with me roaming the city with black eyes and swollen body parts from nights and fights I couldn't even remember. I probably would have spun even more out of control if it weren't for the smell of beef bourguignonne.

A few weeks after the scene at the club, I woke up on Yogi's couch in the haze of that 11:00 A.M. hour, half asleep, half dead, half drunk, half high, half assed. I turned on the TV and started to sink into a show hosted by a dude cooking in a checkerboard-tiled kitchen. As his voice trailed off and my eyes began to roll back under heavy eyelids, I felt a tap on my shoulder and a slap across my face.

"Hey, wake up. Wake up! What the fuck are you doing?"

Very slowly, I started to wake up.

"Why do you act like this? Here, smell this. Try this. Taste this. It's beef bourguignonne. These are herbs. Oregano and basil. *Wake up and get your shit together!*"

Bam. The weights on my eyelids lifted. The room was fuzzy and the TV was still on, but the body in the screen was three-dimensional. Emeril Lagasse wasn't talking to the camera anymore. His eyes were looking straight at me like fucking Mona Lisa's. He was talking to me. And he was shoving oregano and basil under my nose. For one long second, I felt the herbs tickling my nose; I smelled the stew bubbling in the pot. It was exhilarating. Captivating. And bam, just like that, I knew. This was my destiny.

The second passed, and I touched the TV. Emeril was back in the checkerboard kitchen, doing *The Essence of Emeril*, as if nothing had just happened.

Up until that moment, I just didn't see it. I didn't realize how much food was a part of my family, a part of me. I was almost too close to it all, too close to the screen to really see the big picture. But the moment Emeril waved those herbs at me, my whole world clicked into place and I saw what had been in front of my face this whole time: Food. Flavors. *Sohn-maash.* I saw myself in the kitchen. I saw myself at home.

That was it. I made up my mind. I was done with the anger, the shame, the mistakes, the self-pity, the pain. For real this time, I was done. I peeled myself off the couch. Got up, went to the bathroom, and took a hard look at myself. *You fucking low-life SOB. Get your shit together. Get your shit together.*

I got up and left that old me on Yogi's couch. Moved back to the seventeenth hole, and, for the next six months, I stayed strong and focused my energy: I returned to First Investors, where Malvin took me back under his wing. I got back in touch with my clients, took care of their questions, and started navigating the deep labyrinths of the market. I enrolled in a local culinary school, and, two nights out of the week, I honed my knife skills and studied the French method of cooking along with the nine other students in my class. I set my sights on a full-time professional cooking program, learned everything I could, and saved my money.

And, once again, my parents were there. If I was really serious about this, they said, they'd help me. And if I was serious, I had to go to the Harvard of culinary schools—no fucking around this time. We found the Culinary Institute of America in Hyde Park, New York. I had no idea what or where it was. Just that it was in the sticks. As it happened, my cousin was doing his residency in Manhattan and offered up his futon for 250 bucks a month.

I got into the CIA and moved to New York. It was the move that would change my life forever.

I was very lucky, man.

KOREAN-STYLE BRAISED
SHORT RIB STEW

This is that meal from home that every Korean kid says his or her mom does best, the dish that gets packed in CorningWare and taken to parties, the dish that creates some serious lines in the sand over friendship and heated arguments over who seems to know it better or "owns" the best-of-the-best title for it. I don't know whose mom does it best, so try mine.

SERVES 4 TO 6

SAUCE

½ cup chopped scallions

1½ cups soy sauce

¼ cup chopped peeled fresh ginger

½ white or yellow onion, peeled

½ cup garlic cloves, peeled

½ cup sugar

½ cup mirin

½ cup fresh orange juice

½ cup apple juice

4 cups water

4 pounds short ribs, soaked in cold water
   in the refrigerator overnight

VEGETABLES

8 ounces shiitake mushrooms, stems
   discarded

1 cup jarred chestnuts, peeled

1 cup cubed taro

1 cup carrots in large dice

1 cup cubed butternut squash

In a blender or food processor, combine all the ingredients for the sauce except 3 cups of water and puree. Add the pureed sauce, plus the remaining 3 cups water, to a large pot, stir, and bring to a boil.

Meanwhile, remove the soaked ribs from the fridge, drain, rinse, and drain again. Score the ribs across the top of the meat in diagonal slashes. When the sauce has come to a boil, add the ribs. Lower the heat to a simmer and cover the pot.

Let the sauce and the ribs cook for at least 2 hours over low heat, then add the vegetables, replace the cover, and simmer for another 30 minutes or so, until the meat is tender and the vegetables are cooked but retain their integrity.

Serve with rice.

SHARE IF YOU WISH.

SOYBEAN PASTE STEW

My mom's bowls and bowls of stews were what put meat back on my bones after I lost everything. The soybean paste stew was especially comforting: there could be nothing easier, yet nothing more satisfying. Just add some paste to a stock, swirl, add veggies and tofu, boil it all, eat it all. It'll make you rethink everything in your life.

SERVES 4 TO 6

1 pound beef brisket, cut into small chunks
1 tablespoon soy sauce
1 tablespoon minced scallions
1 tablespoon minced garlic
1 tablespoon sliced jalapeño pepper, seeds and all
¼ cup sliced white or yellow onion
1 teaspoon Asian sesame oil

2 tablespoons vegetable oil
3 cups beef stock or anchovy stock (page 21)
2 cups water
¾ cup Korean soybean paste (doenjang)
½ cup shiitake mushrooms, stems discarded
1 cup diced firm tofu
Salt and freshly ground black pepper

In a large bowl, mix the brisket with the soy sauce, scallions, garlic, jalapeño, onion, and sesame oil.

Heat a large soup pot over medium-high heat. Add the vegetable oil and when it begins to smoke, add the brisket mixture. Cook the meat until it browns, about 4 minutes, and you can start to smell its deliciousness. At that point, add the stock and water, the soybean paste, stirring to dissolve it, and the shiitake mushrooms. Bring it all to a boil, then reduce the heat to a simmer and let the mixture simmer, uncovered, for 20 minutes.

Add the tofu and stir gently. Simmer for 20 minutes, then turn off the heat. Add salt and pepper to taste. Serve with a bowl of rice and some kimchi.

JUST ANOTHER EVERYDAY MEAL.

SPICY OCTOPUS

Nothing says Korean bar food more than spicy sautéed octopus or squid. The plate is always huge, the flavors are always over the top, it's always piping hot, and you're always drunk. Is there any other way to eat a meal?

SERVES 2

SAUCE

½ white or yellow onion, peeled

½ Asian pear, peeled, halved, and cored

½ cup kochujang

2 tablespoons soy sauce

1 tablespoon sugar

2 tablespoons chopped garlic

2 tablespoons natural rice vinegar (not seasoned)

2 tablespoons sesame seeds

½ cup water

OCTOPUS

8 ounces baby octopus or squid, cleaned

¼ cup vegetable oil

½ cup scallions in 2-inch batons sticks

¼ cup thinly sliced onion

¼ cup thinly sliced red bell pepper

In a blender, combine all the ingredients for the sauce and puree. Set aside.

Put the octopus in a pot and pour in enough water to cover. Bring it to a boil, then simmer the octopus, uncovered, for about 1½ hours, or until extremely tender. Drain and let it cool for 1 hour at room temperature.

Heat a large pan or wok over high heat. Add the vegetable oil and, when it begins to smoke, add the octopus and get a nice char—this should take about 3 minutes. Immediately add the vegetables and toss for about a minute, until everything is slightly cooked and the vegetables are wilted.

Add the sauce and bring it all together, then turn off the heat and scoop the octopus into a big bowl.

EAT EAT EAT.

KOREAN STAINED-GLASS FRIED CHICKEN

Koreans drink beer. And when we drink beer in Koreatown, we eat fried chicken. Chicken and beer. Sonny and Cher. Ashford and Simpson. But unlike American fried chicken, ours has no flour, no buttermilk, no coating. It is just a skin that cracks like glass and a saltiness that makes you wanna drink more . . . beer.

SERVES 4

BRINE

1½ gallons water

½ cup kosher salt

1 tablespoon black peppercorns

¼ cup sugar

3 garlic cloves, peeled and smashed

¼ cup chopped peeled fresh ginger

Juice of 1 lemon

Juice of 1 lime

Juice of 1 orange

½ cup natural rice vinegar (not seasoned)

4 cups beer—whatever's in your fridge

1 cup whole milk

CHICKEN

1 whole chicken, approximately 4 pounds

2 quarts vegetable oil

Salt and freshly ground black pepper

In a pot large enough to hold 1½ gallons of liquid and all the chicken pieces, combine the ingredients for the brine and cook over high heat for 20 minutes. Drain the brine through a sieve, discarding the solids, return the brine to the pot, and chill it for several hours until cold.

Add the chicken to the chilled brine and soak it overnight.

The next day, remove the chicken from the brine, rinse it in cold water to discard any milk solids, and place on a rack over a sheet pan to dry on your counter for 2 hours, or until it's completely dry.

When you're ready, add the oil to a large, deep pot and heat it to 350°F, or dip a piece of the chicken in the oil—if the oil sizzles, it's ready.

Fry the chicken until each piece is golden brown all over and cooked through, about 10 to 12 minutes.

Transfer the chicken to a paper-towel-lined plate or baking sheet to drain, then season with salt and pepper. The skin should crackle and pop.

Enjoy immediately with some kimchi.

YUZU GLAZED SHRIMP
OVER EGG FRIED RICE

This recipe pretty much sums me up during this chapter of my life: some old habits left over from my youth combined with the gentle, delicate change that was just waiting to happen. And so: egg fried rice—nothing more simple or comforting—combined with beautiful fresh prawns, lightly cooked, then glazed with yuzu.

SERVES 4

GLAZE
1 teaspoon yuzu kosho pepper paste

1 tablespoon fresh lime juice

1 tablespoon fresh orange juice

¾ cup water

RICE
2 tablespoons vegetable oil

2 cups day-old cooked rice

2 tablespoons soy sauce

2 tablespoons Asian sesame oil

1 egg

SHRIMP
2 tablespoons vegetable oil

1 pound large shrimp (16 to 20 count), deveined

Salt and freshly ground black pepper

1 tablespoon butter

Combine the ingredients for the glaze in a small bowl and stir to dissolve.

Heat a large pan or wok over high heat and add 2 tablespoons vegetable oil. Throw in the rice and heat it up, moving it all around until it becomes crispy.

Add the soy sauce and sesame oil and mix to incorporate. Crack in the egg and mix it all around for a minute. Scoop the rice into a bowl and rinse the pan.

Return the pan to the stove and heat it up on high. Add the 2 tablespoons oil.

Season the shrimp with salt and pepper and, working in batches, sear them on 1 side for about 30 seconds. Then, and only then, turn them over to the other side and cook for another 30 seconds. Remove to a plate and repeat for the remaining shrimp.

Return all the cooked shrimp to the pan, and pour the glaze over the shrimp and let it slightly reduce for just a few seconds. Turn off the heat and fold in the knob of butter.

Pour over the rice and **CHOW DOWN.**

HIBACHI STEAK TEPPANYAKI

Before I became a chef, I thought being a chef meant what they did at Benihana. Fire, spatulas, funny hat, shrimp in the pocket, salt and pepper mills shaking up rhythms to the music. I loved the show, and I loved the steak. I spent many birthdays and special occasions at a teppanyaki grill and even worked at one once, cleaning the griddle after the show. No matter where I go as a chef, that hibachi steak, and the whole show that goes with it, goes with me.

SERVES 4

MARINADE
½ cup roughly chopped scallions

1 cup soy sauce

¼ cup chopped peeled fresh ginger

½ white or yellow onion, peeled

½ cup garlic cloves, peeled

1 cup water

½ cup sugar

¼ cup soy sauce

½ cup mirin

½ cup fresh orange juice

½ cup apple juice

½ cup natural rice vinegar (not seasoned)

1 jalapeño pepper

3 shiso leaves

1 tablespoon roasted sesame seeds

STEAK
¼ cup vegetable oil

1 pound skirt steak, pounded ⅛ inch
    thick and cut into 3-inch squares

1 cup thinly sliced onion

1 cup thinly sliced scallions, cut on a bias

1 tablespoon butter

ONE DAY AHEAD

In a blender or food processor, combine all the ingredients for the marinade and puree.

Combine the steak and the marinade in a large resealable plastic bag and let it marinate overnight in the fridge.

THE NEXT DAY

Heat a large pan over medium-high heat and add the oil. Meanwhile, remove the steak from the plastic bag and reserve the marinade. Add the steak to the pan and sear on both sides. Add the onion and scallions and sauté everything for 2 minutes.

Deglaze the pan with as much or as little of the leftover marinade as you wish. Toss in the butter and swirl.

Enjoy immediately with some rice. Or on a toasted roll.

OR FROM YOUR FINGERS LIKE MARK ANTONY ATE GRAPES.

GUMBO

This one's a hat tip to Emeril. My life was as fucked up and twisted and murky as a pot of gumbo, and Emeril saved me that day and didn't even know it! Gumbo to me smells and feels and tastes like the cultures that developed it—the strength, the wisdom, just pure soul.

Filé powder is a thickener sometimes used to make gumbo; no sweat if you don't have it on hand.

½ cup vegetable oil

4 ounces andouille sausage, casing on, chopped

4 ounces dark chicken meat (legs and thighs), chopped

½ onion, diced

½ red, yellow, or green bell pepper, seeded and diced

2 stalks celery, diced

3 garlic cloves, minced

1 jalapeño pepper, seeded and minced

1 cup minced scallions

½ cup sliced okra (use frozen okra if you can't find fresh)

Kosher salt and freshly ground black pepper

1 cup canned diced tomatoes with juice

3 quarts chicken stock

2 bay leaves

4 ounces dark roux

2 cups rice, any kind

12 ounces shrimp, peeled, deveined, and chopped

1 teaspoon filé powder if you have it

Handful of chopped cilantro

Handful of chopped parsley

Juice of 1 lemon

Tabasco or other cayenne-based hot sauce

FOR THE ROUX

½ cup all-purpose flour
8 tablespoons (1 stick) unsalted butter

In a small pot over medium-low heat, melt the butter. Add the flour and cook gently, stirring periodically, until the roux turns a medium-dark brown. This may take 12 minutes. Remove from the heat and cool.

Heat a large pot over high heat for 1 minute, then add the oil. When the oil starts to smoke, add the sausage and chicken to the pot and sauté until you get a nice color on the meat, 3 to 4 minutes.

Add all the vegetables except for the tomatoes and season everything with salt and pepper to taste. Sauté the vegetables until you get a good color on them, about 5 minutes. Then add the tomatoes and cook for 2 more minutes.

Add the stock, bring it to a boil, and then add the bay leaves and cooled roux.

Whisk out any lumps, bring to a boil, reduce the heat to medium, and let it simmer, uncovered, for 20 minutes.

Reduce the heat to low, add the rice, and cook, uncovered, for 30 minutes.

About 5 minutes before the rice is ready, add the shrimp, filé powder if you have it, fresh herbs, and lemon juice, and season to taste again. Throw in a few splashes of Tabasco.

GUNG HO.

CHAPTER 9

NEW YORK, NEW YORK

Winter of 1996. Hyde Park, New York. The first day of culinary school.

A small crowd of kids and their parents—including me and mine—in front of a busy dorm room building, waiting for the resident adviser to arrive and hand out our key cards and room assignments. My family, putting their faith in me one more time, went coast to coast and crossed the country with me. We arrived in Hyde Park via Philly, where we stopped to see

my dad's old stomping grounds. We went up to the University of Pennsylvania to find the little sandwich shops where he worked as a janitor. He showed us his old bike route to and from ABC Studios when he worked for Dick Clark. We touched the Liberty Bell and saw the Declaration of Independence; we ate cheesesteaks in the cold, doing the Philly lean as Cheez Whiz dripped from our fingers. We continued up the coast and ventured through NYC as happy as we could be on our family trip, and then north through the mountains, up the Hudson River to Hyde Park, where naked branches jutted out from brown trees like witches' brooms and the asphalt was covered in dusty black snow.

The dorms were our last stop together, me sitting on my luggage, all of us waiting for the first day of the rest of my life to begin. I turned to the guy nearest to me.

"Hey, I'm Roy. What's up?"

"Oh, hey. I'm Rey, Rey Knight. Good to meet you."

Rey Knight was a young kid from Las Vegas. In fact, as more people piled up at the doors, I realized that everyone was a young kid, somewhere between eighteen and twenty years old. At least six years above the average, I was the clear minority in the crowd. I was restarting college with a bunch of eighteen-year-old Rey Knights. This was going to be interesting.

THE RA FINALLY GOT THERE and handed out our room numbers. I headed inside, walked down a few long hallways, found my number, and opened the door. Dave Matthews was blaring as I walked in. The place was a fucking mess. Socks everywhere. I couldn't see one bit of floor other than what was on the floor.

My program was on a year-round schedule, so students started every other month or so with alternating graduations. So not only was I sharing tight quarters, but my room was already occupied when I showed up. For some fucking reason, I had signed into a four-person room. Two bunk beds and four desks jammed into what was basically a ten-by-ten cinder-block cell. My new roommates were there, hanging out, plus a few more dudes from another dorm room. I don't know if it happened that quickly or if my memory's just hazy, but I don't remember my family anymore after that. It's almost as if they just said good luck and bounced, laughing like hyenas on their way out. I guess it was funny. A twenty-six-going-on-twenty-seven-year-old, sleeping on a bunk bed in a dorm room, surrounded by incense, posters, dirty underwear, and guys not even old enough to drink.

Meanwhile, tucked away in one corner of the room like a caterpillar smoking a peace pipe was a young kid, coolly looking me up and down from under his golden locks. Once things settled down a bit, he grilled me, told me where I was allowed to lay my stuff, pointed to where I would be sleeping, and generally gave me the rundown of how this room "worked." The other dudes nodded along and laughed at his jokes.

He was obviously the top dog, and as much as I already didn't like him, it was way too early for me to challenge him. So I stayed silent and took it all in. Smiled and acted dumb. Made my way across the sea of socks and threw my luggage onto the stripped bunk. Moved to my desk and sank into my chair. Luckily, my desk faced the window, so I took a deep breath, let Dave Matthews, the guys, and the room slowly fade into the background, opened the blinds, and took in my new life. Outside, the majestic Hudson River flowed. Small tugboats broke through the lightly iced waters, and squirrels scurried for scarce snacks in the trees.

I wasn't in Koreatown anymore. Everything was a blank white page.

I was ready to add some color to the scene. I swiveled around and said hello to the guys. It wasn't their fault that they were just a bunch of college kids. It wasn't their fault that this was their first time away from home and they were living it up. So I did what you do in Rome: I grabbed some dryer sheets from my luggage, went to the bathroom, and unrolled the toilet paper. Stuffed the cardboard tube full of Bounce and brought it out. Then, right in front of the guys, I pulled out some weed from another pocket of my luggage, took a monster hit, and blew the smoke through the tube. Flowers.

"Ahhhh, yeah, dude!" they yelled. I had broken bread with a bunch of baking students. We were all good. Except for me and the top dog, that is. He still eyed me carefully from his corner. I ignored him, passed the pipe around, and slipped out. I wanted to see what this campus was all about.

The first dude I met outside was Peter Vafeas. He was as big as an offensive lineman and seemed to be wandering around in the same daze I was in. He was a little bit older than most of the other kids there—around twenty-three, just out of college. We connected right away, and he would become one of my best friends over the next couple years, even up until today. We downloaded each other on

where we came from—L.A. for me, of course, and he from Long Island, New York—and walked around to take in the serenity.

The campus rested on a hill just above the Hudson and sloped downward into the trees. It was centered around Roth Hall, a redbrick castle that used to be a Jesuit seminary and now served as the main building on campus. A bridge took you over to the baking center and kitchens. Every other building on campus was redbrick, too. There was a library, four dormitories, classroom buildings, and a small lake. There were trails and gazebos and a huge parking lot that faced Route 9.

This was the Culinary Institute of America.

THE FIRST DAY OF CLASS was a blur. In the maze of the school, we made our way past the white coats and the cool, confident stares of the second-year students and picked up the supplies for our adventure. Down the hallways for our starched chef's coats, houndstooth cook pants, and paper toques. Another room for textbooks. Then over to another room to pick up our knives—a whole set from a ten-inch down to a paring.

Piled high with books and knives and uniforms, we ran to our rooms, dropped off all our new gear, and went straight to our first class: gastronomy. Gastronomy was in a big corner classroom on the top floor of the redbrick castle; it had beautiful stained-glass windows that faced the Hudson Valley. By the time I got in, it was already packed to the rafters with a hundred or so students. I found Pete and sat down next to him, and we said what up to a bunch of other dudes that would become our crew: Rich Perez, Jesse Gutierrez, Rob Peck, Vinnie Fama, Manny, the list went on.

And if you hadn't noticed, it was all dudes. Back then, it was like three girls for every seventy guys. Not great for the girls. Or the guys.

The classroom was abuzz. We were just now catching our breaths after our Cinderella morning. Everyone was so excited, and no one had any idea what to expect. Then there he was. He walked in like a general, and the room fell quiet. His eyes lit up, and he started pointing at people to sit down, and we did. Then he spoke, in the most regal of ways.

"Welcome to the Culinary Institute of America."

Pause.

"I'm Chef Ron DeSantis. And this is Gastronomy 101."

Chef DeSantis was a certified master chef, a former military chef, a bad-ass muthafucka. He spoke in Shakespearean colloquialisms and walked like a panther. We were all amazed. And we learned. We learned about Carême; we learned about Escoffier. We learned about the brigade system, the history of food, the origins of dishes, how a knife is a carefully constructed balance of blade and handle. I felt like I was an assassin meeting a gun for the first time.

Too soon, the history lesson was over, and they funneled us down to our meal period. This was no joke. One thing about going to a culinary school is that you *eat*: somebody has to eat all the stuff you're making; nothing goes to waste. The CIA food life cycle went from teaching to eating to compost back to knowledge. And we were the perfect, hungry guinea pigs. Every day was a different trip to a Las Vegas buffet. One day it was all the classics, with veal blanquettes and pommes Anna. Another day all the food was out of the international kitchen, with Hungarian goulash and ropa vieja. Then it was all charcuterie, our stomachs filled with sausages, terrines, pâtés, and galantines. Breakfast was always available from the breakfast class. And breads and pastries were everywhere. That food sustained us for our studies. Our chef whites became dashikis, and our knives became dream catchers as we fluttered from class to class, workshop to workshop.

Basic, entry-level classes were set up in seven-, fourteen-, or twenty-one-day blocks, so we had at least a week with Chef Ron DeSantis in gastronomy, plus hot foods, butchering, product identification, breakfast cookery. All the basic cooking techniques were taught in skills class. And this skills class was where, for the first time, I was a model student. I even clicked with the professor, Lou Jones. Yeah, I was that kid who spent time after class with the teacher, hungry for knowledge, asking relevant questions, following up.

In fact, this was the first time since elementary school that I was actually interested in and excited by academics. Everything was coming naturally—I understood the basic elements as if they had been written just for me. I was quick to the knife. The glove fucking fit. The flavors were leaping out of my fingertips and finding a home.

After the classrooms the library was my second home away from home. I got lost in the rows of books, combing the aisles, reading, digesting, reshelving. I picked up everything from histories of early human cooking methods to guides about how to make carved mice out of mushrooms. I got lost in *Culinaria* and its foods from around the world, explored France through Waverley Root, got a crash course on sauces from James Peterson, connected with Native American and Chinese books on cooking, found obscure books on Himalayan and Nepalese cooking. Most nights, I stayed there and read and read till they turned off all the lights. Then trudged back through the snow to my room, where the lava lamp was still burning and the boys were still partying.

And that was the only part that didn't fit. The top dog really didn't like anyone else in his space; truth is, we were both bossy and cocky, and there was just too much ego for one tiny room. Since day one, we had been like two dogs silently fighting for dominance, engaging in a lot of passive-aggressive bullshit like giving each other stares or getting in each other's way accidentally on purpose. Just to piss me off, the top dog and his boys would sit at my desk and use my books to roll joints. Or rummage through my desk and ask, "Who's this in this picture?" or grab a pencil and never return it. When all you got are your books, some photos, and a couple number-twos, that's some major shit. And it worked. It really pissed me off.

But I pulled back. Because of my past, I knew how easy it would be for me to slide into bad behaviors and lose everything over some petty bullshit. I knew I needed structure, and here was a structure built around something I was truly interested in. I couldn't let it slip out of my hands. I couldn't fuck up.

So I pulled the top dog aside, shortened my words, and opened my eyes deep like I do when I'm scolding a cook. Told him in so many words that he had to stop it or I'd end his life. It stopped.

Outside that dorm room, I was making friends. Rich was from Bayside, Queens, and had a vacation home in the Candlewood Lake area just outside of Danbury, Connecticut. At just an hour away, that was a perfect getaway for us. Rob would haul us in his Jeep, and we took impromptu trips up to Montreal to gamble our money away and sink into tits and ass at the strip bars, speaking broken French and eating crusty baguettes. We would get stopped at the border, looking like a band of thieves trying to sneak into the United States. I mean, it was one Korean dude (me), a mutt-looking white dude (Rob), a Mexican dude from Phoenix (Jesse), and a black dude from the Bahamas (Manny), all worn out, all broke, all wired, all smelly. Great fucking times.

AFTER NINE MONTHS OF CLASSES, cooking, and library time, it was time to look for an externship. This was the badge of honor for culinary students; you're either a king or a jester, depending on where you get accepted and where you decide to go. And because everyone's gunning for the same spots in the same precious few restaurants, landing a primo externship was a highly competitive process. You had to bring it.

I had a choice. I could have gone back to L.A. and tried to find something at Patina or Valentino. But I knew I might fall into my old ways again. So I moved to New York. I had to live out the cliché. I had to make it big in Manhattan. No matter what.

I already had a rough idea of the city's neighborhoods and their restaurants. Over the course of the school year, a bunch of us had done short, unpaid stages, immersing ourselves fully in the environment of a professional kitchen, thinking, living, and breathing cookery. Rich and I staged for a while at Aureole, the best restaurant in New York City at the time, with me on the morning shift, prepping potatoes and doing a lot of knife work for the lunch service, and Rich on the evening garde-manger, where he took to chiffonading

like a secretary to a typewriter. We both did a stint at One If by Land, Two If by Sea, then a day at Le Grenouille, set within all the opulence of the red velvet booths and fresh flowers. I stepped into Le Cirque for a day; it had just reopened in the Palace Hotel with a new chef, Sottha Khun, and Jacques Torres madly spinning chocolate and constructing dessert masterpieces. I was really enamored with Patrick Clark at the time, but Tavern on the Green was too high volume for me. All those places just weren't meant to be. Either they were full or they weren't the right fit.

And so me, Rich, and a few other guys pounded New York City pavement. For three days, we followed word of mouth and magazines, researching every nook and cranny for leads on open positions. The only places I didn't really look at were Asian restaurants—back then I thought it was too obvious a career path for a Korean dude who had grown up around stinky tofu and black beans and kimchi and abalone porridge. Instead I looked for places where I could be a French chef. Because in my mind, cooking classic French food would mean that I had arrived, that I had reached the pinnacle of cookery. It would mean I was for real.

After throwing dart after dart, my crew started hitting the bull's-eye. Rich went to a Spanish restaurant called Solera. Someone found a fit at An American Place by Larry Forgione. Other guys went to Gramercy Tavern, Bouley, Nobu, and Daniel. High-class restaurants. As my guys celebrated, I panicked. I was the last kid still waiting to be picked to play for someone's team. On our last day of hunting, I hit up four places. No cigar. It was getting late, and I walked down 51st Street, empty-handed but for one last copy of my résumé, head down, dejected, depressed, and ready to call it a day.

I MOVED TO NEW YORK.
I HAD TO LIVE OUT THE
CLICHÉ. I HAD TO MAKE IT
BIG IN MANHATTAN.
NO MATTER WHAT.

Then, for some reason, I looked up. And right into a restaurant kitchen window. Looking out that window was a chef. It was right before service, almost 5:00 P.M., and he was watching the street traffic, maybe getting a piece of Zen. His face looked familiar—I must have seen him in some magazine. Somewhere, I even knew his name, but I just couldn't place him. I stopped and made eye contact. I grabbed my résumé and showed it to him through the glass, making hand gestures and miming, trying to explain that I was a culinary student. Surely he would understand.

He looked at me. Then, still through the window, he signaled for me to go around and down and up into the restaurant through the staff entrance. I don't know how I understood the directions, but I did. As I made my way around, down, and up, I realized: I was at Le Bernardin. The temple of seafood. One of the best restaurants in the world. And that debonair chef standing in the window was Eric Ripert.

I flew down the stairs to the elevator, then back up to the kitchen, popping out right in the back kitchen next to the prep sinks and three huge walk-ins. Made my way down the hallway, past the pastry kitchen. I found the chef standing in front of the office. He asked to see my résumé.

The résumé was hogwash, filled with everything I had done up to that point, no matter how trivial. So not only my experiences staging at some of the best restaurants in New York, but also my time dishwashing at Leatherby's ice cream shop in high school. The night classes I took at the culinary school in L.A. Books I'd read. Anything to fluff up the space.

But he talked to me. For fifteen minutes right before service, we sat in his office, and he told me his philosophy on food and about the roots of Le Bernardin. The history of Gilbert and Maguy Le Coze, who had founded the restaurant. How the fish arrived and how they had to be treated with care. He talked about what it meant to work there and how the restaurant operated like a symphony. He stressed the importance of dedication and detail and connecting with the food as if it were an extension of your hand. And how I had to decide, really decide, whether I wanted to be part of something special.

We were done with the sit-down. He walked me to the pass, where all the dishes landed for one final inspection before going out to the dining room, and introduced me to the chef de cuisine, Chris Muller. They told me to stand against the wall. And to watch. The place was lit up like Carnegie Hall and as shiny as the rims on my old Blazer. I was right at the pass where Eric himself stood during service. There were maybe a dozen people in the kitchen: the cooks harmoniously worked their stations; the servers took the finished dishes from the pass to the dining room. I watched the plates sail right by me, as if I were Vin Scully calling a game. Whenever my eyes wandered from the kitchen, Chris would snap a finger at me and point out something—he'd explain how the sauce was bacon brown butter or show me how thinly the tuna was pounded so it could absorb the dressing just right. They asked me if I was thirsty and handed me a glass of water. The cooks all smiled at me as they handed dishes to the pass. It was intense but serene. And beautiful. Everyone hitting his or her notes in perfect rhythm. A symphony, just as Eric had said.

Right about then, Eric came to the line and expedited orders as they went in and out: he organized the ticket orders, calling them out to the cooks as they came in, and inspected plated dishes before they went out to the diners, wiping them clean and tasting each and every one before clearing it to go. Chris stepped back onto the line and tutored the cooks. It was a silent dance; this all happened without even a word whispered between them. Chef ran the line for the next thirty minutes or so, then asked Chris to step back on. Chef gestured for me to come to the office.

Gulp.

We went in and sat down, right back where we had started. He asked if I liked what I saw. I blurted out as best I could what I had just seen and experienced. He asked if I could see myself working here. If I'd like to do my externship at Le Bernardin. All of this in the humblest of ways.

My answer was something like "Yesyesyesyesyesyesyesyes."

The dealer had just handed me the best hand in the deck. What poker face?

AFTER CLASSES ENDED for the year, I hopped on the train at Poughkeepsie, rode it out of the Hudson Valley, past West Point, past Sing Sing, and into the bustle of Grand Central Station. It was late summer, early fall 1997, and my makeshift headquarters for the next eight months would be my cousin's living room once again, surrounded by medical school textbooks and that beautiful New York view of another building right outside the window. No big deal. I wasn't there for the view. I entered my first day at Le Bernardin with my rolled-up knife bag, a fresh attitude, and butterflies.

My first order of business was easy enough. I registered with the office upstairs, a small room filled with cubicles and nice people, mostly women, who gave me all the necessary things I needed for payroll and work and such. They sent me downstairs to see the steward. So it was back down the freight elevator to the basement, where I met a very kind man named Fernando. He welcomed me and gave me three sets of my new uniform: white pants and a white chef coat and an apron. He walked me to the locker room, showed me how the system worked, then went on his way, leaving me alone to take a deep breath like a boxer getting into the zone before a fight.

I went upstairs and entered the kitchen.

The kitchen was separated into a few sections: the main area where most of the food was prepped and cooked, an oyster station, and a completely separate section just for pastry. The kitchen was coming off the back end of lunch service, so things were moving a million miles a second. Cooks in full motion, servers taking silver platters with amazingly simple and clean plates of fish on blue-rimmed white china and whisking them to the dining room for the last of the lunch guests.

I said hello to Chef Eric Ripert, but it was Chef de Cuisine Chris Muller who grabbed my attention and took me on a quick tour of the kitchen stations: fish pass, vegetables, canapés, hot appetizers, garde-manger, saucier.

I was to start with Juan at the fish pass. Juan was an amazing dude from the Dominican Republic with tight, gnarly, bristled Afro curls. He was in charge of all the fish that went to each station in the kitchen. On any given day, he could be dealing with monkfish, striped bass, red snapper, skate, scallops, pompano, squid.

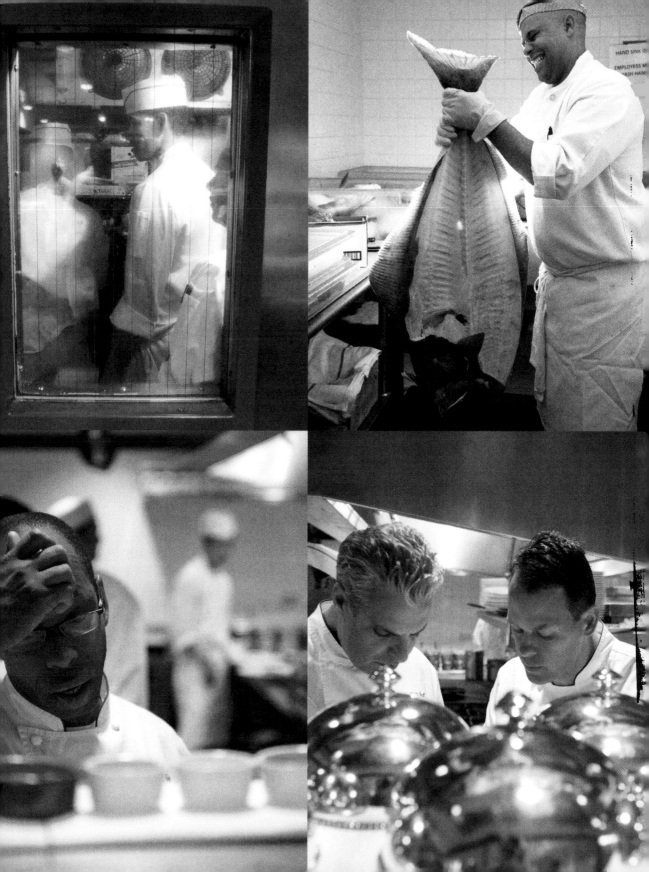

He stood like a watch commander waiting for each ticket to be called so he could start prepping cod for a brandade or slicing yellowfin tuna paper-thin to be cooked rare and draped on a salad of bean sprouts, roasted peanuts, mint, coriander, and a soy-ginger vinaigrette. Juan was a master whistler, and he had a whole vocabulary: he'd whistle to signal the fish that came in; a short or long chirp, like Morse code, depending on the fish. He also whistled to get attention when he needed something and hit another note when he acknowledged what someone needed from him. His whistle was also an indicator of his mood: songs if he was happy, sirens if he was pissed off. Through Juan, I learned all about fish and respecting its proteins.

Just as important was what I was learning about working in a kitchen: organization, follow-through, teamwork, how to open my ears and really hear what people needed. I picked up the fish pass quite well, and they moved me to the vegetable station, where I was paired with the guy who was going to train me. His name was Daniel Holzman—later, he would go on to start up the Meatball Shop in New York, which is now wildly successful.

But at that moment he was supposed to teach me the station. To this day, I remember his entrance: he came into the kitchen, singing with all the confidence in the world. He was no more than seventeen years old, with curly sandy brown hair, all cocky as one can be when one looks just like Justin Timberlake. Even before his first words to me came out of his mouth I couldn't stand the guy.

He started showing me things, but he went too fast. I was overwhelmed

HE WAS ON ME LIKE WHIT
ON RICE, TELLING ME HOW
MUCH I SUCKED, TO PIC
IT UP, THAT SHIT WA
WHACK, THAT I WAS WEA

and needed to catch a breath, a moment to focus so I could get back into the fight. But he was on me like white on rice, telling me how much I sucked, to pick it up, that shit was whack, that I was weak. All I needed was a damn second, and he wouldn't give me that space. Finally, I threw in the towel and told him to hold the fuck up. Asked him to take a walk into the walk-in with me to hash it out. Explained to him in so many words that I was new to this shit and if we were going to work together, he had to give me a fucking break. And that that rat-a-tat military drill was not how we rolled in Cali—I'd catch up quick to this New York style, but it was day fucking one!

He listened. Then he laughed. And I laughed. And from that day forward, we became very close friends. As it turned out, we worked well together because he wasn't as good as he thought he was and I was no good but trying to be better. We would become inseparable.

The vegetable station was responsible not only for all the vegetables and starches in the restaurant but also the family meal. This is the meal we make just for the restaurant staff; served right before service begins, it's the only time when everyone will stop what they're doing and sit down to eat together, even if only for half an hour. And because this time was a precious, rare moment of calm before the doors opened and we all busted our asses trying to capture lightning in a bottle on every plate, it couldn't be something like plain baked potatoes with sour cream on the side. No, it had to be thoughtful and delicious.

Every day, I had two hours to prep all the vegetables for service and to get the family meal on the table. Making it happen was all about timing, and I barely finished every day. Each afternoon at 2:00 P.M. on the dot, I came in and immediately put four or five different pots of stock on the stove to heat or water to boil.

2:05 Assemble, clean, trim, and peel the haricots verts, snow peas, baby carrots, baby turnips, fingerling potatoes, artichokes, spinach, bok choy, asparagus, etc.

2:15 Slice the sweet potatoes very thin and make gaufrettes out of the Idaho potatoes for frying.

2:20 Blanch, shock, and drain the spinach and other vegetables. Roast the portobellos with thyme and garlic.

2:28 Start to prep the family meal with chicken, crustaceans, sides of beef, or whatever was brought in that day. Some days I made couscous or classic chicken fricassee, paella or spaghetti and garlic bread; other days fried rice or chili sambal wings.

3:00 Cut and slice the baby artichoke hearts on a mandoline.

3:10 Slice the marinated artichoke hearts for the hamachi salad. Slice and assemble the portobellos for the portobello tarts or make tomato confit.

3:15 Deep-fry the chips.

3:30 Cook the family meal. Sometimes I fucked up and made something too spicy; I burned couscous once, and the chefs pulled me aside, shaking their heads. *You are the first person to ever burn couscous in New York City.* Great.

4:00 Pick thyme or another pile of herbs or julienne pounds and pounds of ginger. Finish up the family meal. Clean and set up my station for dinner service: cutting board, salt and pepper, herbs, salad bowls, plates.

4:30 Everything stops. Family time. That station better be clean, and the family meal better be up. Aprons come off, and everyone's in line, grabbing their plates and heading downstairs to the big room next to the lockers. Captains in black tuxedos who sat on the chairs and ate at the table. Back waiters in their white tuxedos, mostly from Ecuador and with a big roll of cash that they always seemed to be counting right in front of everybody. The cooks and dishwashers and even the chefs, all sprawled out across the floor. Everyone eating, laughing, talking, zoning. Together. Then it was over before it even started, and we were back upstairs at our stations, hands washed, aprons neatly tied.

4:55 Enter Clint Eastwood. Saloon doors. Whistle, tumbleweeds, toothpick. Stare. Uh-oh. Chef Ripert would walk down each station with Chris or the sous-chef for the line check, spoons in hand, ready to taste everything. We cooks all stood back, bodies still, but eyes moving around rapidly, watching one another's backs to see if anybody had missed anything and, if so, to send signals. Nobody wanted to fail or see their comrades fail. In most cases my station was set, and I shone on the prep side.

5:30 Service begins. 5:30 was when I hit many bumps in the road.

In front of the kitchen was a wall-sized diagram of the dining room. Once a table was seated, the guests were served a complimentary canapé and their table on the diagram was marked with the time. From that exact point forward, everything in the kitchen was set into motion for that table, with dishes timed precisely for each diner, whether the person ordered the chef's tasting menu or a special $160-per-person black truffle tasting menu. Clockwork. But there were no tickets. Le Bernardin used a French system where the chef calls out an order and the cooks respond with a "Oui, chef!" I just tried to remember what was what, how many did I get, how many more do I have to do? Fuck, what did he say?

Every day for the next eighteen weeks, I sweated my balls off. Whether I was on veg or hot apps or amuse, orders would come in hard and fast: seven tuna truffles, nine portobellos, twelve canapés, six artichokes, four spinach, nine haricots verts, six shrimp pizzas, four scallops Julia Child, the monkfish needed its puree, another station was waiting on my peeled asparagus, the sauté needed his carrots to finish his dish.

Some days I soared and ran the station and the food with the precision of a great commis. I constructed whole dishes like portobello tarts and sent them to the pass without a hiccup, sent perfectly cooked mushrooms and shallots to the fish station to be used as the base for the swordfish or monkfish, got the spinach and potatoes to the saucier to sauce and the chef to garnish. Clockwork. But even though I did have those good moments, I was really just a rank amateur trying to keep up with the professionals on Pebble Beach. At least every other week, the speed and detail of the kitchen would hit me hard, and SHANK, it'd be a crucial 350-cover night and I'd swing and miss. I'd lose my swing for days.

On one really bad night of service, I was on deck for the tuna black truffle salad. The knife cuts and layering had to be perfect. The ingredients and the layering of the phyllo dough had to be perfect. And I was trying to be *too* perfect, starting over and over and over and over like a video stuck on a loop, layering and relayering and rerelayering. Others—the whole kitchen—waited and waited and waited, the timetable for the guests' table tick-tick-tocking. Everyone waited patiently until they couldn't take it anymore and told me to hurry the fuck up. I knew what I had to do; I knew how to finish the plate. But I was a deer in headlights. In the heat of the moment, I froze. Forgot what I was doing. My mental mise en place got bent out of shape. I couldn't finish what I'd started, and, worse, I had fucked up the flow of the kitchen. Daniel finally just pulled me off my station and sent me back to the fish pass as Juan whistled my swan song and took my place.

The only highlight of that night was sneaking over to the pastry side, stealing a spoonful of ice cream, and then getting chased out by Florian Bollanger.

When service mercifully ended around 1:30 A.M., I was angry, disappointed, and frustrated with myself and my inability to just fucking execute. We all headed downstairs to the lockers, everyone patting me on the back, saying it was going to be okay, but throwing jabs at me to push me to do better. Then Juan started whistling, and someone else started singing, and Angel started dancing as everyone started to change. Then, almost like a Broadway musical, everyone pulled their pants down at the exact same time, and there it was: all the Dominican Republic dudes in tight tight bright bright tiger-striped bikini briefs in a rainbow of fluorescent colors from purple to pink. And me, the odd man out, the Asian guy with modest boxers, laughing away a hard night of service and ready to hit the town with Danny for more.

The end of the shift at the restaurant was just the beginning of our night. If it was payday, Danny and I usually went straight to some seedy twenty-four-hour check-cashing spot on the West Side Highway in Hell's Kitchen, got our cash, and fueled up with 2:00 A.M. grub before hitting the club. Danny had a deep crew in the city. His boy Mike Chernow was a young phenom in the NYC club scene. They both came out of the *Fame* high school for performing arts and had a crazy group of friends like in the movie *Kids.* Mike worked the door at Limelight, and we would stroll in, no wait no matter the line. We would get with girls and pound shots, then head off to a rave club called Carbon on 55th and 12th, where we'd do hits of E. We'd stumble out at 5:00 A.M., cloaked in kisses and hugs, and head to a diner for a predawn breakfast of milk shakes, burgers, eggs, spaghetti, soup, pastrami, Greek salad, and falafel.

On more mellow nights, Danny and I would go to the pool hall and play until 4:00 A.M., grabbing a slice or a hot dog in between games. Some nights we'd call a Jamaican car service that picked you up on one block, drove around another, and dropped you off again at the same spot, only you'd exit with weed in hand. And we would chill with all the young homies and sassy girls from Riverdale or the Upper West Side and smoke in an alley or on a back stoop or in one of the girls' cars.

That was the life. Even with the stress of the line, I was having a blast. The angry ghosts of self-despair that had haunted me in L.A. didn't follow me to New York. For the first time in a long time, I could smile, just truly smile, and trust the pure, good energy of my environment.

I was becoming a cook in New York City. And it felt fucking great.

POTATOES ANNA BANANA

This was the first dish I perfected as a culinary student, and when I did, I was fucking amazed. It gave me the confidence to believe that I could cook, and that was significant: sometimes you need that little boost, that little moment when you realize that, *Yeah, I can do it.* In school, we learned to make this with one, just one, very thin layer of potatoes, cooked very gently. For my version, I switch it up a bit and make it more rustic and a little more clumsy, with way more layers than my teachers would have wanted, so you can do it at home. But it's still an A+.

SERVES 4 TO 6

4 tablespoons (½ stick) butter
¼ cup vegetable oil
2 medium-size Idaho potatoes (about
    8 ounces), peeled, thinly sliced into
    disks, and held in water

Kosher salt and freshly ground
    black pepper
Couple of sprigs fresh thyme
Couple of garlic cloves, peeled and
    crushed

Preheat the oven to 400°F.

Place a 10-inch cast-iron skillet over very low heat and add the butter and oil to the pan. When the butter has melted, drain and pat dry the potatoes and begin to layer them in the pan in concentric circles, overlapping them a bit. Generously season the first layer with salt and pepper and continue to layer the potatoes, being sure to season the potatoes between layers. The layers don't have to be perfect—they can be a little sloppy, even, so long as they cover the bottom of the pan. And it's okay if the butter and stuff bleeds into everything.

Turn up the heat to medium-high and start to get some action in the skillet. The potatoes on the bottom of the pan will start to brown, and that's what you want. Cook until they're nice and crispy, about 10 minutes (check to see how they're doing by grabbing a spatula and lifting up an edge to take a peek). Then place a plate large enough to cover the pan, or a cookie sheet if you don't have a plate that's big enough, over the pan and flip the skillet so the potatoes are crispy side up on the plate. Being careful, slide the potatoes, crispy side up, back into your pan and return it to the heat.

Cook the potatoes just a little more, then place the thyme sprigs and crushed garlic cloves all over the potatoes. Pop it all into the oven for 5 minutes.

Out of the oven, transfer the potatoes to a plate, remove the thyme and garlic, and enjoy with some Jufran (store-bought banana ketchup) or, if you wish, something fancier.

SEARED BEEF MEDALLIONS WITH SAUCE ROBERT

This just sounded fancy, so I decided to make it for y'all.

SERVES 4

STEAK

1 tablespoon vegetable oil

8 ounces beef tenderloin, cut into
    2-ounce steak portions

Kosher salt and freshly ground black
    pepper

1 tablespoon butter

4 sprigs fresh thyme

4 cloves garlic, peeled and crushed

SAUCE

1 tablespoon butter

¼ white or yellow onion, minced

¼ cup white wine

1 cup demiglace (see page 223)

1 tablespoon Dijon mustard

Kosher salt and freshly ground black
    pepper

Pinch of sugar

Sherry vinegar

Preheat the oven to 350°F.

In a large ovenproof pan, heat the oil over medium-high heat. Season the steak on both sides with salt and pepper. When the oil is smoking, add the steak to the pan and sear the beef until it caramelizes, about 2 minutes per side. You'll know it's ready when the edges start to brown. Transfer the steaks to a sheet pan with a wire rack on it. The meat will be rare in the middle.

Return the pan to the stove over medium heat to make the sauce. Add the butter and onion and cook until the onion is translucent, about 4 minutes. Deglaze the pan with the white wine, then add the demiglace. Reduce the liquid just a tad, then strain the sauce. Transfer the sauce to a clean pan and heat it over medium heat.

Turning back to the steaks, add a smudge of butter to the top of each medallion and shower them all with thyme and a canopy of garlic. Put the pan in the oven and cook them until they're medium-rare, about 3 minutes.

While the steaks are cooking, add a splash of water to the sauce, a little mustard, salt, and pepper, and a tiny pinch of sugar, all to taste. Finish with a tiny splash of sherry vinegar. Taste the sauce. It should be bold, acidic, and delicious.

Once the sauce is perfect, pour it over your steaks and **SPEAK BROKEN FRENCH.**

VEAL STOCK

Nothing says culinary school more than making stocks and mirepoix, along with knowing your mise en place, practicing your butchery, sharpening your knives. These are all building blocks to cooking, and veal stock is one of the most important bricks in that foundation. Once you master it, you can use it for almost anything that calls for stock, and you can strain and season it with salt, pepper, and a touch of sherry vinegar and turn it into a sauce for any beef dish, like the Hibachi Steak Teppanyaki (page 195) and the Seared Beef Medallions with Sauce Robert (page 220).

MAKES 2 QUARTS

5 pounds veal bones, washed
3 tablespoons vegetable oil
½ onion, roughly chopped
2 stalks celery, roughly chopped
1 carrot, roughly chopped
¼ fennel bulb, chopped
¼ whole leek, white part only, washed and cut into rings
1 tablespoon tomato paste

Splash of red wine
1 tablespoon coriander seeds
1 tablespoon whole black peppercorns
½ teaspoon whole cloves
2 bay leaves
Couple of sprigs fresh thyme
Couple of sprigs fresh parsley
Couple of sprigs fresh tarragon

Preheat the oven to 400°F.

Place the bones on a large sheet pan and roast them in the oven until they're brown all over, about 45 minutes.

Heat the oil in a large pot over high heat. Add the vegetables and sauté until they have a deep, dark char. Add the tomato paste and cook, moving everything constantly, for about 3 minutes.

Deglaze the pot with the red wine, then add the veal bones to the pot. Add enough water to cover the bones by a few inches. Add the spices and herbs, bring to a boil, then reduce the heat and simmer for 6 hours, uncovered.

Drain the stock through a sieve and discard the solids. Return the stock to the stove over medium heat and let it simmer for 30 minutes. If you want, you can reduce it by half and make a demiglace, which you can use for any sauce or beef stew.

FREEZE THE LEFTOVERS.

IT'S A WEAPON.

COCONUT CLAM CHOWDER

There are so many bad clam chowders out there, but clam chowder isn't just some ubiquitous bowl of sludge in a Crock-Pot at your local market. It should be something otherworldly. More than that, making clam chowder is a lesson in cooking: it teaches you how to build and layer flavors, and it's a gateway to making different types of cream-based soups. It's a lesson in enjoying those flavors, too.

SERVES 3 OR 4 AS AN APPETIZER OR 2 OR 3 AS THE MAIN COURSE

2 tablespoons vegetable oil

2 ounces pancetta, minced

2 tablespoons minced onions

2 tablespoons minced shallots

2 tablespoons finely diced celery

2 tablespoons minced lemongrass

¼ cup white wine

¼ cup all-purpose flour

One 6½-ounce can chopped clams
    with juice

1 cup coconut milk

1 cup milk

2 cups water

4 ounces Idaho potatoes, peeled, finely
    diced, and boiled for 4 to 5 minutes,
    then held in a bowl of ice water

¾ cup heavy cream

2 tablespoons green curry paste

Juice of ½ lime

10 Manila clams in shells, washed

Kosher salt and freshly ground black
    pepper

Red chile flakes

Fresh Thai basil

Fresh rau ram (Vietnamese coriander)
    or tarragon

In a large pot, heat the oil over medium heat. About 30 seconds after the oil just starts to smoke, add the pancetta. Cook the pancetta until it's light brown in color and some of its fat has rendered, about 4 minutes. Add the onion, shallot, celery, and lemongrass and sauté until they are nicely cooked but still have integrity, about 1 minute.

Deglaze the pot with the white wine and cook to reduce by half. Add the flour, stirring constantly for about a minute, until the liquid thickens up a bit.

Add the chopped clams and their juice, the milks, and the water. Whisk out all the lumps, bring to a very gentle boil, and simmer for 30 minutes. Then add the potatoes and the cream, whisk in the green curry paste, and add the lime juice. Throw in the Manila clams and cover the pot.

As soon as the clams open (in 2 or 3 minutes; toss any clams that don't open), remove the cover and cook for just a little bit as you season the chowder with salt and pepper.

Finish with chile flakes and herbs to taste.

POUR A BOWL FOR YOURSELF
AND ONE FOR THE HOMIES.

POUNDED PORK SCHNITZEL

I make a mean schnitzel, and now so can you.

SERVES 4 TO 6

Four to six 5-ounce pieces boneless
pork shoulder, pounded between sheets
of plastic wrap into steaks about ¼ inch
thick

Salt and freshly ground black pepper
About 1 cup vegetable oil

BREADING
1 cup all-purpose flour
2 eggs, beaten
1 cup panko bread crumbs

ARUGULA SALAD
3 cups wild arugula
1 lemon
Salt and freshly ground black pepper
Really good extra virgin olive oil

Line a few plates or a cookie sheet with paper towels.

Season the pork steaks with salt and pepper.

Set out the flour, eggs, and panko in three separate shallow bowls, in that order.

Place the pork steaks one by one in the flour, dusting them all over. Then dip them in the eggs (coating them thoroughly), and then in the panko (coating them thoroughly), making sure to pat down the crust. Place the pork on a wire rack on top of a sheet pan and let it rest for a few minutes.

Place a large skillet over medium heat and, while it's heating up, add enough vegetable oil to the pan to come about a quarter of the way up. When the oil is just under smoking hot, add the schnitzel and then constantly move it around, shaking the pan to swirl the oil over, around, and on top of the pork. This little bit of wrist action will create a perfect crust.

When the pork is golden brown, flip it over and repeat the swirling action. You should see a froth form—a sign you're on the road to a job well done.

Once lightly browned on all sides, transfer the pork to the paper-towel-lined plates or cookie sheet and season with salt and pepper.

Toss the arugula with a squeeze of the lemon, some salt and pepper, and some olive oil, all to taste.

Move the schnitzels to a large platter and cover with the arugula salad. Drizzle some olive oil all over.

SMILE.

SEARED SCALLOPS WITH CHIVE BEURRE BLANC

If you can pull this off, then you can start to understand the first step in becoming a French chef. The beurre blanc is an amazing thing, and, although simple, it takes a complete focus and attention to transfer that moment into the spirituality of the sauce. It's like catching a butterfly. Magic.

SERVES 2

4 large scallops, connective muscle removed
Salt and freshly ground black pepper
1 tablespoon extra virgin olive oil
2 tablespoons minced shallot
¼ cup white wine
¼ cup natural rice wine vinegar (not seasoned)

8 tablespoons (1 stick) cold butter, cut into pieces
Splash of heavy cream
Juice of ½ lemon
2 tablespoons minced fresh chives

Season the scallops on both sides with salt and pepper.

Heat the oil in a skillet over medium heat and, once it begins to smoke a bit, add the scallops, searing them on each side until a golden crust forms, about 1 minute per side. Remove the scallops from the pan and rest them on a wire rack.

Lower the heat and add the shallot to the same pan. Cook gently, lightly stirring the shallot constantly so it doesn't color. After about 2 minutes, deglaze the pan with the wine and vinegar and reduce until the liquids have nearly evaporated. Turn off the heat and whisk in one piece of the cold butter until it's melted. Repeat for the remaining pieces of butter.

Finish by whisking in a tiny splash of cream, the lemon juice, and a sprinkle of the chives. Taste and adjust the seasoning if necessary.

Spoon the sauce onto a plate and place the scallops on top. Garnish with the remaining chives.

DRINK CHAMPAGNE.

CHAPTER 10

THE PROFESSIONAL

Cali. The sunshine, the blue skies, the tacos, the Mexican culture, the jokes, the vibe. The Veronicas and Rafaels and Eduardos and Sergios. The music of Sinaloa and Tijuana. The jalapeños blistering on the grill. The cars taking their time on the open road.

Right after I graduated from the CIA in 1998, I found myself heading to Borrego Springs, a desert town that could hit 120 degrees on the hottest days and drop to the low 40s on the coldest nights. I was lured there by a recruiter at a job fair, who told me about La Casa del Zorro, a beautiful forty-two-acre resort at the edge of the Sonoran desert, thirty minutes west of the Salton Sea and one hour north of Baja Mexico. There, the best chef in San Diego needed a junior sous-chef, a position that would pay a whopping $28,000 a year.

At first I didn't give it much thought. I was in a groove during my last year of school, absorbing histories and techniques like Neo downloading jujitsu and kung fu in *The Matrix*. I had good grades, was even picked to be the speaker of my class. And so I thought about taking my transcript to a classic French restaurant in New York like Daniel or one of the hottest spots in the city like Nobu or even to Auberge du Soleil in the Napa Valley. But I had just gotten married to a wonderful woman, someone I felt like I had known forever, and supporting us on a cook's wage in a big city would be rough. And something about the restless souls whispering in the hot wind spoke to me. The desert pulled me in like a magnet, and I forgot all about those French kitchens.

BORREGO SPRINGS WAS SO SMALL that there weren't any stoplights and deliveries came in just twice a week. It did, however, have its own small airport, several golf courses, countless hiking trails, and spectacular views. During high season, from November to April, the population spiked from two thousand to ten thousand: the town flooded with golfers, vacationers, bikers, and German tourists escaping the cold to make the desert their winter home or coming to see the fields of blooming wildflowers, gnarly rock formations, and cholla and ocotillo cactus spread across the sand like coral on the ocean floor.

And because the town was accustomed to accommodating all those seasonal guests and workers, La Casa del Zorro had the entire infrastructure set up and ready to go for its new junior sous-chef: a place to stay, electricity and power paid for, sheets and pillows. It was like checking into the military; the only thing that was on my dime was the phone bill.

On my first day of my first job, I walked into the kitchen to meet my "boss." He was a young guy like me, a tall, slender man with dark eyebrows and a very quiet, but very commanding, professional presence. I realized I recognized him from school. Paul Mooring. As it turned out, the chef—the best one in San Diego, the one the recruiter dangled out like a carrot in front of a horse—had quit just a day earlier, leaving Butch Cassidy and the Sundance Kid to run the joint.

Paul and I were in over our heads; neither of us had any business running a kitchen. But we looked each other dead in the eye and made a pact: we were going to turn this place into a world-class resort with the best food we could possibly dish out. Hell, I was a top grad from the Harvard of culinary schools! I knew how to cook.

Or so I thought.

PAUL AND I WERE IN CHARGE of the food program for about 250 rooms and casitas (small, freestanding guest houses), plus breakfast, lunch, and dinner for the resort restaurant. La Casa del Zorro's restaurant had a AAA four-diamond rating and was the only high-end restaurant in town; during the season, then, we were slammed. That's 300 covers for breakfast, 250 for lunch, and 150 for dinner. Plus room service and bar.

We hit the ground running in late autumn, just as the seasonal workers and snowbirds from Montana, Wyoming, Idaho, and the Dakotas were filling the desert with their elbow grease and their cash. We had fifty or so guys on staff, all Latino except for a guy named Mike, a wizard who had worked in every profession known to man. He may very well have been sitting on millions but, like so many drifters and folks in flux, decided to live among the cactus to iron out his soul in solitude. Victor came in the mornings to run breakfast. Rafael was on the line at night. Salvador ran our dish station.

The easiest thing for us to do would have been to bump out what was already on the menu. But it was stuck in the age of surf and turf, salmon with raspberry sauce, pasta primavera. It was old and tired; we were young and fresh. Everything, we decided, had to be made in-house, fresh every day. And so we had seafood delivered overnight directly from Hawaii, bought produce from the Coachella Valley, stacked the club sandwiches with bacon we cured in house, brined and roasted turkeys for turkey sandwiches.

We kept the resort's famous Kit-Fox Salad with its butter lettuce, dates, grapefruit, goat cheese, pecans, and onions in a tart vinaigrette, but we revamped and updated everything else on the menu. We pulled directly from our culinary school playbook and scoured *Art Culinaire* to teach ourselves how to cook fancy, then constructed food based on it, minus the stuffiness, using lots of garnishes and colors and trying to outdo ourselves with every plate. So for breakfast, we had chorizo and tortillas; for dinner, there was lobster, sea bass, lamb chops, and filet mignon with farm-fresh vegetables.

But La Casa del Zorro was a resort, not just a restaurant, which meant we also had to create the lineup for banquets, meetings, and events. And so we learned about banquet event order sheets and got proper event menus up and running: omelet bars and breakfast buffets of sticky buns, croissants, bacon, hash browns, eggs Benedict, tropical fruit platters, granola, pancakes, waffles, smoothies, cereals, charcuterie, cheese platters, carved ham. We even did big holidays and events like Thanksgiving and weddings. This is where I must apologize if you had your wedding at La Casa del Zorro during my tenure between 1998 and 1999: we had no idea what we were doing, but we did the best we could.

And in doing the best we could, I thought we were the best in town. Back in school, especially right after my stint at Le Bernardin, I had gotten a bit cocky, "checking" on my classmates, evaluating their work, questioning their cuts. My friends didn't put up with my bullshit and eventually had to put me in my place. But I still carried some of that big-city swagger to La Casa del Zorro.

This time, though, it was a young, new cook who stopped my swagger in its tracks. It was a busy night. The tickets were stacking up, and we were running low on lamb chops and filets. I instructed a young cook named Kenneth to go to the walk-in and grab a few more chops and filets for service. Kenneth was a half-Filipino, half-white dude with a cinder block for a body, a big beard on a square jaw, bushy eyebrows, glasses, an apron that was always tied up too high, and pants that were always pulled up a bit too short. He had a passion for cooking, but he was still pretty green in the kitchen.

He took off toward the walk-in, but that was the fastest he would move all night. I waited. And waited. The whole kitchen waited. The guests in the dining room were getting antsy. Meanwhile, the orders backed up, the flow of the kitchen was off the rails, and Kenneth was taking fucking forever to find the meats. I yelled and yelled at him across my station, telling him to haul ass so we could get food out the door. The poor guy must have been deep in the walk-in, doing his best, but I should have known better than anyone that when you're nervous and being hollered at, you freeze up and things become a blur. But I didn't care. The pile of unfilled tickets was rising and with it my blood pressure. After taking too damn long, he finally came back with lamb. The frozen lamb we used for our stews.

And I lost it. "You fucking idiot!" I screamed.

The kitchen stopped. Dead silence.

"Don't you even fucking know the difference between lamb chops and lamb leg? That's a fucking rib-eye, you fucking dumb shit."

He stood there. Gordon Ramsay had nothing on me.

"Now get me my muthafuckin' lamb chops and filet *now* or else you are fucking fired, and I will kick your ass out the door back to Montana!"

He fumbled, said sorry, and ran back to the walk-in. A few others went to help him.

Damn, I felt so strong and powerful. Like a king stepping on his villagers, just because he could.

Finally, he brought the right cuts, and I grabbed them while glaring ferociously. Over the next few hours I threw shit around, yelled at everyone, and basically acted out every single cliché of the out-of-control macho chef. As the night wound down, I went out for a cigarette. Kenneth was outside, apron off, toque on his knee, puffing on a Camel. He saw me light up and asked if we could talk. I figured he was going to apologize. Grovel at my feet; tell me how great I was and how embarrassed he was for fucking up so badly. And I had my response all planned out: I was going to generously forgive him. Say, *It's okay, child. One day, years from now, maybe you will be as great as me* . . .

Kenneth's eyes were red and full of tears when he started talking.

"Chef, I really respect you, but where I'm from, we break people's knees for far less than what you did to me in there. I think you have a great way of cooking, but that is no way to treat another human being."

He paused to take a puff.

"You should really look at what you do. Because if you ever do that to me again, you won't finish your sentence."

He didn't lay so much as a finger on me, but I still felt like I had been kicked in the gut. It wasn't that I was scared of him—I'd been in enough fights back in K-Town to erase my fear of a beatdown. What knocked the wind out of me were his tears and honesty. All that time, I thought being a chef meant the white apron, the soigné sauce on the spoon, putting what I thought was my Midas touch on dishes before they went out. Boy, was I wrong. That night, under the pale moon, on the back dock, sitting next to a trash can, I had my after-school-special moment and realized it wasn't the pot throwing and the bullying that made a chef a chef. Even on Grove Street, respect came from working hard, supporting your crew, showing love and leadership, and having their back.

Two grown men broke down and cried right then and there. With all forgiven, we made our way back to the kitchen.

KENNETH WASN'T THE ONLY PERSON at La Casa del Zorro who taught me what it really meant to be a chef. Salvador approached me one day to ask if I could help him with his family business. His cousin and uncle weren't around, and he needed help with a little errand. I'm always down for whatever, so I said yes even though I had no idea what his family business was all about.

At 5:30 the next morning, Salvador was at my door with a smile and a cup of Nescafé. He got behind the wheel in his red pickup, and we headed deep into the Coachella Valley. We drove up to a spot under a grove of date trees where a few guys were hanging out, ready to work out in the fields of dates, grapes, and grapefruit. From there we continued driving, following small cardboard signs marked with crooked arrows and a word written in blocky, uneven letters: *chivo*. Goat. The arrows pointed the way to a whole field of goats. We chose a goat, paid up, hauled him into the pickup, and headed back to Salvador's place in Borrego. It was 8:00 A.M. by then, and the morning dew was already evaporating away in the crisp yolky sun.

Salvador had already prepared his backyard with a hangman's post; a rope was slung over the top and looped into a noose. Nearby, on a small foldout table, were knives, shears, a few empty bottles of Corona, and a saltshaker. We let the goat loose in the yard. Salvador got his utensils ready.

He looked at me. *"¿Listo?"*

"Sí." I had no idea what I had just said yes to.

"¡Vamanos!"

And we went after the goat like Rocky went after the chicken. The goat ran away from us, as goats do. He stopped, turned, and glared back at us, spitting and breathing heavily. Then he headed directly toward me. Just as I blocked his path, Salvador flew in like a lucha libre, landing on the goat with an *oomph,* and got him in a headlock. Just as they rolled over, I saw the goat's eyes. The eyes of fate. He knew what was about to happen.

Salvador and the goat wiggled around on the ground, hugging each other. From there, Salvador told me what to do. He told me to get the rope. I did. He told me to tie the goat's hind legs. I did. He told me to get the Corona bottle, fill it with the salt, then fill it with water. I did. He fed the goat the saltwater like a mother feeding her baby a bottle. For a split second, they actually looked really cute together. Then that second split.

Salvador carried the goat to the hangman's post. We looped the noose around the goat's hind legs and hauled him up. His front legs reached toward the ground, and his horns just cleared the sand. He wriggled a little but was otherwise calm. Salvador went over to the table and grabbed a curved, well-used, but extremely sharp boning knife.

He walked over to the post, looked at me. *"¿Listo? ¡Mira!"*

Right as he said it, he put the blade to the goat's neck. The goat's eyes opened wide, his pupils as large as the sun. Salvador drew the knife across his throat. His neck snapped back. Blood puddled below while Salvador went to work on the belly, sliding the knife from the goat's groin down his torso, splitting the body in one smooth stroke. The skin separated, allowing the organs to dangle out. He talked to me as he worked.

"La botella de agua y sal."

The Corona potion cleansed the internal organs, so there was no odor as the organs spilled into the yard. He gestured me over, and I helped him skin the animal. Once we had skinned the goat and removed his organs, we moved him to a table under a shaded trellis, turned up the radio, and broke the animal down into prime and subprime cuts. We sliced in silence, sometimes looking at each other, sometimes not, hands always moving. Cleaning, trimming, cutting. We wrapped the meat in plastic wrap, packed it into Igloo coolers, and covered everything with ice. Cleaned up, had a beer and breakfast. A cigarette. Two. It was 10:00 A.M.

After breakfast and cigarettes, we loaded up the truck with the Igloos and drove one hour south to Mexicali—or, as some call it, Sexicali—the "other" border town. Filled with some of the best Chinese food on the planet and anything you want at night. In Mexicali, Salvador's family had a *birria* (goat stew) restaurant, and we were delivering the meat to prepare the stew.

We crossed the border and arrived at Salvador's family joint on a small street. I was greeted by warm tortillas and warm, wonderful maternal love. His mom was there, apron on, already cooking; three other members of Salvador's family also were in the kitchen, cooking away and chopping onions, tomatoes. The radio playing Maná, his mom put me to work: we seasoned the meat with oregano, chili powder, chiles, garlic, cumin, salt, and other spices, building flavor on top of flavor. The meat was seared, aromatics were added, and it was left to braise in the stock with its bones until tender. While it braised, we chopped onions and picked cilantro.

All the knife cuts here were rough, the utensils cheap, the aprons stained and patterned with flowers. The ingredients were thrown together without measurements. There were no drawers of spoons for tasting, only fingers and thumbs. The hands were weathered, the faces wrinkled, the laughter free.

For an anal-retentive young whippersnapper of a wannabe chef like me, someone who was trained to cook ever so carefully by the book, being with Salvador's family was a revelation. And a reminder. *This* was cooking from the spirit, from deep-seated instinct. This was dumpling time at Silver Garden.

The birria finished braising, and I dug into a bowl. I felt the energy of the goat transfer into my being. For the first time in my young cooking career, I experienced firsthand the entire circle of life through food, from life to death to life again. I crossed the border a changed man. A more humbled, spiritual man.

A MONTH LATER, Salvador was once again at my doorstep at 5:30 A.M. He had a mug of a Nescafé and his big smile. *"¿Listo?"*

I was.

"Sí. ¡Vamos!"

I MADE SOME WONDERFUL MEMORIES at La Casa del Zorro, but after about a year it was time for me to move on and go out on my own. I didn't go too far: I became the executive chef at the de Anza Country Club, a 500-member golf resort in Borrego Springs, making some $30,000 a year. Not too bad for a thirty-year-old desert cook.

In fact, I thought I was more than not too bad. I thought I was really good. After Le Bernardin, after sailing through the CIA, after creating beautiful dishes at La Casa del Zorro and being put in charge of the kitchen at this country club, I thought I knew most everything, or at least enough to be very confident in my skills. But, as proud as I was of myself, the members of the club didn't really give a shit about my résumé or my skills. They were all retirees about sixty-five years old, who spent half of the year in Canada, the Midwest, or the Northwest, and the other half in Borrego Springs at this club, playing golf and relaxing in the desert. They all paid good money to be members, and they considered the kitchen and the chef to be at their disposal. Especially Mrs. Gates.

Mrs. Gates was the queen bee of the de Anza Country Club. She always came to me with recipes ripped straight out of *Good Housekeeping,* more torn out of the newspaper, some photocopied from old Betty Crocker books. And with each stack of recipes, she would give me explicit instructions on how I was to cook these dishes for her and the other 499 members of the club. These weren't terribly fancy dishes— no, they came straight out of nostalgia. Classic American comfort foods lifted from the Norman Rockwell era, the type of food that gave me such a culture shock in Villa Park when I opened up my friends' wall-sized refrigerators and pantries and found leftover meat loaf and fruit platters. That's what Mrs. Gates and the rest of the club grew up with, and that's what they wanted to eat.

Their perspective refreshed mine, and that calmed me and my ego down. After all, they were allowing me, a Korean kid in a town with barely any other Asians, to cook it for them. And that meant something. With my small crew of five—Eduardo, Wayo, Dora, Pablo, Frank, Miguel—we gave Betty Crocker a makeover. It was exhilarating; I had never cooked dishes like that before. Our general manager, John, was a former chef, and he guided me as I learned how to put my own mark on dishes like pot roast and meat loaf. Corn and New England clam chowders. Deviled eggs and tuna salads. Beef Stroganoff and fried chicken. Cornucopia salads and tuna melts. Potatoes au gratin and macaroni casseroles. We experimented with cooking times, used better butter, threw in fresher herbs and new spices to make everything less bland and more exciting. And so the beef

JACQUES PÉPIN BECAM
PRACTICE, PRACTICE
WAX ON. WAX OFF

Stroganoff had a little more depth of flavor, the pot roast had more herbs and a kick of spice, the garlic for the garlic toast was roasted a little longer than usual. I hoped these dishes would be even better than Mrs. Gates remembered them being. I hoped she would love them.

And she did. They all did. Four nights a week, the 5:00 P.M. rush struck, and we played hit after hit of great American oldies but goodies. I was thanked with fat grandma kisses and big grandpa hugs. As the hot food sparked warm memories, they told me stories of their youth. And that was so special to me, listening to the memories they held so dear, after having lived so much life. The simple things suddenly seemed to matter the most.

Story time usually ended around 7:00, and by 7:30 the place was nothing but crickets. After the season ended in June and most of the club's members went back home to Canada, the Midwest, or the Pacific Northwest, the crickets started chirping by 5:00. That's when we packed up the kitchen and cleaned out the closets, using the rest of the summer to get ready for the return of the crowds in September.

It was on one of those lazy summer days cleaning out the closets that I found something special. The manager of de Anza had a bunch of books stored away in that closet, including Jacques Pépin's *La Technique*. I picked it up, read it cover to cover, then did so again. And again. Reading Pépin made me realize how little I actually knew about the craft of cooking. The CIA gave us a lot, but it had been a crash course. Jacques Pépin became my Mr. Miyagi as he slowed the process down and showed me that cooking takes time, dedication, and practice, practice, practice. Surrounded by mountains that spoke to me through wind and reflection, I spent the summer in the Zen of the kitchen, relearning all the basics. How to hold a knife. How to julienne. How to make foundational sauces. Practice, practice, practice. Wax on. Wax off.

MY MR. MIYAGI
PRACTICE.

TWO YEARS INTO MY COOKING great American classics for Mrs. Gates and crew, the Embassy Suites in Lake Tahoe came calling through a friend, Peter Brinckerhoff, who had become its director. For some reason the guys there thought that a chef who had just spent the last few years cooking for retirees in the middle of a desert was the perfect fit to run a resort that catered to young, active tourists in an action-packed town. But I couldn't turn down the opportunity, even if I may have been in a bit over my head: as much as I loved cooking at the country club, there wasn't much left for me to do. It was time to move on and explore the world outside the desert.

And so in 2001 I said good-bye to the snowbirds and coyotes and left the sleepy, laid-back desert for the high energy of Lake Tahoe. This is a world 6,500 feet above sea level right on the border of California and Nevada, where the water in the lake is clear as glass, the kids learn how to barrel through a half-pipe about the same time they learn how to ride a bike, people hike on their days off instead of watching TV, and locals eat whatever's cheap and whatever's fast—chili bread bowls, wings, pizza—so they can get back to the snow or the water.

And right at the southern tip of the lake is the city of South Lake Tahoe, also known as the South Shore. This is the biggest city in the area, the one you'd hit if you were headed to Heavenly to snowboard or wanted some big-city casino action. And right at South Shore's tip is the Embassy Suites, a four-star four-diamond resort and my new digs.

Pretty quickly, I realized I had to crank my shit up to eleven. At the desert resorts, I was used to taking care of one or two events a day: a big meeting, maybe, or a banquet. The Embassy Suites, though, was a huge operation; on any given day, I'd have to organize and prep for not only a banquet but also a wedding for 200, a reception for 100, ten business meetings with different breakout session schedules. Plus room service for the 400 suites and service for the two restaurants.

But La Casa del Zorro and de Anza Country Club must have taught me something. As it turns out, I was pretty good at the organization needed for this type of high-volume cooking. With a staff of seventy-five people, my sous-chefs, Sal and Jesse, and I put together buffets and deli boards and pasta bars, sometimes even full plate-ups. Together we cooked thousands of meals for every occasion in that kitchen. Weddings, celebrity golf tournaments, corporate gatherings, family vacations. And at Echo, one of the hotel's restaurants, we developed a chef-driven

menu that reflected Northern California's natural beauty and bounty: lots of deep stocks, layered flavors, fresh herbs, first-press olive oil, Marcona almonds, braised short ribs, miso-glazed Hawaiian ono topped with coconut milk relish.

We were a hit. In that town of fast slopes and faster food, we slowed things down, set a new pace for the culinary scene, and even won a few awards. And I set a new pace for myself, too: I'd work all day and most of the night, grab a milk shake from a local casino during my breaks, and still find time to teach classes on gastronomy and banquets at the local community college. I was starting to really find my voice on the plate and as a chef. But there was still so much for me to learn and, two years after I joined the Embassy Suites, a fortuitous trip to Japan would teach me how to dig deeper and cook with an eye for even the smallest of details.

IRON CHEF ROKUSABURO MICHIBA is a legend in the Japanese cooking world. A fucking saint, the very first Iron Chef, and the master to Morimoto. Before Michiba, a long tradition of regionalism meant you couldn't really find regional Japanese dishes outside those specific parts of the country. More than that, chefs mostly used local ingredients; they didn't really incorporate anything that was found outside their area, and they certainly didn't mess with traditional foods or experiment with, say, combining flavors from Hokkaido with those from Osaka. Chef Michiba, though, untapped that regional cooking, broke down those borders, and brought it together to Tokyo.

As it happened, Chef Michiba's daughter had worked for the owner of my hotel some time ago, and they had stayed on friendly terms throughout the years. Friendly enough to ask whether they could send someone—me—to Japan to work alongside her father; this would be both my reward for all of my hard work and a research trip to learn Japanese flavors and technique. My GM, Simeon, and AGM, Stefan, approved. No other American had ever had an opportunity like this to cook in Chef Michiba's kitchen. I'd be the first. A real honor. The owners also had a connection to the Pan Pacific Hotel in the Yokohama Bay, and I'd be sent there, too, to cook in its renowned banquet hall.

But first, Master Michiba. I landed in Tokyo on his seventy-second birthday. We met at his Ginza restaurant, Kaishoku Michiba. When the master shook my hand, I felt the whole universe shift, as if he had transferred his energy to me in a lightning bolt. From that moment forward, it was all work and no play, but that bolt of lightning lit me up all summer long.

The work started every morning around 6:00 or 7:00. Chef Michiba; the chef de cuisine, Yanai-san; the restaurant manager; my translator, Max, and I would go to the Tsukiji market to pick out fish for the day. Huge slabs of tuna and other fish caught those very mornings were laid out on wooden tables, some sliced open for inspection. Everything clean as a whistle.

Chef Michiba usually walked right through the market and went straight to his purveyors. As he approached, the vendors would scurry around in their knee-high rubber boots and heavy blue aprons, hauling out their very best catches of the morning. Chef had first dibs on everything, so it was always fish no one else had yet seen, and wouldn't see, unless he passed on them. If he liked something, he got it, but no money was ever exchanged. His vendors billed him later.

Little sushi bars dotted the market. On one of our morning runs, my hosts took me to one of the most famous ones. They had given the heads-up to the chef that they were bringing a "famous" chef from America, the first ever to work in one of Michiba's kitchens. Great.

The sushi bar was essentially the size of a shoebox, with a small counter barely big enough for fourteen people. There were no plates. No soy sauce. No wasabi. No pickled ginger. No chopsticks. You sat at the counter, you ate with your hands, you drank a cup of hot tea, you got the fuck out.

Our chef that day was the master of the house, about sixty-eight years old. The whole time we were there, he talked with Michiba while setting piece after piece of sushi on the counter. Toro that melted in my mouth. Shiso that was beautiful and pungent. Absolutely amazing seafood, caught just hours before. And all throughout the meal, the old master kept one eye on me. Watching me, scratching his head, then occasionally unleashing a stream of questions in Japanese, which Max translated: "Who are you? Why are you Asian? They said you were American."

I just smiled and nodded, smiled and nodded. Evidently, that didn't impress him. He went back to talking to Michiba, shaking his head, looking at me. He couldn't believe that this Korean dude was the "American" chef everyone was telling him about. I stayed out of it, kept my head down, and ate and ate, one piece at a time, enthralled by the fact that any of this was even happening. Sushi served by a

master in the company of Michiba, with food as our only language in common. Who was I indeed?

AFTER OUR MORNING TRIP to the market, the day really began—and it was a long one. I would be working at Kaishoku Michiba, the chef's main restaurant. It was a small, rectangular space on the eighth floor of an office building across the way from the giant department store Matsuzakaya, on the most celebrated street in Ginza, the highest-rent district of Tokyo. Outside, the city buzzed and bustled, but inside Kaishoku Michiba it was nothing but serene. A long sushi bar with long cutting boards dominated the restaurant; beyond that was the open kitchen that didn't have much more than reach-in refrigerators along one wall and burners and broilers lining the other. There was no walk-in cooler, no back prep area, no separate space for cutting the fish; instead, Styrofoam coffins of fish and seafood packed in ice, all fresh from the morning market, were at our feet as we prepped and cooked, and what was in those coffins was what was available for the day: when it was gone, it was gone. Overall, the kitchen was small, just big enough to fit ten cooks, yet somehow it never felt very cramped.

We had one marathon shift from 7:00 a.m. to midnight, which covered lunch and dinner. It was a trip to work there: nothing went to waste, ever; nothing got brushed aside; nothing was rushed or done nonchalantly or with broad strokes. Even the simplest tasks—peeling tomatoes, filing away the silverware, cutting fish, picking herbs—were treated with respect, handled with care and deliberation. The cooks at Michiba brought a level of detailed focus to their work far greater than that to which I was accustomed. Compared to them, I was a bumbling, clumsy giant with fat thumbs and two left feet.

With my big thumbs and left feet, I pitched in wherever I was needed. In theory, the kitchen had a brigade system similar to that of Le Bernardin and other French kitchens, where each cook had his own place in the hierarchy. But the Japanese way is teamwork over the self. So, regardless of assigned station or official title, we all worked together and everything blended into one harmonious entity. To prep for the ladies who lunched, I filleted fish, learned to pay attention to the nanoseconds that separated a great dashi from a horrible one, made fresh tofu. I cleaned tomatoes, diced fruits, charred mackerel skin, made beef jelly, poached figs,

THE DETAILS WERE
MICROSCOPIC, AND I WAS
JUST STARTING TO LEARN
HOW TO ZOOM IN.

braised fish. Our family meal came at 4:00 P.M., and all the cooks sat down together for what usually was just a quick lunch of curry rice, oden soup, donburi, chirashi, udon, or sukiyaki.

Dinner was a different experience. It was served kaiseki-style, a multicourse meal with a menu that changed every night. During service, I again helped out where needed, trying to be useful and not fuck things up. I prepped bamboo shoots for the yuzu broth that started the meal and then prepared the next course of one-bite sushi and fish, arranging them on the plate so they were perfectly equidistant from each other like numbers on a clock. Next up, courses of broiled fish with somen noodles, octopus, a sampler plate of fish and shellfish, Kobe beef with jelly, then figs, then black sesame flan to end the meal.

I could have stayed for a year and not learned everything I wanted to learn from Master Michiba. But after two weeks at Kaishoku Michiba, it was time to pack up my knives and head to the Pan Pacific Hotel to learn the art of the banquet.

Where other five-star hotels in the Yokohama Bay put their big event halls and ballrooms on rooftops overlooking the city, the Pan Pacific Hotel roof was nothing but cement. Their food hall was in the basement. It was the best banquet in the city. It didn't need a view.

Run by Chef Takayoshi Kawai, a former chef de cuisine for Julian Serrano at Masa in San Francisco, the banquet hall was operated just like an à la carte kitchen, so you could be at a wedding for 300, but the detailed garnishes on each plate made it feel like you were having an intimate dinner for two. And again I picked up on how every flavor, every nuance, every detail was impeccably on point, even in this high-volume setting. Every piece of silverware was organized perfectly in neat drawers, every piece of vegetable seasoned properly. The details were microscopic, and I was just starting to learn how to zoom in.

BEFORE I KNEW IT, I said my *arigatos* to Chef Michiba and his team, and to Chef Kawai and his team, my mind popping with new ideas and flavors. I was ready to take it back to Tahoe, but the Embassy Suites had bigger ideas for me: they needed a regional chef for their brand, and they thought I was the guy to represent their name. I moved up to Sacramento, on the advice of Sandy Murphy, the VP of Hilton, and took over duties to oversee culinary decisions for ten hotels, hundreds of staff members, with an average of $4 million in sales at each property, which stretched from Seattle to San Jose. This was the big time.

My goal was to give our guests a five-star experience for a three-star price, just like how my parents had hustled and flowed with their jewelry in the Pershing Square days. The Embassy Suites' book hadn't been updated since the Reagan years, so I got rid of some of its old, drab cooking techniques and updated everything to 2005. For the Embassy Suites' Sacramento restaurant, we took in-season mushrooms and layered them in quesadillas stuffed with the best cheese and slow-roasted tomato jam, with a side of cauliflower ceviche. Added a West Coast clam chowder loaded with Manila clams, cockles, pancetta cured in-house, shallots, and chives. A foie gras "hamburger" with roasted Fuji apples and a port sauce. Burrata with fresh berries and cracked pepper and olive oil with fennel crostini, a light appetizer that popped like a party in your mouth.

And up and down the coast, we developed an omelet bar with high-quality ingredients—better bacon, better sausage, better potatoes, proper biscuits—so guests could choose their own omelet adventures. We even did a stint on *The Ellen DeGeneres Show* for her special "Ellen in the Park" episode, making custom omelets in eighty-degree heat for her audience. I started to influence the brand on a national scale.

"His parents, Mr. and Mrs. Choi, said, 'We'll name our boy Roy!' " Ellen said, riffing on my name as she introduced me on the show. "Do you enjoy koi, Roy? And when you were a boy, were you coy?"

If she only knew.

THE BEVERLY HILTON GAVE ME an interview, but it was only a courtesy one. I knew what was up. An Embassy Suites Hotel chef—a mid-level brand at best—applying for the chef de cuisine position at a super-high-end flagship hotel on the corner of Santa Monica Boulevard and Wilshire Boulevard in Beverly Hills, 90210? Where presidents stayed and celebrities partied?

Hell, no.

But the area vice president for Hilton recommended that I apply for the job, and after six years at the Embassy Suites, I was looking for a change. I threw my toque into the ring, and the managers there had no choice but to do as their boss said. They put on a whole dog and pony show for me even as they were eyeing someone else, like my interview was just a formality before crossing me off their list.

The interview started in February 2007, lasted three months, and cycled through ten different managers. Even the hotel's telephone switchbox operator and the lady in charge of the hair salon asked me questions. They put me through the ringer, hoping to dampen my interest. But I wasn't ready to throw in the towel. I still had my five-course tasting menu, prepped from scratch, to present and show them what I could do.

On the day of the tasting, all the managers who had given me the runaround were in the room. Waiting for me to fail so they could scrunch up their noses, wrinkle their faces, and politely escort me out of the hotel. I made compressed watermelon with uni and jalapeño gastrique, seared tuna carpaccio with bone marrow and herbs, foie gras with berries and lemon curd and cracklings. Salmon with horseradish. Korean skirt steak with a sesame risotto. That five-course menu was the shot heard 'round the world. Word spread fast. The whole hotel started coming up; everyone wanted to taste it. All the bullshit went away. I got the job on the spot.

I thought it would be perfect for me. The volume was huge. A $35–$45 million food and beverage program, with 200 under my management as the chef de cuisine of the hotel's Circa 55 restaurant and the loungey Trader Vic's. In total, there were five kitchens, plus room service for 570 rooms and the bars in the lobby and pools.

Then there was the caliber of the clientele. When the royal family of Dubai and the king of Morocco visited Los Angeles, they rented whole floors complete with lavish buffets. They didn't use alarm clocks, waking up whenever their bodies woke up, so we always had to be ready to mobilize and feed. Even if they woke up at 3:00 P.M. and wanted breakfast while we were prepping for dinner. The celebrities—

Clive Davis, Alicia Keys, and so on—would just call up for room service and eat in the privacy of their rooms. The newly elected Governator came in and smoked his cigars; Joan Rivers had a lot of lunches, mostly salads; Eddie Vedder and Bruce Springsteen hung out in the hallways. Once, Tom Hanks, playing catch-me-if-you-can with the paps, cut through the kitchen, giving us all a Cali high-five as he made his exit, grabbing a little piece of this or that along the way, saying, "Mmm, this is good! That's good!" And the events were huge: The Billboard Music Awards. The Grammys. The Golden Globes, where celebrities had a three-course plated affair with endive salad, yuzu halibut, chocolate mousse, petits fours.

But as amazing as those meals were, I was having problems. The executive chef of the hotel, Suki Sugiura, and I really liked each other personally, but our positions clashed. The hotel wanted me to transform Circa 55 into a restaurant with simple, clean, delicious, natural, elegant dishes, like Craft or Providence in town, or like Higgins, Wildwood, and Cafe Juanita in the Northwest, and I was itching to do exactly that.

Only problem was, they never told Chef Sugiura about any of these plans. And so he insisted that I cook the menu he had developed: Cobb salad, yuzu halibut, club sandwich, Kobe beef steak with pine mushrooms, salmon with bok choy, smoked ribs, sushi. And I knew I couldn't go up against a chef in a political battle; more than that, at the end of the day, I'm just a cook, loyal to the craft. I had to follow the chain of command, just like I did on the streets. And so that meant I had to follow Chef's lead, not corporate's, even if it meant my own career wouldn't flourish and even if it meant that I'd be constantly caught between the will of the kitchen and the will of the man upstairs. Cobb salad and club sandwiches it was.

The union rules were tough, too. From Borrego Springs to Tokyo to Sacramento, I was used to environments where it was all hands on deck, all the time. The all-union staff at the hotel, though, meant there were strict rules about who could do what and for how long. With those restrictions in place, it was much, much harder to run the kitchen, especially on busy nights and during events.

And so, for all its glory and its history, for all the celebrities and royalties, the Beverly Hilton was fast becoming a huge ocean liner, and I couldn't do anything to turn it as fast as I wanted it to turn.

It was time to jump ship.

BIRRIA

When Salvador put the knife to that goat's neck that day in Borrego, the goat's eyes opened big and wide. Those eyes will forever be tattooed in my soul, and I will forever be linked to birria. It's amazing that an animal that is so important to certain cultures is so underappreciated in the United States, but it doesn't have to be like that: one spoonful of this deep, soulful stew, and you'll start to appreciate it, too.

If you can't find goat meat in your area, try this recipe with lamb.

SERVES 4 TO 6

4 dried guajillo chiles
2 dried ancho chiles
3 garlic cloves, peeled
¼ cup chopped onion
1 jalapeño pepper, seeded
1 scallion
¼ teaspoon cumin seeds
¼ teaspoon dried Mexican oregano
3 whole cloves

1½ tablespoons cider vinegar
1 teaspoon dark brown sugar
½ cup water
2½ pounds goat (leg meat and meaty ribs), cut into 3- to 4-inch cubes
Salt and pepper
½ cup drained canned fire-roasted tomatoes, plus 1 fresh Roma tomato, charred

GARNISH
Limes
Fresh cilantro
Minced white onion

Preheat the oven to 350°F.

Toast the guajillo and ancho chiles in a dry pan over medium heat, until they're smoking and a bit charred on each side. Transfer to a plate.

In the same pan, toast the garlic, then the onion, then the jalapeño, and finally, the scallion, removing each vegetable from the pan before adding the next. You want to toast the veggies until they're smoking and a bit charred.

Grind the cumin seeds, oregano, and cloves together in a spice grinder.

Combine the charred vegetables, ground spices, vinegar, brown sugar, and water in a blender and puree. Rub half of the mixture all over the goat, reserving the other half in the blender. Lightly season the goat with salt and pepper.

Place the goat on a wire rack on a sheet pan and roast it in the oven for about 45 minutes. Remove and transfer the meat to a large pot.

Add the tomatoes to the leftover marinade in the blender and puree. Add the mixture to the pot with the roasted goat and then add enough water to bring the liquid just above the goat. Give it all a good stir, bring it to a boil, then reduce the heat to let the goat simmer, covered, until it's nice and tender, about 1½ hours. It should be really, really soft.

Ladle out bowls of the birria and garnish each bowl with a squeeze of lime, some chopped cilantro, and minced onion. Maybe a little more salt and some dried oregano.

¡LISTO!

CRISPY DUCK BREAST WITH POLENTA AND SWEET AND SOUR MANGO SAUCE

This is a dish that was inspired by *Art Culinaire* and the PBS Great Chefs Series on TV. It's a dish that many young chefs do, trying to be all fancy when they don't even know how to cook yet, like doing a guitar solo but not even being that good at playing the guitar. This is exactly what Paul and I were doing at La Casa del Zorro. Even with all these trappings, though, this combination of mango and duck is pretty damn good. Make sure your skin gets crispy.

SERVES 4

POLENTA

2 cups half-and-half

1 cup water

½ cup polenta

2 tablespoons grated Parmesan cheese

Salt and freshly ground black pepper

SAUCE

½ cup fresh orange juice

½ cup fresh grapefruit juice

2 tablespoons extra virgin olive oil

1½ teaspoons sliced peeled fresh ginger

1 tablespoon sliced garlic

1 tablespoon minced scallions

1½ teaspoons minced jalapeño pepper

½ cup ketchup

1 tablespoon soy sauce

½ cup natural rice vinegar (not seasoned)

2 tablespoons sugar

Flesh of ½ mango

DUCK

2 tablespoons extra virgin olive oil

4 duck breast halves, the skin scored with hash marks and patted dry

Salt and freshly ground black pepper

SLURRY

1 tablespoon cornstarch

1 tablespoon water

PREPARE THE POLENTA

In a pot, combine the half-and-half and the water and bring to a boil. Reduce the heat to a simmer and whisk in the polenta, stirring it continuously with the whisk. Watch out for splashing bubbles—they may burn you.

When the polenta thickens to the consistency of mashed potatoes, after 4 to 6 minutes, add the Parmesan cheese and season with salt and pepper to taste. Set aside and keep warm.

MAKE THE SAUCE

Mix the orange juice and grapefruit juice together and set aside.

Heat a small pan and add the 2 tablespoons of oil. Add the ginger, garlic, scallions, and jalapeño and cook just until aromatic. Add the juice mixture and the rest of the sauce ingredients, bring to a boil, reduce the heat, and simmer, uncovered, for 1 hour.

Puree and strain the sauce. It will keep for days in the refrigerator. Or pack it into small bags and sell it on the street.

TO BRING IT ALL TOGETHER

Put a large sauté pan over medium heat and pour in the olive oil. Season the duck breasts with salt and pepper and cook them slowly, skin side down, until the skin becomes deep golden brown and crispy. Don't rush—the slower, the better.

Once the skin is nice and crispy, turn the duck over and cook. Transfer to a wire rack on a sheet pan to rest.

Mix the cornstarch and the water together in a small bowl. Reheat as much sauce as you want and thicken it a bit with the cornstarch slurry.

Drizzle the sweet and sour sauce around—but not on top of—the duck. To plate, scoop some polenta onto a dish. Slice the duck breasts, which now should be medium-rare, and place them on top of the polenta.

You'll have a crispy skinned duck with polenta and a nostalgic sweet and sour sauce.

BUT IT'S NOT CHINATOWN. IT'S YOUR TOWN. ENJOY.

RED ONION MARMALADE

The de Anza Country Club had a monthly journal for its members, and this was the first recipe I wrote for it. I paired the marmalade with a hamburger recipe and wished my members low scores and happy rounds. This marmalade can be used on my burger (page 301) or on any protein dish as a side condiment.

MAKES ABOUT 1 CUP

2 pounds red onions, sliced
¼ cup olive oil
1 cup red wine
1 cup red wine vinegar
1 cup packed brown sugar

1 teaspoon freshly ground black pepper
½ teaspoon cayenne
Zest (grated) and juice of 1 lemon
Zest (grated) and juice of 1 lime

Combine the onions and olive oil in a large, deep pan and sauté over medium heat, stirring periodically, until the onions are soft and slightly caramelized—about 10 minutes.

Deglaze the pan with the red wine and vinegar. Bring the onions and their liquid to a boil, cooking continuously over high heat until the liquid is reduced by half.

Lower the heat and add the brown sugar, pepper, cayenne, and citrus zest and juice, whisking everything to dissolve the sugar. Cook for 10 to 15 minutes over low heat, stirring periodically. Allow the onions to cool and you're done. It'll keep, covered, for 1 week.

Use on meats or on breakfast toast. YOU CHOOSE.

SIMPLE CLUB SANDWICH

Nothing says golf more than FORE!! Followed by a club sandwich. To me, there is a science to a great club sandwich. Sure, it's simple, but in that simplicity there are certain rules that make it great. Certain forms of architecture that make the sandwich not fall apart or slip around. I hope this recipe can be a road map to that perfect club sandwich.

MAKES 1 SIMPLE SANDWICH

3 pieces sourdough toast
Some mayonnaise
3 slices cooked, crispy bacon
2 leaves dried green leaf lettuce

2 slices tomato
2 slices cooked turkey breast
2 slices Swiss cheese

Slather 1 side of each piece of toast with mayonnaise. Place the bacon, lettuce, and tomato on 1 piece of toast, then top with another piece of toast. Place the turkey and Swiss on the toast and top with the last piece of toast.

Cut into fourths and place one of those colored frilly toothpicks in each triangle.

Eat with Tabasco and ketchup.

YUM.

NOW GO SHOOT
A GOOD ROUND.

EASY DE ANZA COBB SALAD

I really loved Lucy back when I'd watch TV as a tween, and watching her watch William Holden order that Cobb salad got me researching Old Hollywood and the Brown Derby. The Cobb was invented at the Derby, and we had a version of it at de Anza. I don't see Cobb salads much on the menu anymore in these new modern restaurants. I think they're worth it: it's just a matter of time before people realize how good they are when done right with that perfect mix of ingredients.

SERVES 4

VINAIGRETTE

1 cup extra virgin olive oil

½ cup cider vinegar

¼ cup capers, packed in either salt or brine

2 tablespoons minced onion

2 tablespoons chopped fresh parsley

2 tablespoons minced scallions

Salt and freshly ground black pepper to taste

SALAD

Big bowl of mixed greens, like baby romaine, baby butter lettuce, and baby red leaf lettuce

½ cup crumbled blue cheese

2 cups diced cooked turkey

½ cup diced cucumber, peeled and seeded

½ cup diced tomato

½ cup diced hard-boiled egg

½ cup diced cooked bacon

½ cup minced scallions

½ cup diced cheddar cheese

½ cup deep-fried shallots (store-bought fried onion strings are fine)

Combine the ingredients for the vinaigrette in a blender and puree until smooth. Taste and adjust the seasoning if necessary.

Toss the greens in the vinaigrette and place a heaping amount on each plate or in a serving bowl. Gently layer the rest of the ingredients on the greens however you wish.

NOW, WHY WOULD YOU GO OUT AND PAY $14 FOR THIS WHEN YOU CAN MAKE IT YOURSELF?

SIMPLE CHICKEN PICCATA

This was one of the first signature dishes that I perfected as a young chef. And even though it's almost too commonly found in restaurants, and it can be really bad if it's not done right, there is something timeless about capers, lemon, and parsley, something that just brightens up the palate when the acidity matches with the juiciness of the chicken and a touch of cream. This is also a dish to make on a date night, because it's easy and quick and hits a flavor quotient that could possibly get you laid. Just don't break the sauce. . . .

SERVES 4

Four 6-ounce boneless, skinless
    chicken breasts, pounded
    between 2 sheets of plastic wrap
    until ¼ inch thick
Salt and freshly ground black pepper
3 tablespoons extra virgin olive oil
2 tablespoons minced shallot
¼ cup capers packed in brine

¼ cup brine from caper jar
¼ cup white wine
Juice of 3 lemons
3 tablespoons heavy cream
½ cup chopped fresh parsley, plus a
    little more for garnish
2 tablespoons butter

Preheat the oven to 350°F and heat a large sauté pan over medium-high heat for 1 minute.

Season the chicken breasts on both sides with salt and pepper.

Add 2 tablespoons of the olive oil to the pan and sear each side of the chicken breasts, getting good color on each side, about 3 minutes per side. You can do this 2 chicken pieces at a time, being careful not to crowd the pan. When nicely seared, transfer the chicken to a wire rack on a cookie sheet. When all the chicken is seared, place the cookie sheet in the oven until the chicken is cooked through, 4 to 6 minutes.

In the same pan you used to sear the chicken, heat the remaining tablespoon of oil and, over medium heat, cook the shallot just until it starts to color. Quickly add the capers, their juice, and the white wine, moving everything around constantly with a wooden spoon for 1 minute.

Throw in the lemon juice and the heavy cream. Swirl this sauce around for 1 minute; don't reduce it too much.

Taste and adjust the seasoning. Add the chopped parsley and a knob of butter. Swirl the pan vigorously until the sauce has a smooth, velvety texture. It should be loose but viscous.

Remove the chicken from the oven and plate each breast. Pour the sauce over each breast, top with more chopped parsley, and eat.

MANGIA OR MANIA— YOU DECIDE.

FRIED RIBS. WHAT?!

Who fries ribs? Me, that's who. I first thought of frying ribs when I was at the Embassy Suites in Sacramento; they got rave reviews in the local paper. So I've fried ribs, and now you will, too.

SERVES 4 TO 6

BRAISE LIQUID

10 cups water
½ cup garlic cloves, peeled
½ cup chopped peeled fresh ginger
½ onion, chopped
½ cup fresh cilantro stems

1½ teaspoons black peppercorns
½ cup natural rice vinegar (not seasoned)
1 tablespoon kosher salt
1 tablespoon sugar
10 cups water

RIBS

2½ pounds baby back ribs, rinsed and
    scored
2 quarts vegetable oil

SAUCE

½ cup hoisin sauce
¼ cup oyster sauce
½ cup chili garlic sauce
½ cup Chinese black bean sauce
1 cup fresh orange juice

2 tablespoons fresh lime juice
¾ cup water
2 tablespoons Sriracha
1½ tablespoons Chinese mustard powder
1 tablespoon brown sugar

GARNISH

Scallions sliced on a bias
Roasted sesame seeds

ONE DAY AHEAD
In a big pot over high heat, combine all the braise ingredients. Bring the braise to a boil, then add the rack of ribs, making sure the ribs are completely submerged in the water. If the ribs don't fit in your pot, cut them into 2 racks. Reduce the heat and simmer the ribs in the brine for 1 hour. Pull out the ribs and place them on a wire rack on a sheet pan. Allow the ribs to come to room temperature and then transfer them to the refrigerator and leave them there, uncovered, overnight. Discard the brine.

In a big bowl, combine all the sauce ingredients and give them a good whisk.

Heat the vegetable oil to 350°F in a deep fryer or in a large, deep pot. Cut the ribs into individual portions. In batches (so the oil maintains its temperature), fry 'em until the outside gets crispy and develops a deep golden brown color. Pull them out, drain on a paper-towel-lined plate or cookie sheet, and immediately toss with the sauce—enough to generously coat the ribs.

Put the ribs on a plate and garnish with the scallions and a shower of roasted sesame seeds.

YOU'LL HAVE STICKY FINGERS.

FRENCH ONION SOUP

French onion soup was one of my first big lessons in becoming a chef: having the patience to let the onions caramelize just right, understanding the need for great stock, learning the importance of balance and seasoning. Over time, this became one of my signature dishes during my hotel days, and I started to develop my own philosophies and put my own touches on it. My dad was on a Calvados kick for a while, so I knew a lot about this apple brandy and used it instead of more traditional cognac or sherry to really kick up the flavors. Make sure the cheese is nice and brown on top.

SERVES 4 TO 6

3 tablespoons extra virgin olive oil

2 yellow onions, sliced

2 red onions, sliced

Salt and freshly ground black pepper

2 cups Calvados or any brandy

2 quarts veal stock (page 222) or
   beef stock

2 quarts chicken stock

½ loaf French bread, cut into ⅓-inch-
   thick slices, doused in olive oil, then
   toasted in 300°F oven until golden
   brown to make croutons

8 to 10 slices Gruyère cheese

Set a big pot over medium heat and add the oil. Add the sliced onions and swirl them around until they start to caramelize, about 6 minutes. Season them liberally with salt and pepper.

Reduce the heat to medium-low and let the onions cook for about an hour, stirring occasionally. When the onions are really jammy, turn up the heat to high, deglaze the pot with the Calvados, and cook until the brandy is absorbed by the onions and reduced by at least half. Add the stocks, bring to a boil, and then lower the heat and simmer for an hour.

Season to taste again.

Pour the soup into ovenproof crocks and top with croutons and cheese. Broil those crocks for 4 minutes or until they're bubbly and brown.

LOVE.

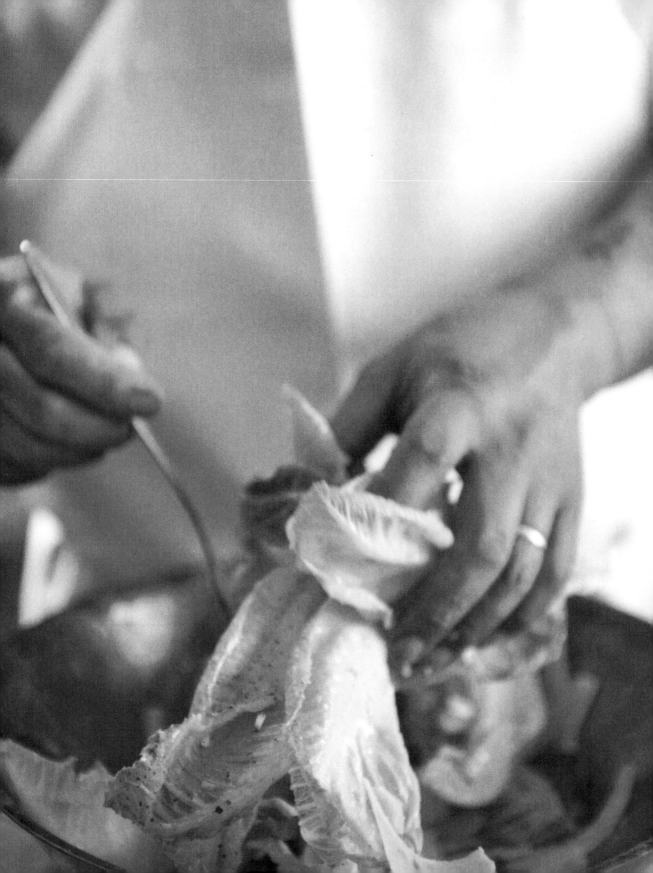

CAESAR SALAD

Yes, it's everywhere, but this one is really good, I swear. Don't omit the shaved Parmesan—the salad won't taste complete until you add it at the end.

Leftover dressing will keep in your refrigerator for up to 5 days.

SERVES 8

DRESSING

3 tablespoons chopped garlic

2 tablespoons chopped anchovies

3 large egg yolks

¾ teaspoon dry mustard

1½ teaspoons freshly ground black pepper

1 cup plus 1 tablespoon extra virgin olive oil

½ cup fresh lemon juice

2 cups mayonnaise

2½ tablespoons Worcestershire sauce

2 tablespoons pureed onion

1 tablespoon water

Good pinch of salt

SALAD

8 romaine hearts, separated into leaves

2 cups shaved Parmesan cheese

1 lemon

Cracked black pepper

Combine all the dressing ingredients in a blender and puree.

Toss the romaine leaves with the dressing, coating with liberal intent.

Plate the leaves and shower each plate with Parmesan, a light squeeze of lemon, and big twists of cracked black pepper from the peppermill.

BE GENEROUS.
THIS IS NOT A TIME
FOR RESTRAINT.

MUSHROOM QUESADILLA

This was one of my hit dishes at the Embassy Suites, and to this day people trip out when they see it. They say, mushrooms in a quesadilla? And I say, yes, mushrooms in a quesadilla, foo; don't trip, just try it. Then they try it and say, Wow! Mushrooms in a quesadilla!!

If you can, splurge on this one and get the fancy mushrooms. It's not like you are gonna do yourself any favors by not going for it. If you're not going to go for it, just don't make it. If you splurge, that simple thing will change your life.

SERVES 4 TO 6

1 cup chanterelle mushrooms
1 cup blue foot mushrooms
1 cup hedgehog mushrooms
About 1 cup extra virgin olive oil
1½ teaspoons kosher salt

1½ teaspoons freshly ground black pepper
Four to six 10-inch flour tortillas
2 cups shredded cheddar cheese

SALSA
Salsa verde (page 119)

GARNISHES (OPTIONAL)
Fresh white or black truffles
Lime, quartered

Trim and slice the mushrooms and toss them into a bowl with 4 tablespoons of the oil, the salt, and the pepper.

In a large sauté pan over high heat, add 6 tablespoons of the oil, and when it starts to smoke, add half the mushrooms or however many will fit in a single layer. Take your time and do it in stages if all of the mushrooms don't fit—if you crowd the pan, the mushrooms will steam instead of caramelizing beautifully. When the mushrooms start to caramelize, after about 6 minutes, transfer them to a wire rack on a sheet pan; then repeat for the remaining mushrooms.

Wipe out the pan or use a griddle, and add just a dab of oil. Heat it just until it starts to smoke. Place a tortilla in the pan and smother it with cheese. Layer the mushrooms over the cheese and continue to cook until the cheese melts and/or the bottom of the tortilla gets crispy and golden brown.

Place another tortilla on top of the cheese and mushrooms and flip.

Add a touch more oil on the fresh tortilla, swirl it around the pan, and cook until crispy.

Remove. Cut. Smother with salsa. Add a squeeze of lime if you like.

Shave truffles.

Eat.

BROILED HALIBUT WITH SOY GLAZE

When I was in Japan, I learned how to make a dashi and how to use that dashi with soy to turn it into a sauce and to use it as a glaze. And while I learned how to cook fish at Le Bernardin, my time at Kaishoku Michiba really solidified all the lessons I learned on how to cook fish just right. This is a simple dish that reflects those lessons—pay attention, stay focused, and you will cook fish the right way each time.

SERVES 4 TO 6

4 to 6 halibut fillets
Salt and freshly ground black pepper
Extra virgin olive oil

Softened butter
2 cups Splash (page 121)
Minced fresh chives for garnish

Preheat the broiler to high and the oven to 350°F (if your oven won't let you use the broiler and the oven at the same time, preheat the broiler first, then turn on your oven after you're done with the broiler).

Season the halibut fillets with salt and pepper on both sides, then dab with oil and smear butter over the top. Place them on a baking sheet lined with aluminum foil and place just under the broiler. You need to watch them now—the fish needs your attention. Keep them there until the tops become nice and deep golden brown, anywhere between 4 and 6 minutes. Move them around as necessary for even cooking.

When it's beautiful on top, transfer the fish to the oven just for a few minutes, until it's translucent in the center.

Meanwhile, reduce the Splash in a pot until it's semiviscous.

Remove the halibut from the oven and glaze it with the Splash. Garnish with minced chives.

Enjoy.

CHAPTER 11

FISH SAUCE

Eight P.M. on a Tuesday night sometime around January 2008 in the dining room of the Beverly Hilton. Room service was cruising along, most of the managers had gone home for the night, there were no major celebrities unexpectedly popping by, nobody trying to escape through our kitchen. A slow night.

I was in the middle of a twelve-hour shift, walking the back hallway toward the huge walk-ins, when my phone rang. A recruiter. Apparently, there was a "major" restaurant project—involving

Southeast Asian cuisine—in the works, from a "major" player in the food industry. The recruiter was looking for someone to help spearhead this "major" restaurant. If I said I was interested, then I could hear more details on what "major" meant and who "major" was.

At any other moment, I probably would have said no outright, hung up the phone, and finished out my service. I had built a career as a hotel chef. I was at the base camp of the profession, climbing the mountain of a worldwide brand and leader in the hotel industry. And I was now father to a beautiful girl, and the job was good security. Just wait a few more years, I told myself, and I'd be the executive chef of a Four Seasons or a Ritz-Carlton. Why ditch almost ten years of work to hop on a dragon that would take me to Southeast Asia?

On top of that, outside my Tokyo summer, I had purposely avoided working in the kitchen of an Asian restaurant. I thought I was proving something to the world by being the Asian chef who never cooked Asian food.

But constantly being caught in the internal politics of the Hilton was taking a toll, and frustration was giving way to misery. And misery has a way of bringing out your desires and forcing you to admit certain truths about yourself. Even if I resisted cooking Asian food professionally, I always dreamed of Thailand and Vietnam, fantasized that I was from Indonesia as I smoked Endo weed. Thai basil, galangal, ginger, tamarind, kaffir lime, fish sauce, chiles, the abalone porridge and kimchi that were waiting for me every morning back at home. Those were all things I loved to smell and loved to eat.

Maybe it was time for me to fess up to myself, stop trying to swim against the tide at the Hilton, and just take the plunge already. I scooted outside to the back dock and told her I was interested.

The "majors" all of a sudden had names: David Overton, the founder of the Cheesecake Factory, had plans to open an Asian concept restaurant, RockSugar, that would explore the countries of Singapore, Vietnam, Thailand, Malaysia, Indonesia, and East India. It would be a magnificent restaurant that departed from the Factory's current corporate identity while creating a brand-new landscape for Asian food. Rather than promoting from within, they wanted to start completely fresh with new chefs and new staff. Mohan Ismail, the Singaporean chef who had opened Spice Market and Tabla, was the corporate executive chef, and they were now looking for a chef de cuisine, which was where I came in. How about it?

Compared to the chug chug chug of the Hilton, this new "major" concept

seemed like a speedboat across the Chao Phraya River in Bangkok. I'd jump from drab fluorescent hallways filled with hotel industry "lifers" into a pool of spectacular vibrancy. Splash! And so I decided it was finally time to taste the rainbow. I told the recruiter to schedule a phone interview and a psychological screening that tested whether I'd be a good fit for the job. Both went well, and I had just one person left to meet: the man himself, David Overton. From my apartment in Hollywood, it was an easy drive up Highland to the 101 Freeway, past the Hollywood Bowl and then over the dangerous interchange near Universal Studios, where the 101 meets the 170. Then through the Valley and on and on for an hour until I finally found the Lost Hills exit and made my way to the Cheesecake Factory's corporate headquarters in Calabasas Hills. I pulled up to the huge building, parked, turned off my talk radio, took a deep breath, and went in.

I was sent upstairs to meet Mr. Overton. As I went up up up the huge set of stairs, I felt like Kung Fu Panda, taking one fateful step after another, ready to tackle my destiny even if I didn't have a clue about what to expect. Along the walls, models of the mysterious Asian restaurant project and posters of signature Cheesecake Factory dishes were displayed like proud family portraits. After a few flights, I finally reached the center of the cheesecake. Mr. Overton's kind assistant walked me into a tranquil office full of books and Buddhas.

David Overton greeted me with huge, open arms and then sat me down. A true gentleman, he made our meeting less of an interview and more of a long conversation. He told me about his travels through Asia, how he had studied Buddha and Shiva, and his vision for a huge restaurant filled with the soul of Southeast Asia. We went over my résumé and talked about how I wanted to cook the foods of the countries that peppered my dreams.

After talking for over an hour, it was time for a walk. We went downstairs, and I met all the players on the team: Chef Mohan Ismail, who talks fast and works faster. Chef Robert Okura, whom I had read about in culinary school and who had

I WAS A COG IN THE MACHINE, A REPLACEABLE PART

helped develop the foundation of the Cheesecake Factory. A few vice presidents here and there. We made our way down to the test kitchen, a true training, research, and development HQ for Chef Maxwell Smart, et al. I was impressed. After exploring the kitchen, we reached the end of the tour. Right then and there, Mr. Overton turned to me and offered me the job. No need to talk to anyone else, no waiting for months, no runaround. We shook hands, and it was a done deal.

I drove straight back to the Hilton and put in my notice. I thought leaving there would be bittersweet, but it wasn't bitter or sweet. In fact, it wasn't really anything. And that's when I realized that even though I had worked so hard to get to that celebrity palace, it really meant nothing to me. I was a cog in the machine, a replaceable part. And that was okay. In fact, it made for the easiest good-bye I had ever had: at every other place—Borrego Springs, Tahoe, Tokyo, Sacramento—it was like the end of *Lord of the Rings* 3, a neverending scene of farewells and good-byes and hugs and kisses. Quitting the Beverly Hilton, though, was simple. Hasta la vista, baby.

THREE MONTHS. I had just three months in the RockSugar test kitchen to get up to speed on a project that had been in development for two years. My job there was to be Chef Ismail's chef de cuisine, the Number One to his Jean-Luc Picard. We hit it off pretty good right off the bat, and I got to work understanding his ideology and style. He had spent the last few years developing key flavors built around his mother's cooking, matching them with the strong technique he had learned from Floyd Cardoz at Tabla and from Gray Kunz and Jean-Georges Vongerichten at Spice Market. And what he created for RockSugar blew my mind: braised short ribs with lemongrass, Malaysian chile sauces, gentle sambals, clay pot chickens, and shaking beef. Savory caramel sauces and stocks for phở. Everything with fresh herbs and quality spices that were always, always freshly ground. In total, eighty to ninety dishes would comprise the final menu, a huge number.

For three months, I practiced and practiced dozens and dozens of recipes. And I loved it. The more I worked with the foods and embraced the ingredients, the more I bridged the gap between what I loved and what I thought I was supposed to do as professional chef. Everything clicked.

Meanwhile, opening crews from other Cheesecake Factories were brought in to start the construction. The scope of the restaurant matched the ambition of the menu: a giant, 7,500-square-foot glass box with seats for 250 guests located right at the front of the huge office towers of Century City Plaza, a high-end outdoor shopping mall. There would be extremely high ceilings. An enormous Buddha watching the diners from on high. Massive red doors. Teak imported from Thailand. Computer screens on the kitchen line instead of tickets—a big deal for 2008. Gardens in the front. Every whisk, each packet of sugar was part of the restaurant master plan—nothing more and absolutely nothing less.

Then seemingly out of thin air, *poof,* we had the full command station: point-of-sale systems, computers, computerized recipe stations, an office, and full staff, all ready to go. We cleaned the restaurant and filled the massive walk-ins with produce and proteins. We put together a kitchen staff of forty-five to fifty people, and, under my order, we trained and trained and trained. Tweaked the recipes, practiced the recipes. Then trained some more to perfect formulas and build muscle memory so it all would be effortless once it was game time. Because when shit got real, the volume for the restaurant would be tremendous, and there wouldn't be time to think. We couldn't be anything less than perfect.

Then, boom. Open for business.

Covered in sweat and fish sauce, we bumped out plate after plate. Caramel shrimp and Indonesian fried rice. Samosas and bang bang chickens. Green curries and spicy, pungent satays. All huge dishes, served family style.

The crowds were amazing from the get-go. The fact that RockSugar was a restaurant in a mall didn't seem to matter; the place was packed, and we somehow cleared 1,500 covers a day. Reservations were available only at 6:15 or 9:45; otherwise, forget it. Go to Mozza. I had never seen so many people in one restaurant in my life. It looked like a club. Word got out, and the celebrities started coming in full force. Megan Fox at lunch. The Beckhams for dinner. Halle Berry in the private dining room.

At first, I was on it. Tickets in, dishes out. But the pace was relentless. Order after order. Table after table. Shaking beef after shaking beef. And sure enough, soon it was me shaking in my boots. With the hours I put in at the test kitchen, plus the stress of the first opening weeks, my tires were spinning and there wasn't much rubber left.

I wasn't losing my traction so much because of the volume—no, I was just too damn close to the flame. At the Hilton, we'd prepare as much food as on any night at RockSugar, but the pace and pressure at the hotel was steadier. An even keel. At RockSugar, though, there was the eighty-plus-item menu book. The multiple layers of ingredients. The frenzied pace of the restaurant, the tight storage spaces, the numbers analyzed without mercy. The place was just too damn big. The pressure became too damn much. Everything moved too damn fast. And like Lucy at the chocolate factory, I just couldn't keep up with what was coming down that conveyor belt and finally fucking cracked.

What was once second nature all of a sudden became as foreign to me as the Persian alphabet. I fucked up crabs while cleaning them. I fell behind on prep lists. I couldn't run the line and tell my cooks who needed what, when, and where. The recipes I had practiced over and over and over again during the test kitchen phase seemed to disappear from inside my head. I could feel the frustration of Mohan and the others. Mohan gave me a few talking-tos, one on one, chef to chef, man to man. But his voice was too far off in the distance, and I couldn't connect. I hadn't been this incompetent since my first years as a beginner cook.

So I did what I did when I was a beginner cook and crashing at Le Bernardin: tried to find my swing again through sheer muscle. I clocked in earlier and clocked out later than anyone else, spending fifteen hours a day going over recipes, looking at prep, cleaning, studying, rearranging the walk-in, organizing the pantry. Anything I could do. But it didn't work. Things didn't get better—they only got worse. I was sinking fast in a quicksand trap, and the more I fought it, the faster I sank. I'd come to work in a daze, fumble through work in a daze, and leave in a daze.

Three months of my being dazed and confused later, Mohan asked me to join him in the private dining room for a meeting. It was midmorning, right before lunch. I knew I was beaten up and things weren't going well, but I figured this would be one more one on one. Maybe Mohan had some new ideas on how to improve, simplify.

I entered the dining room. From the east, the sun hovered above Santa Monica

Boulevard and crept up on my neck. Corporate was already there, waiting for me at a big table. They asked me to join them and sit. I sat. A big manila envelope waited in front of me. The room was calm as they told me they had to let me go.

You know those cartoons where someone's jaw drops to the ground? You could have swept dust into my mouth. I couldn't believe it. I was working fifteen to eighteen hours a day. How could I be fired? I was dedicated, obviously. Loyal, no question. Who would fire me? They saw my confusion and backtracked a little so I could process what was going on. They went through all the good things we had accomplished together, all the stuff we had perfected in the test kitchen, how great a launch we had had. And then they said it again.

Fired.

There were no questions about whether I wanted to stay or wanted to go. It wasn't my decision to make. In the envelope were a small severance and my final documents. I couldn't speak. Tears rolled down my face. *We shall escort you out. Please do not disturb the staff.* They were very polite and professional. My time was done. The door was thattaway.

Faster than I could understand what had just happened, I was out on the fake boulevard of the outdoor mall, holding my books and my knives like I was back in culinary school. But instead of being excited about going to a redbrick castle to learn from the very best, I was dumbfounded, surrounded by the long legs of Beverly Hills MILFs, their Louis Vuitton purses and little blue bags full of little blue boxes, everyone staring at me like I was some alien.

I ran to my car and threw up. I couldn't breathe. I didn't know what to do. So I just drove. Went up the coast to Santa Barbara, trying to figure out what had just happened. What to say to my wife and my daughter. When I finally got back home, I still didn't have an answer. So I didn't say anything for a couple days and played like nothing had happened. Just dressed up and left for work like I normally did. But instead of going to Century City, I drove around the entire city, numb. Three dazed days of eating nothing, drinking nothing, being nothing.

Then on the fourth day, I finally told my wife everything. Being the person that she is, she understood. She didn't know why I had lost my step or the circumstances of the firing, but she just understood that I had fucked up. And that there was no time to dwell on the past. We packed our bags, took a trip to San Diego, and got lost at Legoland for a few days.

Then I came back to L.A. and tried to rebuild the blocks of my career. Any other time, the firing would have been a minor, shitty setback, but just a setback. I probably still could have picked myself up and found something somewhere. Except this was 2008. The economy was turning to shit. I started with my old contacts first, but no luck. No one was hiring. And even though I was reluctant to reach back out to Hilton, I swallowed my pride and gave them a call. They weren't too happy about my having left, and, anyway, they didn't have anything available.

I called headhunters and recruiters and hit websites and classifieds. Monster .com. Craigslist. Jobfinder.com. Every daily and weekly in town. Nothing. I did some consulting work in San Rafael, but that was just enough to pay the rent. Money was running out, and bills were piling up.

Then, a glimmer of hope. A recruiter came through and scheduled a 1:00 P.M. interview for me at the Viceroy. Perfect. I got this, I thought. I showed up for the meeting at 1:00 on the dot, all suited up with résumé in hand, ready to meet with the main guy and shake hands for another job well done. Then it was 1:15. He'd be right with me, I was told. 1:30. I could hear him yelling in the office, then a phone slamming. He poked his head out of his door. The meeting wasn't gonna happen that day, he told me curtly, then put his head back into his office and slammed the door. I picked up my jaw and got up to reschedule my interview. I didn't need to reschedule, they said. They'd call me back.

They never called me back. Goddamn it.

I went back to the classifieds and found something at a Simi Valley country club. They were looking for someone who could do country club food: Club sandwiches. Caesar salads. Spaghetti Bolognese. Hamburgers, hot dogs. Garden salads with Italian vinaigrettes. Breakfast burritos. Clam chowder. A piece of cake, I thought. I could do all this stuff in my sleep. Man, I was a CIA grad, I had worked the line at Le Bernardin, I did nothing but country club food for years, I cooked with the Iron Chef in Japan, I was the chef at the Beverly Hilton. In. The. Fucking. Bag.

But I must have talked gibberish at the interviews, manifesting the wrong thing at the wrong time. Instead of showing how I was a confident, eager chef, I probably looked like a desperate guy in an old wrinkled suit, his wrinkled soul on his sleeve, holding out a wrinkled résumé, asking—almost expecting—a job. Of course I didn't get the job.

By then, it was late autumn. I couldn't even get an entry-level chef position that paid $35,000 a year. The more I looked, and the more I was rejected, the angrier I became. I felt betrayed. Cooking didn't want me, *fine*. I didn't want anything to do with cooking. Maybe I wasn't ever really good at it anyway. Maybe my knees were giving out, and it was time for me to stop running the bases, finally retire and move on to the next thing. Just like I had done my whole life.

So I thought about my other options. Maybe I could go back to my childhood dream of being a tour guide, driving a bus with a Janet Jackson microphone. Opening a door with a swing handle and showing people the beauties of L.A. Taking them down our streets and alleys and corners and blocks, pulling curbside so they could see, breathe, and almost taste our City of Angels. What the hell, right? I was only thirty-eight. I could re-create and live in my adolescent dream. Why the fuck not?

My mind made up, I packed my knives away. I was in the middle of shifting gears, all set to go pound the star-studded pavement on Hollywood Boulevard and see how I could start driving one of those tour buses, when my phone rang.

"Yo, whatcha doin', dawg?"

It was Mark Manguera from my Hilton days. And he wanted to talk to me about a crazy idea.

EGGPLANT CURRY OVER RICE

I think eggplant is overlooked here in America. Sure, we do the whole Parmesan thing, but overall, not many people enjoy eggplant as much as I think we should. Maybe it's because we think we gotta eat it by itself, the same way we eat carrots and broccoli and every other vegetable, as if we gotta eat that shit steamed, making funny faces in the name of health. Fuck that. Mix this eggplant up with some curry and fish sauce and coconut milk, serve it over some rice with hot sauce, and you'll stop making that funny face.

SERVES 4 TO 6

CURRY PASTE

2 tablespoons minced shallots

2 Thai bird or serrano chiles, minced, (including stems and seeds)

1 lemongrass stalk, white part only, minced

2 tablespoons minced galangal

1 tablespoon minced peeled fresh ginger

2 kaffir lime leaves

2 teaspoons ground coriander

2 tablespoons chopped fresh cilantro

2 tablespoons minced garlic

2 tablespoons green curry paste

EGGPLANT

¼ cup vegetable oil

4 tablespoons water

One 14-ounce can coconut milk

6 Thai eggplants or 2 Japanese eggplants, cut into medium-size dice

Salt and freshly ground black pepper to taste

Limes, halved

Combine all the ingredients for the curry paste in a blender and puree.

In a pan over medium heat, heat the oil and, when it's smoking, sauté the curry paste for a few minutes. Thin it out with 4 tablespoons water, then add the coconut milk. The mixture will become a little soupy.

Add the diced eggplant and cook it all for another 5 minutes. Taste the curry and adjust for seasoning.

Serve over rice with a squeeze or two of fresh lime.

CHICKEN SATAY
WITH PEANUT SAUCE

Chicken satay is usually bland and dry dry dry. But the true satays of the world, the ones you'll find throughout the streets of Malaysia, Singapore, and Thailand, come off the charcoal moist, smoky, and bursting with amazing flavor. This one's an ode to the flavors and the work of those satay vendors.

SERVES 4 TO 6 AS AN APPETIZER

MARINADE
2 tablespoons fish sauce
2 tablespoons soy sauce
1 teaspoon ground cumin
2 shallots, minced
½ cup coconut milk
2 tablespoons pineapple juice
1 tablespoon condensed milk

1 tablespoon palm sugar
2 tablespoons chopped fresh
    cilantro
1 tablespoon cognac
1 tablespoon sambal oelek
    (chile paste)
2 tablespoons roasted sesame seeds

CHICKEN
Bamboo skewers soaked in water
1½ pounds boneless, skinless chicken
    breasts, cut into 8- to 12½-thick strips
Salt and freshly ground black pepper

PEANUT SAUCE
½ teaspoon chopped lemongrass
½ teaspoon chopped garlic
½ teaspoon chopped peeled fresh ginger
Splash of water
½ tablespoon vegetable oil
½ cup peanut butter

½ tablespoon soy sauce
½ cup coconut milk
½ tablespoon sugar
½ tablespoon sambal oelek (chile paste)
1 tablespoon fresh lime juice

GARNISH
Fresh cilantro
2 limes, quartered

Combine all the marinade ingredients in a blender and puree. Transfer the marinade to a flat-bottomed dish (like a casserole dish) large enough to hold the chicken.

Place the chicken in the marinade for at least 3 hours.

Meanwhile, prepare the peanut sauce. In a blender, combine the lemongrass, garlic, and ginger with a splash of water and puree to make a paste.

In a small pot, combine the paste with the oil, peanut butter, soy sauce, coconut milk, sugar, sambal oelek, and lime juice. Cook very gently over low heat, stirring constantly, for about 2 minutes. Turn off the heat and allow the sauce to cool.

Remove the chicken from the marinade and skewer. Heat a grill to medium-high heat. Season the chicken skewers with salt and pepper, then grill the skewers until the chicken is charred.

Serve with the peanut sauce, fresh cilantro, and lime wedges.

COCONUT RICE

Sometimes we get caught up with our ways and think that rice can be cooked only with water. But water is just a liquid medium. Try cooking rice with chicken stock or lobster stock or even coconut milk mixed with stock, as I do here. Make rice fun and different.

2½ cups jasmine rice
½ cup coconut milk
½ teaspoon kosher salt
2 tablespoons julienned peeled fresh
    ginger

2 cups water
3½ cups chicken stock

GARNISH
Limes
Papaya, chopped

Rinse the rice thoroughly, at least 5 times, until the water runs clear.

In a medium-size pot with a tight-fitting lid, combine the coconut milk, salt, ginger, water, and stock. Add the rice, bring to a boil, reduce the heat, and simmer, covered, for 12 to 15 minutes, until cooked. Fluff it up and serve with limes and fresh papaya.

YOU MAY NOT NEED ANYTHING ELSE.

CARDAMOM MILK SHAVED ICE

Once you make granita at home, you can forget the whole homemade Popsicle game: this is way more fun. There is something really special about how flavored ice shaves off itself and breaks up into crystals and how that reacts on your tongue. Just like a kiss.

SERVES 6

One 14-ounce can condensed milk, plus a little more for garnish

3½ cups water

One 14-ounce can coconut milk

½ teaspoon ground cardamom

3 tablespoons cold brewed coffee

1 teaspoon roasted and crushed sesame seeds

1 tablespoon fresh lime juice

Grated zest of 1 lime

GARNISH

Fresh or canned lychee

Fresh mint leaves

Combine the condensed milk, water, coconut milk, cardamom, coffee, sesame seeds, lime juice, and zest in a big bowl and give it a good whisk. Run the mixture through a sorbet machine or freeze it in a pan, running a fork through it every 30 minutes until frozen.

Scoop and serve the shaved ice in a bowl with the lychees, the mint, and a little more condensed milk drizzled over top.

AHHHH.

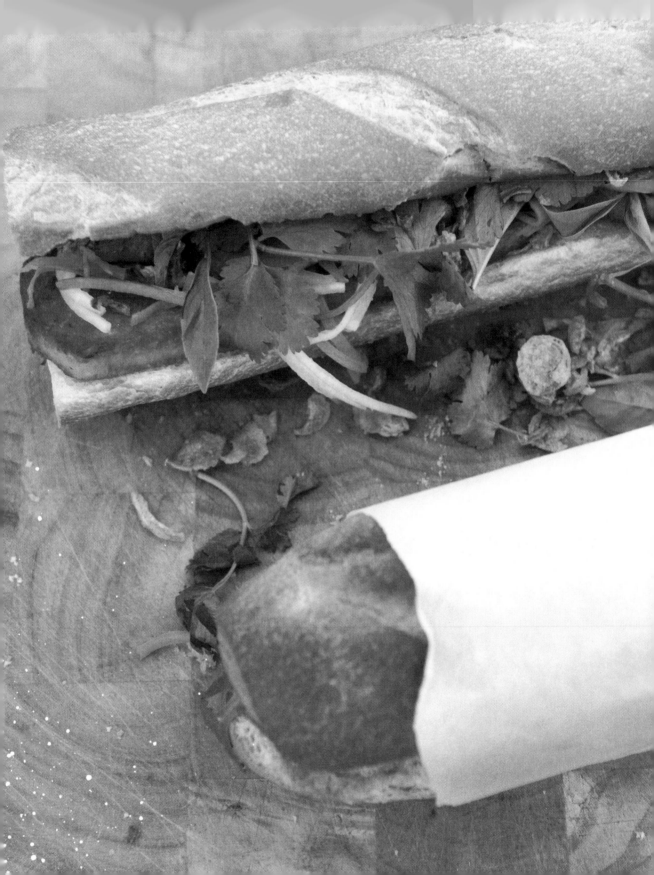

SPAM BÁNH ME

The first time I ate a bánh mì sandwich was in Orange County's Little Saigon back in high school, on my way to the Asian Garden Mall to pick up some Euro disco CDs. I went across the street from the mall to a little sandwich shop that was filled with people and a line out the door. I didn't really know what I was getting into, but it seemed simple enough. Cheap, line, sandwich, wrapped in paper. How could I go wrong? My version pays respects to the traditional sandwich, pickled veggies and all, but with some Spam thrown in for something a little different.

MAKES 4 SANDWICHES

PICKLES

1 cup julienned daikon

1 cup julienned carrots

½ cup natural rice vinegar (not seasoned)

1½ teaspoons salt

1 tablespoon sugar

1 cup water

SANDWICHES

4 demibaguettes

½ cup mayonnaise

1 tablespoon Maggi seasoning

1 tablespoon Sriracha

Butter, softened

1 teaspoon vegetable oil

1 can Spam, cut into 8 thin steaks

Fresh cilantro sprigs

Fresh Thai basil or opal basil leaves

Fried shallots (store-bought)

Limes

Place the daikon and carrots in small bowl. Combine the vinegar, salt, sugar, and water in a small pot. Bring the mixture to a boil, then turn off the heat and let it cool until it's warm. Pour over the daikon and carrots and let it sit for at least 30 minutes and up to 2 hours.

Cut the baguettes in half but keep them intact. In a small bowl, mix the mayonnaise with the Maggi seasoning and the Sriracha. Set aside.

Slather the cut sides of the baguettes with softened butter and toast them in your toaster oven or in a pan over low heat until they're nice and crispy. Set aside.

Heat the oil in a skillet, add the Spam, and cook over medium heat until it's golden brown in color. Transfer to paper towels and reserve.

Slather the buttered sides of the baguettes with the spicy mayonnaise. To build the sandwiches, place the Spam on the bottom half of each baguette, then top with the pickled daikon and carrots and add a layer of cilantro and basil. Top with the fried shallots and a squeeze of lime and close up the baguette.

CRUNCH!

HAINAN CHICKEN, KIND OF

Hainan chicken is a treasure in Southeast Asia, and people can get real territorial over the "right" way to make the dish. I'll be first to tell you, though, that my version is more of a riff on the dish rather than the real thing. I think I got it right, kind of . . .

SERVES 4 TO 6

One 5-pound chicken
3 tablespoons kosher salt
1 cup chopped peeled fresh ginger
1 cup roughly chopped scallions
1 cup garlic cloves, peeled and smashed
1 tablespoon coriander seeds

1 cup roughly chopped fresh cilantro
1 lime, quartered
2 kaffir lime leaves
One 3-inch cinnamon stick
Splash of Maggi seasoning
Splash of dark soy sauce

GARNISH
Handful of chopped cilantro
Jar of chili garlic sauce for the table

Rinse and dry dry dry the chicken. Coat it with the salt all over and let it sit for a few minutes as you bring enough water to cover the chicken to a boil in a big pot.

Once boiling, add everything but the chicken to the pot. Bring it to a boil again, then add the chicken and reduce the heat to produce a low simmer.

Cook the chicken, uncovered, low and slow, until tender, about 1 hour.

Remove the chicken and soak it immediately in an ice-water bath. Chill the chicken until the meat is still warm but the skin is cold, then remove it (it's okay if the chicken is a little wet from the ice bath). Strain the broth (you can use it to make rice if you wish).

Serve the chicken by itself or over rice with the cilantro and the chili garlic sauce.

CRÈME BRÛLÉE

The crackle of the burned sugar, the creamy inside, vanilla beans speckled throughout, the feeling when scraping the inside of the ramekin after finishing most of it, the idea of sharing with friends at the table. I love crème brûlée, and the pandan leaf gives it an extra layer of sweet flavor. I hope this recipe makes you love again, too.

You'll need a kitchen blowtorch to burn the sugar.

SERVES 4 TO 6

5 cups heavy cream
Seeds scraped from ½ vanilla bean
One 12-inch strip pandan leaf

1 cup sugar
14 egg yolks, beaten
Superfine sugar for sprinkling

Preheat the oven to 325°F.

Combine the cream, vanilla seeds, pandan leaf, and half the sugar in a pot. Bring the mixture to a slight boil, then lower the heat to simmer.

Combine the egg yolks and the other half of the sugar in a large bowl and beat thoroughly, for about 2 minutes.

Ladle by ladle, add the cream to the egg yolks, whisking constantly so the hot cream doesn't cook the yolks (this process is tempering the cream). When everything is combined, add the mixture back to the pot and cook it over very low heat until it's slightly thick and coats the back of a spoon. Make sure to keep it at low heat so as not to scramble the eggs.

Fill 4 to 6 ramekins with this mixture—crème anglaise—and place them in a large roasting pan filled with an inch or so of water. Place the pan in the oven and bake for 45 minutes.

When the ramekins are ready, remove them from the oven and from the water bath. Let them cool, then refrigerate for 2 hours.

Sprinkle the tops of the ramekins with sugar, then use the blowtorch to melt and burn the sugar until golden brown. Cool and allow the surface to harden.

ENJOY YOUR DESSERT.

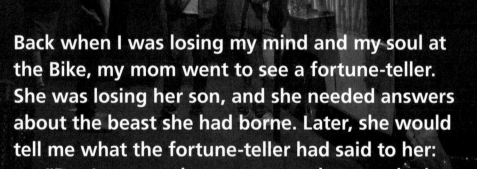

CHAPTER 12

WINDSHIELD

Back when I was losing my mind and my soul at the Bike, my mom went to see a fortune-teller. She was losing her son, and she needed answers about the beast she had borne. Later, she would tell me what the fortune-teller had said to her:

"Don't worry about your son, because he is going to be surrounded by people in a parking lot, in a party, always. Surrounded by smiling faces and warm laughter. He will be there in the party and at the center somewhere. Don't worry if he is not smart. Don't worry about making him what you think he needs to be. Just feed him. Feed him food and knowledge. Just love him."

IT COULDN'T HAVE HAPPENED any sooner.

"Yo, I heard you lost your job. Who gives a fuck?!"

The voice on the line was so carefree, so fearless, so nonchalant. It was exactly what I needed to hear at that moment. Still, I was surprised to hear from Mark after a couple years; at the Beverly Hilton, we had always been on the same wavelength, always able to bust on each other in a second, but mostly it had been a work friendship. Outside the hotel, we didn't really hang.

"Fuck it, man, it's just a job," he continued. "Come meet me for some coffee in K-Town. We'll chill and look at some honeys. And I got something to ask you."

A promise of freedom, a little humor. A cup of coffee would be a nice escape, even if only for a few hours. Going to Hollywood to check out the tour buses could wait. We met up at a café in my old stomping grounds, Koreatown. As we sat on the patio sipping caramel lattes and squishing cigarettes into an ashtray full of coffee grinds, Mark told me about an idea. I sat and listened. And listened.

And chalked it all up to ridiculousness and went home. The idea didn't really have any substance; it was a pencil sketch at best. It seemed so trivial, in fact; the kind of thing you listen to and forget, mindlessly nodding along to a guy trying to sell you on a time-share because you're bored and just trying to be polite.

But I couldn't sleep. The idea gnawed at the edges of my dreams. Maybe it wasn't so trivial after all. The next morning, I saw it. As if it had always existed. Because it always had.

In a heartbeat, Mark and I were at Kaju Market in Koreatown. Up and down the aisles, it was as if my fingers knew all the ingredients to a recipe my mind hadn't yet written. Vinegars and chile pastes. Scallions, onions, cilantro, ginger, garlic, masa, manteca de cerdo, short ribs, soy sauce, oranges, limes, romaine, cabbage, sesame seeds, kochujang, kochukaru.

The idea, as Mark presented it over lattes and cigarettes, was to put Korean BBQ in a taco. "Wouldn't it be delicious?" he said. And that was all he proposed, a basic outline in black and white. But it was enough. Enough to lead me back to the box of crayons that I had tucked away for the last ten years while I was busy climbing

the ladder, enough for me to know exactly what colors to use to fill in that outline.

I did a beta test of the salsa roja on my own, then hit the market again to tweak it and pick up more ingredients. I got everything I needed for the improved salsa, plus everything for the taco itself—marinated short ribs, tortillas, onions, cilantro, limes, cabbage, lettuce, scallions, sesame seeds—and made my way to Mark's kitchen in his tiny Koreatown apartment. Spread all the groceries out and started to color in our outline of a taco. I didn't know exactly what the picture would look like when I was done, but the technical details didn't matter right then. As I chopped and layered ingredients, visions of Silver Garden, Pershing Square, my childhood refrigerator, cruising in Whittier, Grove Street, transient life, the desert bubbled up and started flowing through me like a tidal wave. I was possessed. *Sohn-maash.*

I had it.

It was about four inches in diameter. One and a half bites at most. Oily but crispy. Made of fresh corn, but never grainy. Filled with meat that felt like it had been chopped all day by the same cleaver over and over again on a worn wooden block, then thrown on a plancha and sizzled to a crusty sticky juicy niblet of life. Showered with chopped onions and more handfuls of chopped cilantro than you can imagine. Lime juice everywhere. And salsa roja, smoky and pungent.

There it was. Los Angeles on a plate. Maybe it wasn't everyone's L.A., but it was mine. It was Koreatown to Melrose to Alvarado to Venice to Crenshaw crumpled into one flavor and bundled up like a gift. The elements looked like city blocks. The flavor tasted like the streets. And the look said home.

AFTER A FEW WEEKS of scoping out purveyors and cutting cash-only deals directly with sources all over Downtown L.A. for the best-quality produce and meat, we were ready to roll. On a cold night just before Thanksgiving in 2008, I got behind the wheel of a beat-up 1980s Grumman catering truck with a decal of the number 69 on the windshield.

My hands wrapped around the steering wheel like Arthur's on the sword in the stone. I gunned the engine. With the crew riding in the back, we set out to Silver Lake and East Hollywood, the energy of the city showing us the way.

We drove and parked, drove and parked, drove and drove. Those first nights were slow. But I was mad determined. I knew in my bones that our style would find a home with the people of L.A., from the cholos in white tees and Dodger-blue caps to a crew of gangsters at a picnic, guns down for a hot minute, to everyone at your grandma's birthday party. So, no matter whether those youngsters threw up gang signs at us near Rampart, no matter whether young Korean girls mocked us in front of Hodori, no matter whether club kids cracked jokes at our square wheels, no matter whether the wanderers in Hollywood would even look at us, no matter what anyone thought about a couple of random guys rolling up in this creaky-ass Grumman—no matter all that. In my mind's eye, I could see the empty corners filled with people. People with their guard down, ready to relax, ready to smile. They would be strangers, but excited to be friends. I knew people would love what we had.

And sure enough, one by one, the youngsters pulled back their gang signs. The Korean girls came over to check us out. The club kids needed to satisfy their munchies. As the corners filled up and people came out to eat together on the curb, the food slowly and steadily took on a life of its own. It began to taste Indonesian, look Mexican, feel Korean. It spoke to hipsters, comforted families, filled eager bellies. It breathed L.A. All the way.

As for me, I was finally in full bloom. I was finally home. I didn't feel the need to defend or define myself, didn't have to be anyone in particular anymore. Not a success. Not a career climber. Just me. A fucked-up, restless kid from L.A. who had morphed into a thug who had become a chef who had cooked his way up a ladder, only to fall into the arms of the streets. Through that windshield during that first week, I saw a city that didn't know it was hungry and a reflection of a guy who was free.

The fortune-teller was right, you know. Because here I am.

Standing in a parking lot. Surrounded by friends.

Smiling.

BEEF CHEEK TACOS

Cabeza—or beef cheek—tacos are some of the best things this planet has to offer as food. I ate so many of these and other tacos growing up in both L.A. and Orange County that they became part of me and, in a way, prepared me to cook my own tacos. Splash some salsa verde on there, and that's it: SoCal, and especially L.A., on a plate.

MAKES 8 TO 10 TACOS

BRINE

2 tablespoons kosher salt
Juice of ½ lemon
Juice of ½ orange
Juice of 1 lime
½ cup sugar
3 garlic cloves, peeled and smashed
½ cup red wine vinegar

½ cup whole dried chiles de árbol
1½ whole dried guajillo chiles
1 cup roughly chopped fresh cilantro
2 quarts water
1 pound beef cheeks, cleaned (ask your
   butcher to do this for you)

SALSA VERDE

1½ tomatillos, charred
1½ cups roughly chopped fresh cilantro
1½ serrano chiles, with seeds
1½ jalapeños peppers with seeds,
   charred

Juice of 1 lime
2½ garlic cloves, peeled
½ cup roughly chopped scallions,
   charred
½ cup natural rice vinegar (not seasoned)

¼ cup vegetable oil
8 to 10 corn tortillas
Salt and freshly ground black pepper
   to taste

GARNISH

Chopped white onions
Chopped cilantro

In a large pot, combine all the brine ingredients. Bring the brine to a boil, then remove from the heat and let it cool. Add the beef cheeks to the cooled brine (if you add the meat to the hot brine, the meat will cook instead of marinate). Place the pot in your fridge and marinate the beef cheeks, uncovered, in the brine overnight.

The next morning, set the beef cheeks (still in the brine) over high heat and bring to a boil, then reduce the heat to a simmer and cook, uncovered, until the beef cheeks are tender, about 1 hour.

Remove the beef cheeks from the pot, discarding the brine, and let them cool. Once the cheeks have cooled, roughly chop them into small pieces.

Combine all of the ingredients for the salsa in a blender or food processor and puree.

Heat the oil on a griddle or in a skillet and cook the tortillas over medium heat for 30 seconds to crisp up, then flip. Remove the tortillas and add the beef cheeks to the griddle or skillet, cooking for about 2 minutes, until the meat is caramelized. Season with salt and pepper.

To bring everything together, stack 2 tortillas on a plate and top with beef cheeks. Spoon salsa all over the beef. Garnish with onions and cilantro.

EAT MANY.

ROY'S BURGER

Long before our truck started, my dream was to have a small burger stand with stools around a horseshoe counter, patties sizzling on a well-seasoned griddle, a machine that served Orange Bang, the *Los Angelas Times* scattered everywhere, Vin Scully calling the Dodgers game on the radio. That was my dream; that *is* my dream. It's just that the lines got long for this truck, and here I am today. Although I may never get that dream of having a lazy greasy spoon, I do have this burger that would have been in that dream. So here you go. My burger from my imaginary burger stand.

THIS RECIPE IS FOR ONE PERFECT BURGER.
MAKE AS MANY AS YOU WISH.

1 burger bun
1 tablespoon soft butter
One or two 4-ounce burger patties,
   depending on your appetite
2 tablespoons vegetable oil
Salt and freshly ground black pepper
2 slices sharp cheddar cheese
1 teaspoon yellow mustard

1 tablespoon mayonnaise
1 thin slice red onion
2 thin slices tomato
1 large shiso leaf
1 leaf butter lettuce
Handful of roasted and crushed
   sesame seeds
Tapatío hot sauce

Slather the inside of the bun with butter and set aside.

Heat a grill or griddle. Brush the burger patties with a bit of oil and season with salt and pepper. Cook them for just a couple minutes on each side for medium-rare, then, with the patties still on the grill, place the cheese slices on each to melt.

Meanwhile, in a dry pan over medium-low heat, toast the bun butter side down until the butter becomes golden brown and crispy, then slather the inside of the bun with mayo and mustard.

Place the patty or patties on the bun and on top of the melted cheese, layer, in this order, the onion, tomato, shiso leaf, and lettuce. Top it all off with a sprinkle of sesame seeds and hot sauce.

IF YOU WANT TO BE FANCY AND MAKE YOUR OWN, THIS IS MY FAVORITE BURGER BLEND:

10 PERCENT BEEF BONELESS SHORT RIB
10 PERCENT BEEF TRITIP
30 PERCENT BEEF CHUCK
25 PERCENT PORK SHOULDER
25 PERCENT PORK BUTT

CLOSE AND ENJOY ON A WARM CALI DAY.

L.A. CORNER ON THE COB

As I roamed around the city looking for the ingredients for what would be the taco, I always ran across people selling corn slathered with mayonnaise with chili powder, Cotija cheese, a squirt of lime, and done. I'd been around these street vendors my whole life, but I saw them so often during this time that I got to seeing them as spiritual guides of sorts, showing me the way. In any case, this is a much better way to do corn on the cob than just BBQing 'em on the grill. Enjoy!

MAKES 4 CORNER COBS

4 ears corn, shucked
3 tablespoons vegetable oil
2 tablespoons butter, softened
Pinch of kosher salt

¼ cup mayonnaise
1 cup grated Cotija cheese
Pinch of cayenne
2 limes, halved

Heat a griddle over medium heat. When it's hot, add the oil.

Stick a wooden chopstick or skewer into the end of each ear to make a corn lollipop. Slather the ears of corn with butter and season them with salt.

Sear the ears on the griddle, turning them over as needed, until they're lightly browned on all sides, about 2 minutes.

Once the ears are cooked, slather them with mayo and shower them with Cotija cheese. They should be completely covered in mayo and cheese.

Dust the cayenne all over the ears, followed by a squeeze of lime.

EAT.

IMMEDIATELY.

KIMCHI AND PORK BELLY STUFFED PUPUSAS

When we started the truck, my closest friend was a lady from El Salvador who had worked with me at RockSugar and then became my only cook on the truck. I had known about the pupusa game before, but she taught me a few things, and I've never looked back.

If fresh masa isn't available in your area, feel free to use instant corn masa mix.

MAKES 6 TO 10 PUPUSAS

MARINADE

½ onion, peeled and quartered

½ Asian pear, cored and quartered

½ cup kochujang

2 tablespoons soy sauce

1 tablespoon sugar

1 tablespoon minced garlic

1 tablespoon Asian sesame oil

1 tablespoon fresh lime juice

½ cup water

PUPUSAS

1 cup kimchi (page 19 or store-bought), minced

1 tablespoon butter

About ¼ cup vegetable oil

1 tablespoon roasted sesame seeds

½ cup salt

½ cup sugar

1 pound pork belly, whole, skin off (ask your butcher to do this for you)

8 ounces fresh masa

ON THE TABLE

Your favorite hot salsa

Pickled jalapeños

Preheat the oven to 500°F.

Combine the ingredients for the marinade in a blender or food processor and puree. Pour the marinade into a large bowl and set aside until the pork is ready.

In a pan over medium heat, caramelize the kimchi in the butter and a touch of the oil until it's lightly browned, about 2 minutes. Sprinkle in the sesame seeds, then remove from the pan and set aside to cool.

Mix the salt and sugar together and rub the mixture all over the pork belly. Let the pork sit on your counter for a couple hours, uncovered, to cure it.

Place the cured pork on a wire rack in a sheet pan, with the side where the skin was removed facing up, and roast in the oven for about 20 minutes, or until it's slightly

brown. Turn the oven down to 200°F and let the pork cook for 3 hours. Check to see if the meat is tender; if not, let it cook for another hour, checking on it every 15 minutes to see if it's done.

Remove the pork from the oven and let it rest until it has cooled to room temperature (keep the oven on). When the pork is cool, cut it into small chunks and place it in the marinade. Coat the pork with the marinade and set aside while you heat a pan over medium heat. Add 2 tablespoons of the remaining oil; when it starts to smoke, sear the marinated meat in the pan until it's nice and caramelized, about 4 minutes. Remove to cool.

Meanwhile, on a cutting board, rub a tiny dot of the remaining oil between your hands and scoop enough masa into your hands to roll into an egg-sized ball. Create a deep well in the center of the masa ball. Place 2 tablespoons of the pork and 2 tablespoons of the kimchi in the well, then roll the masa around it to enclose it in a ball. Flatten the pupusa and repeat until you have as many as you would like, up to 10.

On a pancake griddle or a nonstick pan, add a touch of the remaining oil and heat over medium heat until just under smoking. Sear the pupusas on each side until they're crispy, about 2 minutes. Stick them in the oven for a hot minute, just until the middles of the pupusas are warm to the touch.

Eat piping hot with the hot salsa and pickled jalapeños.

WELCOME TO L.A.

L.A. DIRTY DOG

The East Coast has the pizza slice, and the South has Waffle House. Pittsburgh got them roadside sandwiches; Buffalo, you got wings; and all you other cities, y'all got your drunk food, right?! In L.A., when it's 2:00 A.M. and we're stumbling out of the club, we got dirty dogs off a shopping cart cooked on sheet pans lit by Sterno underneath. Even fine-ass bitches get down on dirty dogs; don't front.

MAKES 4 HOT DOGS

2 tablespoons vegetable oil
½ onion, sliced
1 red bell pepper, seeded and sliced
1 green bell pepper, seeded and sliced
Salt and freshly ground black pepper
4 hot dogs, split lengthwise so they won't
    burst when cooked

4 slices bacon
4 soft hot dog buns
Mayonnaise
Ketchup
Mustard
Tapatío hot sauce

Heat the oil in a pan or on a griddle over medium heat, add the onion and peppers, and sauté with a touch of salt and pepper until they're slightly caramelized, about 4 minutes. Remove.

Wrap each hot dog tightly in a strip of bacon. In a pan over medium heat, slowly cook your hot dogs, moving them continuously to cook them evenly, until the bacon is nice and brown but still soft, about 4 minutes. Remove.

Toast the inside of the buns in a bit of that bacon fat.

Place a hot dog in each bun and slather it with mayonnaise, then top with the peppers and onions. Squeeze on the ketchup and mustard to taste, then a splash of the Tapatío.

YOU SHOULD BE DRUNK.

SESAME-SOY SALAD DRESSING

So easy, so good, so quick. After all those tacos, corn cobs with mayo, dirty dogs, and burgers, go eat a mixed greens salad or something, would ya?!

MAKES ABOUT 2 CUPS

½ cup soy sauce

½ cup natural rice vinegar (not seasoned)

¼ cup mirin

¾ cup plus 2 tablespoons vegetable oil

½ cup chopped scallions

1½ teaspoons minced, peeled fresh
  ginger

1½ teaspoons minced garlic

1½ teaspoons roasted sesame seeds

2 tablespoons sugar

½ cup water

Pinch of kosher salt

Combine all the ingredients in a blender or food processor. Puree it all together. Dress up your salad.

CHAPTER 13

VEGETABLES
1-2-3

These are the B-sides, a little section I wanted to put in for those days when you wanna cook just enough for you and maybe a friend, but don't wanna go all the way in. A 1-2-3 to make it easy to have great snacks, sides, or a decent meal or two. All on the fly.

ASPARAGUS

White vinegar

2 eggs

Kosher salt

6 large asparagus, stalks trimmed
and peeled

1 tablespoon extra virgin olive oil

1 tablespoon butter

½ lemon

2 tablespoons shaved Parmesan cheese

1½ teaspoons roughly chopped fresh
flat-leaf parsley

Cracked black pepper

Put a few inches of water into a small pot, add a splash of white vinegar, and heat until the water begins to simmer. With the heat on medium-low, swirl the water with a wooden spoon and, while the water is swirling, carefully crack in each egg and cook until the eggs coagulate, about 2 minutes. Pull them out with a slotted spoon and set aside.

Bring a big pot of water to boil and season it with salt. Meanwhile, ready a big bowl of ice water.

Blanch the asparagus in the boiling water for 2 to 3 minutes, until it's slightly tender but still has its color—keep it bright green. Remove the asparagus from the pot and shock it in the ice water.

Heat the oil in a large sauté pan over medium heat and add the asparagus, cooking until its slightly colored on all sides, about 3 minutes. Transfer to a paper towel and then to a plate.

Throw the butter into the pan and let it brown slightly. Season the butter with some salt and a squeeze of the lemon. You're done. Pour it all over the asparagus.

Garnish with the poached eggs, shaved Parmesan, and parsley.

CRANK THE PEPPERMILL UNTIL I SAY STOP.

BABY BOK CHOY

¼ cup extra virgin olive oil

1 pound baby bok choy, stalks separated, washed and spun dry

¼ cup fresh orange juice

2 tablespoons natural rice vinegar (not seasoned)

2 tablespoons soy sauce

1 tablespoon chili garlic sauce

1 teaspoon sugar

1 tablespoon butter

1 tablespoon sliced scallions

1 teaspoon roasted sesame seeds

Heat the oil in a pan over high heat.

When it's smoking, add half of the baby bok choy and sauté the vegetable for a minute, then add the other half. Sauté the bok choy until it's caramelized, about 3 minutes, then remove to a plate.

Deglaze the pan with the orange juice and the vinegar, then add the soy sauce. Cook for just a few seconds, then swirl in the chili garlic sauce and sugar. Cook for about 45 seconds more, reducing the sauce slightly.

Turn off the heat and add the butter, stirring it in to finish the sauce. Pour it around the bok choy and garnish the plate with the sesame seeds and scallions. Eat.

BROCCOLI RABE

Kosher salt

1 pound broccoli rabe

1 tablespoon olive oil

1 lemon

1 tablespoon red chile flakes

1 cup ricotta cheese

Prepare a big gallon-size bowl of ice water.

Bring a large pot of water to a boil and season with salt. Place the broccoli rabe in the water and cook until tender, about 3 minutes. Remove and shock immediately in the ice water.

Remove the broccoli rabe from the ice bath and pat dry. Season the broccoli rabe with the olive oil and salt. Heat a grill or grill pan and, when it's hot, char the rabe. Transfer to a plate.

Squeeze the lemon all over the rabe and sprinkle on the chile flakes. Spoon some ricotta cheese over everything and eat immediately.

BRUSSELS SPROUTS AND KIMCHI

3 tablespoons extra virgin olive oil
8 ounces brussels sprouts, halved
1 cup minced kimchi (page 19 or
    store-bought)

1 tablespoon butter
Salt and freshly ground black pepper
1 lemon
2 tablespoons minced shiso leaves

Heat a pan over medium heat until it's smoking. Add the oil and the brussels sprouts.

Move the pan around, caramelizing the sprouts, 5 to 7 minutes. Add the kimchi and toss.

Get some good color on everything, about 7 to 10 minutes, then add the butter. Swirl and season everything with salt, pepper, a squeeze of the lemon, and a sprinkle of the shiso leaves.

Enjoy immediately.

ROASTED CAULIFLOWER

8 ounces cauliflower
Extra virgin olive oil
Salt and freshly ground black pepper

Pinch of ground cumin
Chopped fresh herbs (optional)

Preheat the oven to 400°F.

Break up the cauliflower into florets and discard the stalk. Coat the florets with oil and season them with salt, pepper, and cumin.

Place the florets on a sheet pan and roast in the oven for 20 to 25 minutes, or until they're medium brown and crispy. Take out of the oven and, if you wish, douse with more extra virgin olive oil and the chopped herbs.

ROASTED MUSHROOMS

8 ounces any mushrooms you want,
   stemmed
1 cup olive oil
½ bunch fresh thyme

Cloves from 1 head garlic, peeled
Extra virgin olive oil
Salt and freshly ground black pepper

Preheat the oven to 500°F.

Soak the mushrooms in the olive oil and season with salt and pepper. Remove the mushrooms and lay them in a single layer on a sheet pan lined with foil. Discard the oil.

Sprinkle them all over with thyme and garlic, then roast it all in the oven for 20 to 25 minutes, or until they're all completely brown. Enjoy.

QUICK SPINACH SOUP

2 cups chicken stock
¼ cup plus 2 tablespoons miso
5 tablespoons soy sauce
9 ounces spinach (about 5½ cups),
    washed

4 ounces tofu, cut into cubes
Salt and freshly ground black pepper

Warm the stock in a pot over medium heat and whisk in the miso and soy.

Add the spinach to the pot and bring the mixture to a boil. Reduce the heat and simmer, uncovered, for 5 minutes.

Add the tofu to the pot and cook, uncovered, for 2 more minutes.

Taste and adjust the seasoning with salt and pepper if necessary. Enjoy with rice.

ROASTED SWEET POTATOES

4 sweet potatoes, washed
Salt

Preheat the oven to 350°F.

Wrap the sweet potatoes in foil, then bake them until they're tender, about an hour.

Unwrap and eat the potatoes directly out of the foil, scooping out the flesh and sprinkling with salt to taste.

SLOW-ROASTED TOMATOES

8 ounces Roma tomatoes, cut in half
½ cup olive oil
Salt and freshly ground black pepper

½ bunch fresh rosemary
½ bunch fresh oregano

Preheat the oven to 200°F.

Coat the tomatoes in the olive oil and season them with salt and pepper. Lay them on a sheet pan, cut side up. Sprinkle the herbs all over the tomatoes.

Place the sheet pan in the oven and cook for 2 to 3 hours, until the moisture from the tomatoes has been released.

Remove from the pan and eat with everything.

ZUCCHINI FRITTER OMELET

4 tablespoons extra virgin olive oil
2 medium zucchini, grated
Salt and freshly ground black pepper

1 teaspoon butter
2 eggs, whisked

Heat a pan over medium heat and add 2 tablespoons of the oil. Place the grated zucchini in a single layer in the pan and cook until it gets a little color, about 3 minutes. Flip.

Season the zucchini with salt and pepper, then add the butter.

Once the butter begins to brown slightly, pour the whisked eggs over the zucchini in the pan and cook. Drizzle in the other 2 tablespoons of olive oil as they're cooking and let the eggs cook until they're slightly firm, about 2 minutes.

Fold the eggs over once to create your omelet and enjoy.

WATERMELON AND GOAT CHEESE

½ watermelon, sliced
Pinch of kosher salt
1 lime, halved
1 cup goat cheese

Cracked black pepper
½ cup toasted cashews
2 tablespoons extra virgin olive oil

Season the watermelon with salt and lime juice.

Lay the watermelon on a plate and crumble goat cheese all over it, along with the pepper, cashews, and olive oil.

SIMPLE SIMPLE SIMPLE.

BUTTER PINEAPPLE

¼ cup extra virgin olive oil
½ pineapple, peeled, cored, and cut into
   thick rings
¼ cup sugar

¼ cup rum
Splash of fresh orange juice
2 tablespoons butter

In a large nonstick pan over medium heat, heat the oil until it's smoking. Place the pineapple in the pan in a single layer and caramelize on each side, which should take about 4 minutes. You may have to do this in stages if there isn't enough room to fit all the rings, transferring each batch of finished rings to a plate.

Once all the pineapple rings are caramelized, return them to the pan and add the sugar. Caramelize the sugar just slightly, then deglaze with rum. Reduce a bit and splash in the OJ.

Fold in the butter TO COAT AND SHINE.

SALTED MANGO AND CUKES

1 lime, halved
2 mangoes, peeled and sliced
½ cucumber, peeled and sliced

2 teaspoons kosher salt
Pinch of cayenne

Squirt the lime all over the mangoes and cukes, then season them with salt. Dust with cayenne as you wish. Eat. Enjoy.

THE RULES

TOOLS

The recipes in this book bounce to the tune of each chapter. Collectively, they make an album, and to play this album, you probably don't need anything too different from what you already have. So, if you ain't got that much to begin with, *which I get, my brothers and sisters,* then you can just mix everything up in an old plastic bowl. Or cut a plastic 2-liter Coke bottle and use that. On the real, the

food in this book always tastes better when it's made with cheap-ass tools like 99-cent-store plastic bowls, mismatched utensils, and wooden spatulas. Then you can cook the dishes with anything from an elaborate stovetop to the hood of your car on a hot Cali day.

Wherever you get what you get, these are the tools that will come in handy and connect you to the spirit of the food.

So here's the list of things you may need:

- Big plastic buckets for marinating
- Plastic bowls and strainers for washing vegetables and making kimchi
- Wooden cooking spoons and spatulas
- Aluminum foil
- Pans
- Big pliers for grabbing hot soup cauldrons
- Rubber gloves
- Spoons (the kind you eat with)
- Chopsticks
- Kitchen scissors
- Cutting board
- Knife
- Yesterday's newspaper to catch vegetable peels
- Blender
- Electric griddle
- Charcoal hibachi
- Big glass jars or Mason jars
- Tupperware
- Flower-patterned apron
- Rice cooker
- Some gossip to dish out while you peel garlic

ESSENTIALS

As a basic rule, try to hit some farmers' markets in your town to supplement your staple veggies (ginger, garlic, and scallions) with other types beyond run-of-the-mill onion, celery, and carrots. In Southern California, just east of San Diego County on the Mexican border, lies the Imperial Valley, where many Korean-run farms grow acres of soy sprouts, mung bean sprouts, melons, chile peppers, sesame, mustard plants, ginseng, chestnuts, persimmons, pomegranates, Mandarin oranges, sweet potatoes, and pears.

If you don't have access to those kinds of farms, try foraging. Dandelion greens and mustard greens probably grow right next to your highways and behind those chain-link fences in abandoned lots. Scour backyards for fruit trees; keep an eye out for garlic chives. Wild food grows everywhere. You just have to look.

Beyond fresh fruits and vegetables, this list of essential ingredients will help you cook Korean food, or your version of Korean food. There is a lot more you can get to stock your cupboards and fridges, but this is a good start. Tear our cuisine up, mess around, take chances, mix and match. These things will bring joy to your life and liven things up. Then you too might be eating rice e-v-e-r-y d-a-y.

> *NOTE:*
>
> BUY WHAT YOU CAN BUY, BUT IF YOU'RE FEELING LOST, THE HAITAI AND MONGO BRANDS ARE GOOD FOR KOCHUJANG, DOENJANG, AND KOCHUKARU.

RICE

My boy PK has this joke where an Asian kid goes to his Caucasian friend's house and realizes that his family eats bread every day. "You eat bread e-v-e-r-y d-a-y?" Yeah, we eat rice every day, and our differences make us that much more similar to each other.

Now, for Koreans, there ain't no uncle named Ben. There are two major rice grains in Asia, so let's get to the long and the short of it.

Korea, Japan, Tibet, Mongolia, and a big part of China more or less eat short-grain rice that's high in starch. It sticks together and can be pounded into glutinous cakes. It also sticks to your bones, so it's perfect for cold weather.

As it gets warmer and you head toward the equator, the grain becomes long and loose. Countries like Vietnam, Thailand, Laos, Myanmar, Cambodia, Indonesia, Singapore, Malaysia, the Philippines, Taiwan, and parts of southern China eat jasmine long-grain rice packed in big burlap sacks. Perfect for pounding into noodles or paper for wraps.

Then you got basmati as you head farther west through India.

The most important step in cooking rice is how you wash it. Our Western mentality gets us in the habit of washing fruits and vegetables because they are dirty; washing rice, though, comes from a totally different place. Wash your rice to cleanse, not to clean. Run cold water through the rice and massage the grains, transferring all your energy to the rice as the rice transfers its own energy to you. Try to feel every single grain as you swirl the water.

Drain the water and do it again. Get deeper with it, turn off your phone, fuck the world for a minute.

Drain the water and do it again.

And again.

And again.

Minimum 3 times, up to at least 5 times, and more if you'd like and are feeling kinky about it.

Fill the vessel back up with water till it rises about an inch above the surface of the rice and cook.

I hope that you explore the beauties and spirituality of rice. Really, it's therapy for every day of your life.

SOY SAUCE

Soy sauce is a fermented liquid made from soybeans, yeast, and wheat flour, and it's our cultural olive oil. You just can't cook without it, so it's very important always to have a bottle somewhere in your home. There are different varieties for cooking, steeping, marinating, and finishing. I like Kikkoman, but explore and discover what suits your taste.

SESAME OIL

Nutty, viscous, delicious. Sesame oil is not really used for cooking per se; instead, it's a vital element in sauces and marinades. It is an essential component of dumpling fillings. It's the final splash on a bowl of bi bim bap. You use it sparingly, so don't skimp on the

quality by getting a blended version or some other cheap-ass product. Respect yourself and buy the best that tastes the best to you. Me, I like Kadoya's sesame oil.

GARLIC

Oh, if I could count the ways . . .

Bottom line: you need garlic in your kitchen to cook Korean food or any food in this book. There was a time, back in the day, when some chefs tried to give garlic a bum rap. Like they were over it. Like garlic was the easy way out.

I'm glad that didn't fly.

Garlic is onion's evil cousin, my homie. It's good for your skin and bad for your breath. You choose your fate.

Get it where there are heaps of it in markets and not where they sell five bulbs lined in a pretty plastic mesh bag on a pretty shelf with a pretty label. American supermarkets trap garlic in a cage, but it ain't no circus animal. Garlic needs to breathe. It's gotta hang and stretch its legs in big piles of stank.

If you really wish, you can use the peeled stuff from Gilroy packed in jars or bags, but getting the whole bulb and smashing it, peeling it, and chopping it is a wonderful thing to do.

Smashing, peeling, chopping. It's a ritual. Make it a part of your life.

SCALLIONS AND GINGER

Ginger Garlic Scallion. The trinity. The mirepoix of a wok. The foundation of flavor. One of my professors at the Culinary Institute of America used to always say, "GGS!" Anyone who went to the CIA back in the day knows Danny Lee. Rest in peace, my brother. Chef Lee always reminded us of our GGS. He'd pop around corners like John Turturro in *Mr. Deeds*: "GGS, don't forget!" Light fire, oil, GGS, go!

KOCHUKARU

Long red peppers dried on mesh mats in the dry heat, then ground into coarse flakes. Life is good.

You need this stuff. Kochukaru is to Korea what duck fat is to Gascony. There is no way to imagine that it would never be around. It keeps for a long time, so buy a bag and store it. You need it for kimchi, sauces, marinades—everything. We don't use much salt in Korean cooking, as the soy provides that saline element, so kochukaru is almost like our salt.

KOCHUJANG

Dry peppers, grind the peppers, keep some ground, then use the rest to make into a paste. That is what kochujang is. It's a fermented product that combines chile powder, soybeans, and a bunch of other aromatics and is allowed to develop into this amazing postapocalyptic glue that binds food together. You absolutely need it for stews and marinades. This stuff keeps till your kids get to college.

DOENJANG

You can call it miso just like you can call a girl a ho: that is, you can't. It just ain't right to do that to this funky paste. Miso is miso and doenjang just ain't the Korean version of it. No, this is a mashed-up soybean fermentation that can turn water into a meal. Seriously. Try it and get back at me. A scoop of doenjang and some water, heat, boil, reduce, eat. Delicious. You can use it for dips on vegetables or make stews. Like kochujang, this stuff is almost indestructible, so keep it in your fridge and mark it as an heirloom.

DAIKON RADISH

The Korean type is short, fat, and stubby, like me. The Japanese type is long and slender. Either way, it's delicious and integral to build a base flavor. It's also good for crunchy snacking.

Peel it and cut into cubes for ggakdugi, a spicy kimchi. Shred it into salads. My favorite is to slice and braise it in soy or to throw it into beef stock for that extra layer of flavor.

TOFU

Soak soybeans, crush and heat them, then coagulate with seawater. Soft, silken, hardened, pressed, stinky.

People sometimes hate on tofu, saying it has no taste. If you think like that, it's game over. So let's shatter that thinking and restart.

Tofu is an amazing product, just like cheese is an amazing product. Sometimes I like to look at tofu as if it were a cheese, with different varieties like burrata and fresh ricotta. If you do that, you'll cook and treat it with care, working to enhance the flavor with delicate and concentrated touches. And you'll understand that tofu is not supposed to be eaten like a steak, the way it's offered in many whack-ass vegetarian restaurants. No, try dicing that tofu and putting it in a stew with anchovies, shrimp, clams, pork shoulder, dwenjjang, and zucchini. Y-U-M! Or slowly braise it, covered with soy sauce, minced scallion, ginger, sesame seeds, and kochukaru.

Silken, cook it in a stew with spicy red pepper paste, oysters, beef, and garlic. You see? This ain't Tofurky.

Asian markets have refrigerator cases just for tofu. I love to use the Pulmuone tofu brand.

RICE VINEGAR

Get a natural brown rice vinegar like Marukan's rice wine vinegar. Not that seasoned crap.

DRIED SEAWEED

Dried seaweed is used for many things and comes in many forms: the salted versions are great for eating with rice or making rolls. Then there is the actual kelp that is dried as is, and you use that as a base for a broth or in a special birthday soup, mixed with beef and cooking soy sauce. We eat that soup instead of cake.

DUMPLING WRAPPERS

Dumpling wrappers are my thing, yo. It's like having pasta around at your fingertips. Fill 'em, then boil, fry, steam, or stew. Delicious.

SPAM

Spam. Gotta have Spam.

MAPLE SYRUP

Get pure maple syrup from Vermont or New Hampshire. The pure syrup will always, always trump the fake "non-pure" versions, so get the pure one and then experiment with the different grades and shades to find your favorites.

CANNED FRUIT

I use canned fruit a lot in my cooking; ain't no shame in that. I like Dole's canned fruits.

CULTURAL SHIT

The farmers in Korea, who have such a profound understanding of soil, land, and growth, have shown us visionary ways to approach a meal: eat with passion and heart. These cultural rules are about respect and ritual, and they connect us to the harvest.

You don't have to follow any of these rules and regulations, and if you grew up with certain cultural codes, I pardon you for breaking them if you wish. Just remember that whether you stick by the rules or scorn them, there *is* a proper way to prepare and eat food.

- Elders are served first. Don't eat till they start.
- Elders leave the table first. Don't get up until they get up.
- Don't stick your chopsticks straight into the rice. That means death, and not in a cool, Goth, Siouxie and the Banshees sort of way. No, it's just straight up rude, a low-level spit in death's face.
- Don't point your chopsticks at people. That shit's also rude.
- Slurp your noodles at a voracious pace.
- Eat all your rice.
- No measuring cups or measuring spoons when cooking. Use your palm instead.
- Taste with fingers.
- Chew each bite twenty times.
- Eat slow; drop the deuce fast.
- Thank each other for the meal before you eat and again after the meal.
- Double, triple dip.
- Eat with your mouth open; talk with your mouth full.
- Reach across the table.
- Wipe sweat with a folded napkin.
- Sit straight.
- Eat a lot.
- Talk about what you're going to eat for the next meal, even—and especially—if you haven't yet finished this one.
- Cook with your soul.

INDEX

Note: Page references in *italics* indicate recipe photographs.

A

Abalone Porridge, *20,* 21
Almond Cookies, Chinatown, 69
An American Place by Larry
    Forgione (restaurant), 207
Anchovy(ies)
    Caesar Salad, *264,* 265
    Stock, 21
de Anza Country Club, 237–39,
    255, 257
Appetizers. *See also* Snacks
    Chicken Satay with Peanut
      Sauce, 284–85
    Chips and Dip, 90
    Coconut Clam Chowder, *224,* 225
    Dumpling Time, 38–39, *39*
    Korean Carpaccio (Sort of), *40,* 41
    Mushroom Quesadillas, *266,*
      267–68
Apples
    Fruit Roll Ups and Downs, 88
Asparagus, *312,* 313

B

Bacon
    Easy de Anza Cobb Salad, 257
    Simple Club Sandwich, 256

Bananas
    My Milk Shake, *162,* 163
    Windowpane Smoothies, 67
Bánh Me, Spam, *288,* 289
Beans
    Pork and, 115
    Potato Pancakes, 44
Beef. *See also* Veal
    Carne Asada, *108,* 109
    Casino Prime Rib, 170–71
    Cheek Tacos, *298,* 299–300
    Chili Spaghetti, 24–25
    Dumpling Time, 38–39, *39*
    Hibachi Steak Teppanyaki, 195
    Jerky, 110, *111*
    Kalbi Plate, 164, *165*
    Korean Carpaccio (Sort of), *40,*
      41
    Korean-Style Braised Short Rib
      Stew, *186,* 187
    L.A. Dirty Dog, 309, *309*
    Lebanese Bee's Knees, *60,* 61–62
    Medallions, Seared, with Sauce
      Robert, 220, *221*
    Phở for Dem Hos, 172–73
    Roy's Burger, 301
    Soybean Paste Stew, 188, *189*

Beverly Hilton Hotel, 247–49,
    271–72
The Bicycle Club, 142–48
Birria, *250,* 251–52
Black Mike (in Grove Street Mob),
    96
Blueberry Pancakes (variation), 140
Bobbitt, Danny, 99
Bob's Big Boys (restaurant), 24
Bohemian (bar), 181
Bok Choy, Baby, 314
Border Grill (restaurant), 151
Bouley (restaurant), 207
Brinckerhoff, Peter, 240
Broccoli Rabe, 314
Brown, Ryan, 96–99, 100–102
Brussels Sprouts and Kimchi, 315,
    315
Burger, Roy's, 301
Bustamante, Carlos, 99
Buttermilk Pancakes, 140

C

Cabbage. *See* Kimchi
Caesar Salad, *264,* 265
Cal State Fullerton, 123–24
Campanile (restaurant), 151

Caramelization, note about, 45
Cardamom Milk Shaved Ice, 287,
    287
Cardoz, Floyd, 275
Carne Asada, *108,* 109
Carpaccio, Korean (Sort of), *40,* 41
Carrots
    Korean-Style Braised Short Rib
        Stew, *186,* 187
    Spam Bánh Me, *288,* 289
Casino Prime Rib, 170–71
Cauliflower, Roasted, 316
Cerro Villa Junior High School,
    79–85
Cheese
    Asparagus, *312,* 313
    Broccoli Rabe, 314
    Caesar Salad, *264,* 265
    Easy de Anza Cobb Salad, 257
    French Onion Soup, 263
    Goat, and Watermelon, 321
    L.A. Corner on the Cob, 302, *303*
    Mushroom Quesadillas, *266,*
        267–68
    Perfect Instant Ramen, *132,* 133
    Pizza, Dough to Sauce, 138–39
    Roy's Burger, 301
    Simple Club Sandwich, 256
Cheesecake Factory, 272–75
Chernow, Mike, 217
Chicken
    Fried, Korean Stained-Glass, 192
    Gumbo, *196,* 197
    Hainan, Kind of, 290, *291*
    Kung Pao, Papi Style, *116,*
        117–18
    Piccata, Simple, 258–59
    Satay with Peanut Sauce,
        284–85
Chiles
    Beef Cheek Tacos, *298,* 299–300
    Birria, *250,* 251–52

Chorizo and Eggs, 64–66, *65*
Eggplant Curry over Rice, 282,
    283
Salsa Verde, 119, *119*
Salsa Verde for Beef Cheek
    Tacos, *298,* 299–300
That's So Sweet, 91
Chili Spaghetti, 24–25
Chinatown Almond Cookies, 69
Chips and Dip, 90
Choi, Roy
    attends Culinary Institute of
        America, 185, 199–206
    Chevy Blazer automobile, 103–7
    childhood birthday parties,
        13–14
    college years, 123–28
    detox in Mission Viejo, 176–77
    early childhood, 5–17
    eating and drinking in Los
        Angeles, 150–51, 179–84
    elementary school years, 34
    externship at Le Bernardin,
        208–17
    financial problems, 153–57
    gambling activities, 142–50,
        152–57
    high school years, 93–107
    junior high school years, 79–85
    Korean taco food truck, 294–97
    parents' backgrounds, 6–9
    parents' jewelry business, 47–59
    and Salvador's goats, 234–37
    Silver Garden restaurant years,
        27–37
    Times Square YMCA experience,
        128–31
    Villa Park years, 73–85
    work at de Anza Country Club,
        237–39
    work at Embassy Suites, 240–41,
        246–47

    work at First Investors, 177–78,
        181, 185
    work at Kaishoku Michiba,
        244–45
    work at La Casa del Zorro,
        230–34
    work at Pan Pacific Hotel,
        245–46
    work at RockSugar, 272–79
    work at the Beverly Hilton,
        247–49, 271–72
    work options after RockSugar,
        279–81
    work with Chef Michiba, 241–44
Choi Family Treehouse, 32–34
Choi Jewelry, 59
Chorizo and Eggs, 64–66, *65*
Chowder, Coconut Clam, *224,* 225
Cilantro
    Salsa Verde, 119, *119*
    Salsa Verde for Beef Cheek
        Tacos, *298,* 299–300
    That's So Sweet, 91
Cinnamon
    Ghetto Pillsbury Fried
        Doughnuts, 134–35, *134–35*
    Horchata, 120
City Café (restaurant), 151
Clam(s)
    Abalone Porridge, *20,* 21
    Chowder, Coconut, *224,* 225
Clark, Patrick, 207
Clifton's Cafeteria (restaurant), 57
Cobb Salad, Easy de Anza, 257
Coconut milk
    Cardamom Milk Shaved Ice, 287,
        287
    Chicken Satay with Peanut
        Sauce, 284–85
    Coconut Clam Chowder, *224,*
        225
    Coconut Rice, 286

Eggplant Curry over Rice, 282, *283*
Windowpane Smoothies, 67
Commerce Casino, 149
Condiments
Kimchi, *18,* 19
Magic Fish Dip, 86, *87*
Red Onion Marmalade, 255
Salsa Verde, 119, *119*
Salsa Verde for Beef Cheek
Tacos, *298,* 299–300
Sesame-Soy Salad Dressing, 310
Splash, 121
That's So Sweet, 91
Cookies, Chinatown Almond, 69
Corn
L.A. Corner on the Cob, 302, *303*
Crème Brûlée, 292
Cucumbers
Instant Pickled, *42,* 43
Salted Mango and Cukes, 322
Culinary Institute of America (CIA),
185, 199–206
Cultural rules, Korean, 331
Curing, note about, 307
Curry, Eggplant, over Rice, 282, *283*

D

Daikon radishes
about, 329
Spam Bánh Me, *288,* 289
Daniel (restaurant), 207
Dean, Garrett, 96
DeGeneres, Ellen, 246
DeSantis, Ron, 203–5
Desserts
Butter Pineapple, 322
Cardamom Milk Shaved Ice, 287,
287
Chinatown Almond Cookies, 69
Crème Brûlée, 292
Ghetto Pillsbury Fried
Doughnuts, 134–35, *134–35*

Pecan Pie, 70, *71*
Salted Mango and Cukes, 322
Dips
Chips and, 90
Fish, Magic, 86, *87*
Dirty Dog, L.A., 309, *309*
Doenjang, about, 329
Dong Il Jang (restaurant), 13
Doughnuts, Ghetto Pillsbury Fried,
134–35, *134–35*
Drinks
Horchata, 120
My Milk Shake, *162,* 163
Windowpane Smoothies, 67
Duck
Breast, Crispy, with Polenta and
Sweet and Sour Mango Sauce,
253, 253–54
Fat Fries, Twice-Cooked, 22
Dumpling Time, 38–39, *39*
Dumpling wrappers, about, 330

E

Eggplant Curry over Rice, 282, *283*
Egg(s)
Abalone Porridge, *20,* 21
Asparagus, *312,* 313
Chorizo and, 64–66, *65*
Easy de Anza Cobb Salad, 257
Fried Rice, Yuzu Glazed Shrimp
over, 194
Ketchup Fried Rice, *136,* 137
Korean Carpaccio (Sort of), *40,*
41
Perfect Instant Ramen, *132,* 133
Pork Fried Rice, *158,* 159–61
Zucchini Fritter Omelet, *320,*
321
The Ellen DeGeneres Show, 246
El Taurino (restaurant), 181
Embassy Suites, 240–41, 246–47,
267

F

Fama, Vinnie, 203
Feninger, Sue, 151
First Investors Corporation, 177–78,
181, 185
Fish. *See also* Anchovy(ies);
Shellfish
Broiled Halibut with Soy Glaze,
269
Dip, Magic, 86, *87*
the Fonz, 12, 17
Frank (high school friend), 83
French Onion Soup, 263
Fries, Twice-Cooked Duck Fat, 22
Fruit. *See also specific fruits*
canned, cooking with, 330
Roll Ups and Downs, 88
Windowpane Smoothies, 67

G

Garlic
buying, 328
Kimchi, *18,* 19
Roasted Mushrooms, 316
Spaghetti Junction: The $4
Spaghetti That Tastes Almost
as Good as the $24 Spaghetti,
166, 167–69
That's So Sweet, 91
Gates, Mrs., 238–39
Gehr, Frank, 96
Ghetto Pillsbury Fried Doughnuts,
134–35, *134–35*
Ginger, cooking with, 328
Goat
Birria, *250,* 251–52
and Yellow Rice Stew, *112,*
113–14
Grains. *See* Polenta; Rice
Gramercy Tavern (restaurant), 207
Greens
Caesar Salad, *264,* 265

Greens *(continued)*
    Easy de Anza Cobb Salad, 257
    Pounded Pork Schnitzel, 226
    Quick Spinach Soup, 317, *317*
Grove Street Mob, 94–107
Gumbo, *196,* 197
Gutierrez, Jesse, 203, 206

H

Hainan Chicken, Kind of, 290, *291*
Halibut, Broiled, with Soy Glaze,
    269
Happy Days, 17
Herbs. *See* Cilantro; Thai basil
Hibachi Steak Teppanyaki, 195
Hodori Restaurant, 181
Holzman, Daniel, 212–13, 217
Horchata, 120
Hurry Curry (restaurant), 181

I

Ice cream
    My Milk Shake, *162,* 163
Ingredients, 325–30
    canned fruit, 330
    daikon radish, 329
    doenjang, 329
    dried seaweed, 330
    dumpling wrappers, 330
    garlic, 328
    ginger, 328
    kochujang, 329
    kochukaru, 328
    maple syrup, 330
    rice, 325–27
    rice vinegar, 330
    scallions, 328
    sesame oil, 327–28
    soy sauce, 327
    spam, 330
    tofu, 329–30
Ismail, Mohan, 274, 275, 277–79

J

Janzen, Steve, 99
Jerky, Beef, 110, *111*
Johnnycakes (variation), 140
Jones, Lou, 205
Juan (at Le Bernardin), 210–12
Juhn, Paul "Yogi," 142, 178–81

K

Kaishoku Michiba (restaurant), 242,
    244–45
Kalbi Plate, 164, *165*
Kawai, Takayoshi, 244
Kenneth (at La Casa del Zorro),
    232–34
Ketchup Fried Rice, *136,* 137
Khun, Sottha, 207
Kimchi, *18,* 19
    Brussels Sprouts and, 315, *315*
    and Pork Belly Stuffed Pupusas,
    304, 305–7
    Stew, 45
Knight, Rey, 200
Kobawoo House (restaurant), 181
Kochujang, about, 329
Kochukaru
    about, 328
    Kimchi, *18,* 19
Korean cultural rules, 331
Korean taco food truck, 294–97
Korea University, 124–27
Kudra, Matt, 103
Kung Pao Chicken Papi Style, *116,*
    117–18
Kunz, Gray, 275

L

La Brea Bakery, 151
La Casa del Zorro, 230–34
Lagasse, Emeril, 184–85
Lamb
    Lebanese Bee's Knees, 60, 61–62

La Technique (Pépin), 239
Lebanese Bee's Knees, 60, 61–62
Le Bernardin (restaurant), 208–17,
    269
Le Cirque (restaurant), 207
Lee, Danny, 328
Le Grenouille (restaurant), 207
Los Angeles
    Asian population in, 11
    Jewelry District, 48–50
    during 1960s, 9, 11
    West Anaheim region, 28–30,
    36–37
    West Hollywood region, 15–16

M

Magic Fish Dip, 86, *87*
Main dishes
    Abalone Porridge, *20,* 21
    Beef Cheek Tacos, *298,* 299–300
    Birria, *250,* 251–52
    Broiled Halibut with Soy Glaze,
    269
    Carne Asada, *108,* 109
    Casino Prime Rib, 170–71
    Cheese Pizza, Dough to Sauce,
    138–39
    Chicken Satay with Peanut
    Sauce, 284–85
    Chili Spaghetti, 24–25
    Chorizo and Eggs, 64–66, *65*
    Coconut Clam Chowder, *224,*
    225
    Crispy Duck Breast with Polenta
    and Sweet and Sour Mango
    Sauce, *253,* 253–54
    Easy de Anza Cobb Salad, 257
    Eggplant Curry over Rice, 282,
    283
    French Onion Soup, 263
    Fried Ribs. What?!, *260,* 261–62
    Gumbo, *196,* 197

Hainan Chicken, Kind of, 290,
    291
Hibachi Steak Teppanyaki, 195
Kalbi Plate, 164, *165*
Ketchup Fried Rice, *136,* 137
Kimchi and Pork Belly Stuffed
    Pupusas, *304,* 305–7
Kimchi Stew, 45
Korean Stained-Glass Fried
    Chicken, 192
Korean-Style Braised Short Rib
    Stew, *186,* 187
Kung Pao Chicken Papi Style,
    116, 117–18
L.A. Dirty Dog, 309, *309*
Lebanese Bee's Knees, *60,* 61–62
Mushroom Quesadillas, *266,*
    267–68
Perfect Instant Ramen, *132,* 133
Phở for Dem Hos, 172–73
Pork and Beans, 115
Pork Fried Rice, *158,* 159–61
Pounded Pork Schnitzel, 226
Roy's Burger, 301
Seared Beef Medallions with
    Sauce Robert, 220, *221*
Seared Scallops with Chive
    Beurre Blanc, 227
Simple Chicken Piccata, 258–59
Simple Club Sandwich, 256
Soybean Paste Stew, 188, *189*
Spaghetti Junction: The $4
    Spaghetti That Tastes Almost
    as Good as the $24 Spaghetti,
    166, 167–69
Spam Bánh Me, *288,* 289
Spicy Octopus, *190,* 191
Yellow Rice and Goat Stew, *112,*
    113–14
Yuzu Glazed Shrimp over Egg
    Fried Rice, 194
Zucchini Fritter Omelet, *320,* 321

Mango
    and Cukes, Salted, 322
    Sauce, Sweet and Sour, 253–54
    Windowpane Smoothies, 67
Manguera, Mark, 281, 294–97
Manny (CIA friend), 203, 206
Maple syrup, buying, 330
Marmalade, Red Onion, 255
Matsuhisa, Nobu, 151
Matsuhisa (restaurant), 151
Meat. *See also* Beef; Pork
    Birria, *250,* 251–52
    curing, note about, 307
    Lebanese Bee's Knees, *60,*
        61–62
    Spam Bánh Me, *288,* 289
    Veal Stock, 222–23
    Yellow Rice and Goat Stew, *112,*
        113–14
The Meatball Shop (restaurant), 212
Michiba, Rokusaburo, 241–44
Milk
    Cardamom, Shaved Ice, 287, *287*
    Horchata, 120
    Shake, My, *162,* 163
Milliken, Mary Sue, 151
Mooring, Paul, 230–32
Mountain Café (restaurant), 21
Muller, Chris, 209, 210
Murphy, Sandy, 246
Mushroom(s)
    Kimchi Stew, 45
    Korean-Style Braised Short Rib
        Stew, *186,* 187
    Quesadillas, *266,* 267–68
    Roasted, 316

N
Nobu (restaurant), 207
Noodles
    Perfect Instant Ramen, *132,* 133
    Phở for Dem Hos, 172–73

Normandie Casino, 148–49
Nuts
    Chinatown Almond Cookies, 69
    Pecan Pie, 70, *71*

O
OB Bear (restaurant), 181
Octopus, Spicy, *190,* 191
Oil, sesame, about, 327–28
Okra
    Gumbo, *196,* 197
Okura, Robert, 274–75
Omelet, Zucchini Fritter, *320,* 321
One If by Land, Two If by Sea
    (restaurant), 207
Onion
    Red, Marmalade, 255
    Soup, French, 263
Ortega, Martin, 95–96
Osmail, Mohan, 272
Overton, David, 272–75
Oysters
    Kimchi, *18,* 19

P
Pag (in Grove Street Mob), 99
Pancakes
    Blueberry (variation), 140
    Buttermilk, 140
    Johnnycakes (variation), 140
    Potato, 44
Panchan, about, 28
Pan 9 games, 144, 146
Pan Pacific Hotel, 245–46
Paramount Studios, 17
Pasta. *See* Noodles; Spaghetti
Peaches
    Windowpane Smoothies, 67
Peanut Sauce, Chicken Satay with,
    284–85
Pecan Pie, 70, *71*
Peck, Rob, 203

Peppers. *See also* Chiles
    Chorizo and Eggs, 64–66, *65*
    kochujang, about, 329
    kochukaru, about, 328
    L.A. Dirty Dog, 309, *309*
Perez, Rich, 203, 206–7
Phở
    at The Bicycle Club, 144–46
    for Dem Hos, 172–73
Phoenix Bakery, 58
Pickled Cucumbers, Instant, *42*, 43
Pie, Pecan, 70, *71*
Pineapple
    Butter, 322
    Fruit Roll Ups and Downs, 88
    Windowpane Smoothies, 67
Pizza, Cheese, Dough to Sauce,
    138–39
Poker playing, 146–49
Polenta and Sweet and Sour Mango
    Sauce, Crispy Duck Breast
    with, *253*, 253–54
Pork. *See also* Bacon
    and Beans, 115
    Belly and Kimchi Stuffed
        Pupusas, *304*, 305–7
    Chorizo and Eggs, 64–66, *65*
    Dumpling Time, 38–39, *39*
    Fried Ribs. What?!, *260*, 261–62
    Fried Rice, *158*, 159–61
    Gumbo, *196*, 197
    Kimchi Stew, 45
    Lebanese Bee's Knees, *60*,
        61–62
    Schnitzel, Pounded, 226
Porridge, Abalone, *20*, 21
Potato(es)
    Anna Banana, *218*, 219
    Chips and Dip, 90
    Pancakes, 44
    Sweet, Roasted, 318
    Twice-Cooked Duck Fat Fries, 22

Poultry. *See* Chicken; Duck; Turkey
Pupusas, Kimchi and Pork Belly
    Stuffed, *304*, 305–7

Q

Quesadillas, Mushroom, *266*,
    267–68

R

Ramen, Perfect Instant, *132*, 133
Rice
    Abalone Porridge, *20*, 21
    Coconut, 286
    cooking, 327
    Eggplant Curry over, 282, *283*
    Fried, Egg, Yuzu Glazed Shrimp
        over, 194
    Fried, Ketchup, *136*, 137
    Fried, Pork, *158*, 159–61
    Gumbo, *196*, 197
    Horchata, 120
    types of, 325–26
    washing, 326
    Yellow, and Goat Stew, *112*,
        113–14
Rice vinegar, 330
Ripert, Eric, 208–10
Robinson, Curtis and Ken, 99
Röckenwagner (restaurant), 150
RockSugar (restaurant), 272–79
Rodney (high school friend), 81
Roy's Burger, 301
Ryan, Nolan, 76–78

S

Salad Dressing, Sesame-Soy, 310
Salads
    Caesar, *264*, 265
    Cobb, Easy de Anza, 257
Salsa Verde, 119, *119*
Salsa Verde for Beef Cheek Tacos,
    298, 299–300

Salvado (at La Casa del Zorro),
    234–37
Sandwiches
    Club, Simple, 256
    L.A. Dirty Dog, 309, *309*
    Lebanese Bee's Knees, *60*,
        61–62
    Spam Bánh Me, *288*, 289
Satay, Chicken, with Peanut Sauce,
    284–85
Sauces
    Mango, Sweet and Sour, 253–54
    Pizza, 138–39
    Salsa Verde, 119, *119*
    Salsa Verde for Beef Cheek
        Tacos, *298*, 299–300
    Splash, 121
    That's So Sweet, 91
    Yogurt, 61–62
Scallions, cooking with, 328
Scallops, Seared, with Chive Beurre
    Blanc, 227
Scherr, Malvin, 177
Seafood. *See* Fish; Shellfish
Seaweed, dried, about, 330
Semaza, Mike, 96
Sesame oil, about, 327–28
Sesame-Soy Salad Dressing, 310
Shaved Ice, Cardamom Milk, 287,
    287
Shellfish
    Abalone Porridge, *20*, 21
    Coconut Clam Chowder, *224*,
        225
    Gumbo, *196*, 197
    Kimchi, *18*, 19
    Seared Scallops with Chive
        Beurre Blanc, 227
    Spicy Octopus, *190*, 191
    Yuzu Glazed Shrimp over Egg
        Fried Rice, 194
Shep (in Grove Street Mob), 96

Shrimp
 Gumbo, *196,* 197
 Yuzu Glazed, over Egg Fried Rice, 194
Side dishes
 Asparagus, *312,* 313
 Baby Bok Choy, 314
 Broccoli Rabe, 314
 Brussels Sprouts and Kimchi, 315, *315*
 Caesar Salad, *264,* 265
 Coconut Rice, 286
 L.A. Corner on the Cob, 302, *303*
 Potatoes Anna Banana, *218,* 219
 Potato Pancakes, 44
 Quick Spinach Soup, 317, *317*
 Roasted Cauliflower, 316
 Roasted Mushrooms, 316
 Roasted Sweet Potatoes, 318
 Slow-Roasted Tomatoes, 318, *319*
 Twice-Cooked Duck Fat Fries, 22
 Watermelon and Goat Cheese, 321
 Zucchini Fritter Omelet, *320,* 321
Silver Garden (restaurant), 27–37
Simple syrup, preparing, 41
Smoothies, Windowpane, 67
Snacks
 Beef Jerky, 110, *111*
 Cardamom Milk Shaved Ice, 287, *287*
 Fruit Roll Ups and Downs, 88
 Ghetto Pillsbury Fried Doughnuts, 134–35, *134–35*
 Horchata, 120
 Instant Pickled Cucumbers, *42,* 43
 Kimchi and Pork Belly Stuffed Pupusas, *304,* 305–7
 Mushroom Quesadillas, *266,* 267–68

My Milk Shake, *162,* 163
Windowpane Smoothies, 67
Solera (restaurant), 207
Soups
 Coconut Clam Chowder, *224,* 225
 French Onion, 263
 Perfect Instant Ramen, *132,* 133
 Phở for Dem Hos, 172–73
 Spinach, Quick, 317, *317*
Sour cream
 Chips and Dip, 90
Soybean Paste Stew, 188, *189*
Soy sauce
 about, 327
 Sesame-Soy Salad Dressing, 310
 Splash, 121
Spaghetti
 Chili, 24–25
 Spaghetti Junction: The $4, That Tastes Almost as Good as the $24 Spaghetti, *166,* 167–69
Spam Bánh Me, *288,* 289
Spinach Soup, Quick, 317, *317*
Splash, 121
Squash
 Korean-Style Braised Short Rib Stew, *186,* 187
 Zucchini Fritter Omelet, *320,* 321
Stews
 Birria, *250,* 251–52
 Braised Short Rib, Korean-Style, *186,* 187
 Gumbo, *196,* 197
 Kimchi, 45
 Soybean Paste, 188, *189*
 Yellow Rice and Goat, *112,* 113–14
Stocks
 Anchovy, 21
 Veal, 222–23
Strawberries
 Windowpane Smoothies, 67

Street City Minis, 105–7
Sugiura, Suki, 249
Sweet Potatoes
 Roasted, 318
 Twice-Cooked Duck Fat Fries, 22
Swoboda, Edward, 48

T

Tacos, Beef Cheek, *298,* 299–300
Taro root
 Chips and Dip, 90
 Korean-Style Braised Short Rib Stew, *186,* 187
Tavern on the Green (restaurant), 207
Thai basil
 Salsa Verde, 119, *119*
 That's So Sweet, 91
 Twice-Cooked Duck Fat Fries, 22
That's So Sweet, 91
Tofu
 about, 329–30
 Dumpling Time, 38–39, *39*
 Kimchi Stew, 45
 Quick Spinach Soup, 317, *317*
 Soybean Paste Stew, 188, *189*
Tomatillos
 Salsa Verde, 119, *119*
 Salsa Verde for Beef Cheek Tacos, *298,* 299–300
Tomatoes
 Pizza Sauce, 138–39
 Simple Club Sandwich, 256
 Slow-Roasted, 318, *319*
 Spaghetti Junction: The $4 Spaghetti That Tastes Almost as Good as the $24 Spaghetti, *166,* 167–69
Tommy (Martin Ortega's uncle), 99
Tommy's Burgers (restaurant), 12–13, 22
Tools, 323–24

Torres, Jacques, 207
Torres, Robert, 104
Tortillas
  Beef Cheek Tacos, *298,* 299–300
  Mushroom Quesadillas, *266,* 267–68
Turkey
  Easy de Anza Cobb Salad, 257
  Simple Club Sandwich, 256

V

Vafeas, Peter, 201–3
Veal Stock, 222–23
Vegetables. *See also specific vegetables*
  Asparagus, *312,* 313
  Baby Bok Choy, 314
  Broccoli Rabe, 314
  Brussels Sprouts and Kimchi, 315, *315*
  how to char, 114
  Kung Pao Chicken Papi Style, *116,* 117–18
  Quick Spinach Soup, 317, *317*
  Roasted Cauliflower, 316
  Roasted Mushrooms, 316
  Roasted Sweet Potatoes, 318
  Salted Mango and Cukes, 322
  Slow-Roasted Tomatoes, 318, *319*
  Zucchini Fritter Omelet, *320,* 321
Villa Park, Orange County, 73–85
Villa Park High, 93–107
Vinegar, rice, 330
Vongerichten, Jean-Georges, 275

W

Water Grill (restaurant), 150
Watermelon and Goat Cheese, 321

West Anaheim region, 28–30, 36–37
West Hollywood region, 15–16
Winkler, Henry, 12, 17

Y

YMCA (Times Square), 128–31
Yogurt Sauce, 61–62
Yorkshire Grill (restaurant), 53–54
Yuca
  Twice-Cooked Duck Fat Fries, 22
Yuzu Glazed Shrimp over Egg Fried Rice, 194

Z

Zucchini Fritter Omelet, *320,* 321

ABOUT THE AUTHORS

ROY CHOI was born in Seoul, Korea, and raised in Los Angeles, California. He graduated from the Culinary Institute of America and went on to cook at the internationally acclaimed Le Bernardin. He was named Best New Chef by *Food & Wine* in 2010. Choi is the co-owner, cofounder, and chef of Kogi BBQ, as well as the restaurants Chego!, A-Frame, Sunny Spot, and POT. He lives in Los Angeles, California.

TIEN NGUYEN writes regularly about Los Angeles foods and personalities as the senior food writer for *LA Weekly* and has contributed to *Time Out Los Angeles* and the Daily Beast. She lives in Los Angeles, California.

NATASHA PHAN oversees innovative business development and brand communications for multiple restaurants, including Kogi BBQ, Chego!, A-Frame, Sunny Spot, and POT. In 2013, the L.A. native was named one of Zagat's 30 Under 30, an award distinguishing her influence in the food industry.